# Demand-based Data Stream Gathering, Processing, and Transmission

Jonas Traub

AF285015

Bibliografische Information der Deutschen Nationalbibliothek: Die Deutsche Nationalbibliothek verzeichnet diese Publikation in der Deutschen Nationalbibliografie; detail-
lierte bibliografische Daten sind im Internet über http://dnb.dnb.de abrufbar.

Herstellung und Verlag: BoD – Books on Demand, Norderstedt
ISBN: 978-3-7526-7125-4

# Acknowledgements

This book is a modified and extended version of my dissertation submitted to Technische Universität Berlin in 2019. I wish to thank my advisors Volker Markl, Asterios Katsifodimos, Sebastian Breß, and Tilmann Rabl for their feedback and support which led to this thesis. I also thank Manfred Hauswirth, Volker Markl, Amr El Abbadi, and Albert Bifet for being part of my committee and for providing highly valuable feedback.

Many more people have been guiding and supporting me in the past years. In general my thanks go the whole Databases and Information Management Group (DIMA) at TU Berlin and DFKI. In my first year, I received great support to get started from my colleagues Sebastian Schelter, Max Heimel, Christoph Boden, and Alexander Alexandrov. I thank Paris Carbone and Seif Haridi for our close cooperation, continuing the line of research we started when I wrote my master's thesis at KTH. I was always blessed with a nice atmosphere in the office with most sofas. This was mainly the merit of Asterios Katsifodimos, Sherif Sakr, and Alexander Renz-Wieland who shared the office with me.

I coauthored a total of thirteen publications and experienced great team work in achieving our research goals. My thanks go to all the authors of these publications: Ahmed Awad, Kaustubh Beedkar, Tobias Behrens, Janis von Bleichert, Sebastian Breß, Paris Carbone, Bonaventura Del Monte, Morgan Geldenhuys, Dimitrios Giouroukis, Philipp Marian Grulich, Felipe Gutierrez, Seif Haridi, Fabian Hueske, Julius Hülsmann, Jeyhun Karimov, Asterios Katsifodimos, Clemens Lutz, Volker Markl, Tilmann Rabl, Alejandro Rodríguez Cuéllar, Viktor Rosenfeld, Manuel Renz, Till Rohrmann, René Saitenmacher, Sherif Sakr, Nikolaas Steenbergen, Tim Stullich, and Steffen Zeuch.

Many of the achievements presented in this thesis were made as part of SENSE and related projects. These projects would not have been possible without the great work of my student assistants. Jannis von Bleichert was the first member of the SENSE team and contributed to our first prototypes. Andreas Osowski contributed to the initial C++ implementation of our sensor node system. Tim Stullich contributed to the implementation of the fault-tolerance features in the SENSE project and to the implementation of the operator logic on sensor nodes. Philipp M. Grulich was a great support for the development of the Scotty framework and the $I^2$ demonstration. Together, we achieved the best demonstration award at EDBT 2017 and gave two talks at FlinkForward. Julius Hülsmann was a great partner for discussing all mathematical problems related to time coherence guarantees and their optimization. His commitment and dedication to the project have my deep respect and appreciation. Zbigniew Jerzak from SAP guided us in the early stages of the SENSE project and provided an industrial point of view.

I am glad that I had the chance to advise highly motivated, exceptional bachelor and master students. I wish to thank Chiao-Yun Li for her work on automatic tuning of read-time tolerances, Vianney de Cibeins for his design of a benchmark for adaptive data collection, Yusuf Güven Toprakkiran for his investigation of machine learning techniques in heterogeneous computing environments, Alejandro Rodríguez Cuéllar for his work on window aggregate sharing for out-of-order stream processing, Jerred Blankenburg for his performance analysis on complex event processing engines, Robin Rabe for his evaluation of cloud-dased stream processing systems, and Alexander Dadiani for his catalogue of sampling algorithms for sensor data. I am thankful that these students made advising theses one of the most satisfying tasks I had during the time of my doctoral studies.

As part of my teaching duties, I was responsible for our evaluation server, which validates students' submissions using unit tests. I want to thank Alexander Alexandrov for implementing this system in the first place. I also want to thank Naveed Kamran, Vianney de Cibeins, and Taifun Wiechert for continuously implementing new features. I thank Martin Kiefer for taking over the responsibility for the system and our system administrator Lutz Friedel who helped with technical issues of all kind.

I am grateful for the support I received with all administrative issues from Claudia Gantzer, Melanie Neumann, Katrin Jung, and Anna Weymann, our excellent secretary team. I appreciate the work of our academic director Ralf Kutsche who does a great job in managing all teaching duties and turned out to be an excellent badminton player.

I thank my parents Sonja and Thilo Traub, my sisters Saskia Traub and Jenny Trumpfheller, and my grandparents Wolfgang Traub and Renate Schuck for their trust in me and for giving me the confidence required to pursue a doctoral degree. I further thank Stephan Wypler for being the best possible co-tenant in the past years.

Throughout my doctoral studies, my wife Melanie Kuffner was my closest person. She was on my side, no matter if I was in a bad mood before deadlines, overworked, or stressed out. She was the one who took my mind off things if needed and I cannot imagine the past years without our shared vacations, free time, cooking evenings, and bike tours. Whenever life gave me lemons, Melanie taught me to make lemonade!

# Abstract

The Internet of Things (IoT) consists of billions of devices which form a cloud of network-connected sensor nodes. These sensor nodes supply a vast number of data streams with massive amounts of sensor data. Real-time sensor data enables diverse applications including traffic-aware navigation, machine monitoring, and home automation.

Current stream processing pipelines are demand-oblivious, which means that they gather, transmit, and process as much data as possible. In contrast, a demand-based processing pipeline uses requirement specifications of data consumers, such as failure tolerances and latency limitations, to save resources. In this thesis, we present an end-to-end architecture for demand-based data stream gathering, processing, and transmission.

Our solution unifies the way applications express their data demands, i.e., their requirements with respect to their input streams. This unification allows for multiplexing the data demands of all concurrently running applications. On sensor nodes, we schedule sensor reads based on the data demands of all applications, which saves up to 87% in sensor reads and data transfers in our experiments with real-world sensor data.

Our demand-based control layer optimizes the data acquisition from thousands of sensors. We introduce time coherence as a fundamental data characteristic, which is the delay between the first and the last sensor read that contribute values to a tuple. A large scale parameter exploration shows that our solution scales to large numbers of sensors and operates reliably under varying latency and coherence constraints.

On stream analysis systems, we tackle the problem of efficient window aggregation. We contribute a general aggregation technique, which adapts to four key workload characteristics: Stream (dis)order, aggregation types, window types, and window measures. Our experiments show that our solution outperforms alternative solutions by an order of magnitude in throughput, which prevents expensive system scale-out.

We further derive data demands from visualization needs of applications and make these data demands available to streaming systems such as Apache Flink. This enables streaming systems to pre-process data with respect to changing visualization needs. Experiments show that our solution reliably prevents overloads when data rates increase.

# Zusammenfassung / German Abstract

Im Internet der Dinge (engl. Internet of Things/IoT) fungieren Milliarden von Geräten als Sensorknoten und formen eine Datenwolke (engl. Cloud). Diese Sensorknoten produzieren in Echtzeit eine Vielzahl von Datenströmen mit enormen Datenmengen und ermöglichen somit verschiedenste Anwendungen, wie die Automation von Gebäuden, die Überwachung von Maschinen und eine Navigation auf Basis aktueller Verkehrsdaten. Momentan werden in der Regel bedarfsunabhängig so viele Sensordaten wie möglich erhoben. Im Gegensatz dazu steht ein bedarfsorientiertes System, welches Anforderungsspezifikationen von Datennutzern, wie zum Beispiel Fehlertoleranzen und zulässige Latenzen, verwendet, um Ressourcen zu sparen. Die vorliegende Arbeit stellt eine Ende-zu-Ende Architektur vor, mit der Sensordaten bedarfsabhängig erhoben, übertragen und verarbeitet werden können.

Der Datenbedarf einer Anwendung ergibt sich aus den Anforderungen an die Eingabedatenstöme. Die vorgestellte Lösung vereinheitlicht die Spezifikation des Datenbedarfs, sodass der Bedarf aller laufenden Anwendungen gebündelt werden kann. An Sensorknoten können so Lesevorgänge abhängig vom gemeinsamen Bedarf aller Anwendungen ausgeführt werden. In Experimenten ergab sich dadurch eine Einsparung von bis zu 87% des Datenverkehrs.

Ein neuartiges Sensorkontrollsystem optimiert die Datenerhebung von einer Vielzahl von Sensorknoten und etabliert die zeitliche Kohärenz als essentielle Eigenschaft von Datentupeln. Die zeitliche Kohärenz beschreibt die Verzögerung zwischen dem ersten und letzten Lesevorgang, der Sensorwerte zu einem Tupel beisteuert. Eine umfassende Untersuchung zeigt, dass das System zu tausenden Sensorknoten skaliert und auch bei variierenden Rahmenbedingungen effizient ist. Zur Optimierung der Performanz von Systemen zur Datenstromenanalyse wird eine allgemeine Aggregationstechnik vorgestellt. Diese passt sich automatisch an die zeitliche Sortierung von Datenströmen, die Art der Aggregationsfunktionen, die Art der Fenster und die Dimensionen, in denen Fenster definiert sind, an. In Experimenten verzehnfachte dieser adaptive Ansatz den Datendurchsatz im Vergleich zu alternativen Techniken.

Abschließend betrachtet die vorliegende Arbeit den Datenbedarf von Anwendungen, die Datenstöme in Echtzeit visualisieren. Dabei wird der Datenbedarf von Visualisierungseinstellungen abgeleitet, welche von Benutzern jederzeit interaktiv verändert werden können, und dann Systemen zur Datenstromanalyse, wie zum Beispiel Apache Flink, bereitgestellt. So können diese Systeme große Datenmengen bedarfsorientiert und in Echtzeit vorverarbeiten. Experimete zeigen, dass die gezeigte Lösung auch bei steigenden Datenraten eine Systemüberlastung verhindert.

# Contents

# 1

# Introduction

## 1.1 Motivation

Real-time sensor data is the basis for many applications, such as dynamic traffic control, smart manufacturing, and early warning systems. Such applications connect our infrastructure with state-of-the-art information and communications technology to optimize, secure, and individualize our everyday life. For example, a navigation software can use real-time traffic data to individually optimize suggested routes based on current traffic conditions; smart factories can monitor machine data to predict failures and prevent accidents; and weather services can detect seismic activities to issue tsunami warnings.

We observe a trend towards an *Internet of Things (IoT)*, leading to billions of network-connected devices which supply vast amounts of real-time sensor data [193]. This growth has even lead to a production shortage on electronics components - especially sensors [91, 92]. *Driven by the fast growth of the IoT, the goal of this thesis is to efficiently gather, transmit, and process sensor data from a large number of sensor nodes, and to make it available to a large number of applications in real-time.*

To meet real-time requirements of applications, stream analysis systems, such as Apache Flink [35] and Apache Storm [177], process data in stream processing pipelines. A *stream processing pipeline* is a series of concurrently running operators for data gathering, data transmission, and/or data processing. Each operator of a stream processing pipeline continuously consumes input data from its preceeding operator(s) and immediately transmits output data to its succeeding operator(s) [169]. This reduces the end-to-end latency compared to processing batches of data in consecutive stages [49].

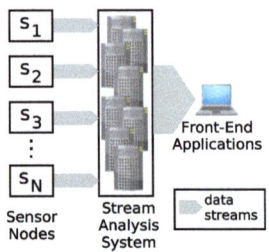

FIGURE 1.1:
A typical demand-oblivious
processing pipeline in the IoT.

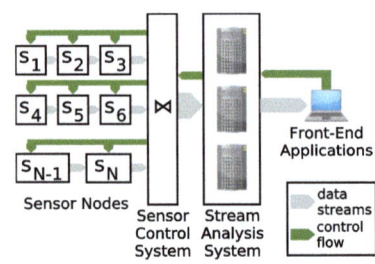

FIGURE 1.2:
Demand-based data stream gathering,
processing, and transmission.

Current stream processing pipelines are demand-oblivious, which means that systems gather, transmit, and process as much data as possible without considering the data demand of data consumers (Figure 1.1). The *data demand* of a data consumer (e.g., a front-end application or an operator in a processing pipeline) is the minimum number of data points which allows for providing a desired functionality (e.g., computing an aggregate with a desired precision). An operator of a processing pipeline is *demand-based* if it utilizes requirement specifications (e.g., failure tolerances) of data consumers to reduce resource utilization (e.g., to reduce network traffic).

Demand-oblivious pipelines cause several problems in the IoT: *(i)* sensor nodes transfer large amounts of data which causes high network traffic, often charged by (mobile) network providers. *(ii)* Processing all these data requires large clusters for stream analysis systems which leads to high scale-out costs. *(iii)* Front-end applications, which visualize data in real-time, are exposed to high velocity result streams which causes overloads and application crashes when data rates increase.

The fast growth in the number of sensors and the resulting vast volume of data are grand challenges in the IoT [40, 108, 127]. We address these challenges with an architecture change towards *demand-based data stream gathering, processing, and transmission.*

We introduce control interfaces between sensor nodes, stream analysis systems, and front-end applications, and unify the way in which applications express their data demands (Figure 1.2). We further provide a sensor control system which orchestrates sensor nodes in adaptive pipelines and joins values of all sensors to concise sensor data tuples, reducing the number of concurrent input streams at central system components. The result is an end-to-end architecture which optimizes state-of-the-art stream processing technology based on the data demands of applications.

## 1.2 Research Problems and Contributions

In this section, we state the research problems addressed in this thesis and outline our contributions. The following chapters will then discuss our contributions in detail.

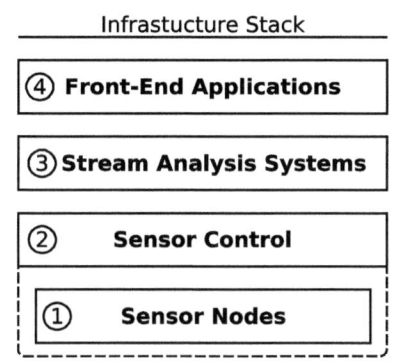

FIGURE 1.3: Infrastructure Stack.

Figure 1.3 shows our infrastructure stack. At the bottom of the stack are distributed sensor nodes ①, which capture sensor data and transmit it to upstream systems. Sensor nodes are managed by a sensor control layer ②. The resulting data streams are processed by stream analysis systems ③, which perform central data analysis (e.g., correlation detection among sensors) on compute clusters. Users access the results of the analysis through front-end applications ④ which offer domain-specific user interfaces.

Modern cars are a good example of sensor nodes with thousands of sensors [54]. Manufacturers deploy sensor control systems to collect sensor data from their fleets and to feed back current traffic information [116]. Stream analysis systems allow for analyzing sensor data in real-time to facilitate diverse applications such as red light aware cruise control [143], traffic prediction [48, 148], and locating parking spots [209]. All these applications share the same data sources (connected cars) but have different data demands.

We introduce techniques to express the data demand of an application, and methods for combining data demands. This allows for sharing computations among applications and prevents redundant data transmissions. On the sensor node layer ①, we introduce an on-demand read scheduling technique which operates based on the data demands of all running applications. We further introduce a sensor control system ② which continuously monitors performance characteristics, tunes configuration parameters, and reacts on failures automatically. In stream analysis systems ③, we improve the performance of a major bottleneck, namely windowing and aggregation, and enable computation sharing among concurrently running stream processing jobs. Finally, we show through an example application ④ how interactive visualizations can expose their data demand to streaming systems. These systems can then adapt to changing visualization settings (i.e., data demands) with low latency and without a need to restart cluster applications.

### 1.2.1 Layer 1: Sensor Nodes (Chapter 2)

Current stream analysis systems such as Apache Flink [7, 35], Apache Storm [177], or Apache Spark [205] require data at high frequencies to serve all possible use-cases. This is suboptimal because it forces us to read and transfer sensor values beyond the data demand of applications. We call this problem *oversampling*:

┌─ *Problem 1: Oversampling on Sensor Nodes* ──────────────────────────────

The *data demand* of a query is the minimum number of data points which allows for answering a query with the desired precision. *Oversampling* is reading or transmitting additional data points that are not required to achieve the desired precision.

└──────────────────────────────────────────────────────────────────────────

The massive growth in the amount of sensors makes *oversampling* a critical problem. The *available data of a sensor* is the maximum number of samples a sensor node can acquire from a sensor. For example, if a sensor node (e.g., a smart phone or a Raspberry Pi) can collect samples from a sensor (e.g., a photo cell or an accelerometer) at a 10kHz frequency, the available data are ten thousand samples per second. As the number of available sensors in the IoT increases rapidly, systems cannot transfer and process all available data with maximal frequencies any more. We thus need to trade-off sampling rates against scale out and data transfer costs.

In order to prevent oversampling, sensor nodes need to adapt their sampling rates on-the-fly. For example, sensors which experience anomalies should provide detailed data (high sampling rates). However, most sensors, which do not experience anomalies at the moment, should reduce their sampling rates. Thus, at any time, we process high frequency data from a few sensors but we reduce sensor reads and data transmissions for the majority of sensors to prevent unnecessary costs.

┌─ *Problem 2: Missing Adaptivity* ────────────────────────────────────────

Existing systems lack support for adapting sampling rates on-the-fly depending on anomalies in sensor data and the combined data demands of multiple queries.

└──────────────────────────────────────────────────────────────────────────

We contribute a technique that optimizes communication costs while maintaining the desired accuracy. Our technique schedules sensor reads across large numbers of sensors based on the data demands of a large number of concurrent queries. We introduce user-defined sampling functions (UDSFs) to overcome the oversampling problem. UDSFs define the data demand of queries and facilitate various adaptive sampling techniques, which decrease the amount of transferred data. Moreover, we share sensor reads and data transfers among queries. Our experiments with real-world data show that our approach saves up to 87% in data transmissions in a practical use case.

## 1.2.2 Layer 2: Sensor Control (Chapter 3)

Stream analysis systems combine data streams from many distributed sensors to derive insights in real-time. Currently, these systems assume that sensor nodes have synchronized clocks, which assign accurate timestamps to measurements. However, this assumption does not hold in the IoT where diverse sensor nodes such as smart phones and single board computers are operated by many different organizations and users. In this case, sensor nodes may travel between timezones, use diverse synchronization techniques, and connect to different reference clocks. Thus, events with the same timestamps are not necessarily recorded at the exact same time and data tuples have an unknown *time incoherence*. This incoherence can lead to undetected application failures, such as false correlations and wrong predictions.

---
*Problem 3: Time Incoherence*

Sensor values from distributed sensors, which have the same timestamps, are not guaranteed to be recorded at the same time because sensor node clocks are affected by clock drifts, imprecise clock synchronization, and other failures.

---

In this thesis, we introduce time coherence as a fundamental data characteristic. Time coherence measures are an addition to common time synchronization techniques. They allow for monitoring the synchronization precision, for detecting synchronization failures, and for quantifying the imprecision of sensor node clocks. The *time coherence* of a data tuple is the time span in which all values contained in the tuple have been read from sensors. We explore concepts and algorithms to quantify and optimize the time coherence of sensor data tuples that combine values from a large number of distributed sensor nodes. For each tuple, we provide a guaranteed time coherence which is independent of clock synchronization among sensor nodes.

Current stream analysis systems combine data from many distributed sensors centrally. Thus, they receive individual sensor measures in the form $\langle time, value \rangle$ from many data steams and join them to tuples in the form $\langle t, v_1, \ldots, v_n \rangle$. This central correlation has four major issues: *(i)* it misses edge computing opportunities, *(ii)* it provides no time coherence guarantees, *(iii)* it relies on costly stream joins, and *(iv)* it results in a vast amount of parallel network connections at the streaming system.

---

**Problem 4: Scaling to huge Numbers of Sensors**

With the rise of the IoT, we aim to join measurements from thousands of sensors. Therefore, we are facing the performance limits of central stream joins with respect to throughput, latency, and network utilization.

---

We explore architectures for gathering data tuples from huge numbers of distributed sensors. Our technique adapts data gathering and processing pipelines automatically to optimize resource utilization and time coherence while maintaining guaranteed upper limits for time incoherence. We show that our solution scales to thousands of sensors, operates efficiently under latency and coherence constraints, adapts to changing network conditions automatically, and avoids central bottlenecks caused by stream joins.

### 1.2.3 Layer 3: Stream Analysis Systems (Chapter 4)

Our sensor control layer prevents a bottleneck caused by central stream joins (see above). Another bottleneck in stream analysis systems are window discretization and aggregation. Window aggregation is a redundancy-prone operation. Overlapping (sliding) windows and concurrent queries regularly share data and the corresponding aggregate computations. The many-to-many mapping between applications and sensors in the IoT makes this redundancy a critical problem which leads to an expensive system scale-out.

---

**Problem 5: Redundant Aggregate Computation**

Large computation overlaps caused by sliding windows and multiple concurrent queries lead to redundant computations which limit throughput and scalability.

---

Existing aggregation techniques focus on reducing latency, eliminating redundant computations, and minimizing memory usage. However, each technique operates under different assumptions with respect to workload characteristics such as properties of aggregation functions (e.g., invertible, associative), window types (e.g., sliding, sessions), windowing measures (e.g., time- or count-based), and stream (dis)order.

---
**Problem 6: Limited Applicability of Efficient Aggregation Techniques**

Existing efficient aggregation techniques are limited by different assumptions with respect to workload characteristics. Violating the assumptions of a technique can deem it unusable or drastically reduce its performance.

---

In this thesis, we introduce a general technique for window aggregation based on the concept of stream slicing. Our technique automatically adapts to workload characteristics to improve performance without sacrificing its general applicability. As a prerequisite, we identify workload characteristics which affect the performance and applicability of aggregation techniques. Our experiments show that our general stream slicing technique outperforms alternative concepts by up to one order of magnitude. Our solution is generally applicable to all data flow systems which adopt a tuple-at-a-time processing model (e.g., Apache Storm, Apache Flink, and other Apache Beam-based systems).

## 1.2.4 Layer 4: Front-End Applications (Chapter 5)

Front-end applications for live data visualization experience the same issues as stream analysis systems with respect to massive amounts of streaming data in the IoT. The amount of available data frequently makes it impossible to visualize all data points at the same time in front-end applications.

---
**Problem 7: Visualization Overload**

Due to the massive amount of available real-time data, it is impossible to visualize all data points at the same time. Streaming data to front-end applications without appropriate pre-processing results in an overload which causes applications to crash.

---

Because we cannot visualize all data points at the same time, it is important to allow for interactive data exploration in the IoT. To this end, we need to connect front-end applications with pre-processing jobs, which run on stream analysis systems, in order to synchronize data pre-processing with changing visualization needs.

---

*Problem 8: Missing Interactivity*

Stream processing pipelines of current systems do not adapt to changing visualization needs. This makes it hard to allow for interactive and graphical data exploration without causing visualization overload and/or heavy cluster utilization.

---

We present $I^2$, an interactive development environment for front-end applications and corresponding pre-processing jobs. $I^2$ coordinates running cluster applications and corresponding visualizations such that only the currently depicted data points are processed and transferred. To this end, we generalize M4 [93], an algorithm for the visualization of time series, to enable real-time visualization of data streams. M4 is proven to be correct and minimal in terms of transferred data. Moreover, we show how cluster programs can adapt to changed visualization properties at runtime to allow interactive data exploration on data streams.

Our experiments show that the amount of transferred data, the memory utilization, the CPU load, and the frame rate remain constant when $I^2$ is active. Without $I^2$, the visualization becomes unresponsive due to the massive amount of arriving data which needs to be filtered and aggregated in dashboard applications.

## 1.3 High-Level Architecture

We provide an end-to-end architecture, which affects all layers of the infrastructure stack presented in Section 1.2. We present a novel system for operating sensor nodes (Layers ① and ②) and extend stream analysis systems (Layer ③) with novel algorithms to address new requirements posed by the IoT. Finally, we introduce an interactive development environment which connects front-end applications (Layer ④) with stream analysis systems (Layer ③). It is important to highlight that our architecture is modular. Thus, sensor nodes, sensor control, stream analysis systems, and front-end applications can run independently of each other but are connected through unified interfaces. The modular design allows for replacing layers (e.g., changing the stream analysis system) and for skipping layers (e.g., applications can also request data from sensor nodes directly). To simplify the explanation, we present our architecture based on an example processing pipeline (Figure 1.4 on Page 9).

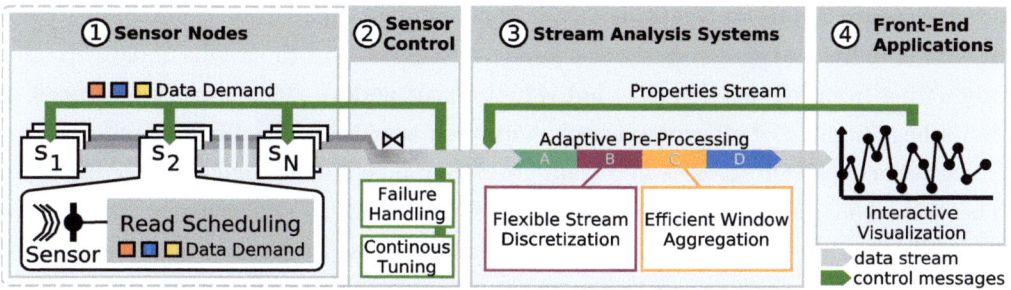

FIGURE 1.4: Architecture overview of on-demand data stream processing.

① **Sensor Nodes** ($s_1$, $s_2$, ..., $s_N$) are the origin of data streams ( ) (left of Figure 1.4) and transmit live sensor data to upstream layers of our infrastructure stack. The core of each sensor node is a sensor read scheduler (shown for $s_2$) which decides when to read values from sensors and when to transmit them. We introduce an on-demand scheduling technique which produces tailored data streams based on data demands ( ) expressed by data consumers. For each sensor, we perform read scheduling such that sensor reads and corresponding network traffic are shared among users and queries. One of our contributions is to unify the way in which data consumers express their data demands. In Figure 1.4, the control layer ② derives and posts data demands as control messages ( ) based on performance metrics and observed failures. In general, any user, streaming system, or application can submit their data demand to any sensor node and will receive the requested data stream.

② **The Sensor Control Layer** manages the data acquisition from huge numbers of sensors located at distributed sensor nodes. Thereby, the control layer solves scalability and data quality issues which arise when operating huge numbers of sensors. The control layer continuously monitors performance metrics and trades latency and result precision against resource utilization making sure that all application requirements are met.

The control layer arranges sensor nodes in pipelines to prevent scalability issues (Problem 4 in Section 1.2.2). As part of the control layer, we join (⋈) sensor values $(v_1, v_2, \ldots, v_N)$ from distributed nodes $(s_1, s_2, \ldots, s_N)$ to combined sensor data tuples in the form $\langle t, v_1, v_2, \ldots, v_N \rangle$. Our solutions supports acquisitional query processing [120] to apply data transformations within sensor node pipelines. For example, one can compute spatial aggregates [43, 63, 156] to receive result tuples in the form $\langle t, agg(v_1, v_2, \ldots, v_N) \rangle$. Each result tuple provides a time coherent snapshot of sensor values taken at time $t$.

③ **Stream Analysis Systems** receive coherent data tuples from a joint input stream instead of individual sensor values scattered over hundreds or thousands of data streams originating from IoT devices (i.e., individual sensor nodes). This prevents the need to join a huge number of streams centrally and, thus, avoids a central bottleneck.

Another typical bottleneck in stream processing pipelines are temporal aggregations. The IoT trend poses new challenges in this context: Many concurrently running application (i.e., queries) aggregate the input stream based on many different window specifications (e.g., different sliding windows [83], session windows [5], user-defined window [36], and data-driven windows [75]). We solve these challenges with a multi-query windowing ( B ) and aggregation (  ) framework which is highly efficient and flexible with respect to window types. Our solution shares partial aggregates among all queries, including all window types, and thereby prevents redundant computation steps. We conduct an extensive experimental evaluation which shows that our solution scales seamlessly to thousands of concurrent windows and outperforms existing solutions by one order of magnitude in terms of throughput.

④ **Front-End Applications** such as browser-based dashboards and smart phone apps visualize live-data and allow for monitoring current events. However, front-end applications cannot display all available IoT data at the same time because the amount of data would immediately overload the visualization application. Thus, front-end applications rely on data pre-processing steps ( A B C D ) such as filtering and aggregation which are performed on stream analysis systems. We present $I^2$, an interactive environment for visualization supported development of stream analysis applications. $I^2$ establishes an interface between stream analysis systems and front-end applications. Through this interface, front-end applications propagate current visualization properties (  ) to running pre-processing jobs in stream analysis systems. This enables stream analysis systems ③ to pre-process data adaptively and to minimize the output data with respect to visualization needs. We introduce a four step data reduction ( A B C D ): The first step handles data arriving out-of-order ( A ). The second step discretizes the stream to windows ( B ), before windows are aggregated in the third step (  ). Finally, we apply an additional data compression ( D ). With $I^2$, users can explore live data in an interactive visualization while pre-processing jobs adapt at runtime to data demands of the visualization and deliver tailored data streams.

## 1.4 Impact of Thesis Contributions

**Research Publications.** The primary results of this thesis have been presented in the following peer-reviewed publications at international top-tier venues:

1. **Jonas Traub, Sebastian Breß, Tilmann Rabl, Asterios Katsifodimos, Volker Markl:** *Optimized On-Demand Data Streaming from Sensor Nodes.* ACM Symposium on Cloud Computing (SoCC), 2017.

2. **Jonas Traub, Julius Hülsmann, Tim Stullich, Sebastian Breß, Tilmann Rabl, and Volker Markl:** *SENSE: Scalable Data Acquisition from Distributed Sensors with Guaranteed Time Coherence.* https://arxiv.org/abs/1912.04648, 2019.

3. **Jonas Traub, Philipp Grulich, Alejandro Rodríguez Cuéllar, Sebastian Breß, Asterios Katsifodimos, Tilmann Rabl, Volker Markl:** *Efficient Window Aggregation with General Stream Slicing.* International Conference on Extending Database Technology (EDBT), 2019.

4. **Jonas Traub, Philipp M. Grulich, Alejandro Rodríguez Cuellar, Sebastian Breß, Asterios Katsifodimos, Tilmann Rabl, Volker Markl:** *Scotty: Efficient Window Aggregation for out-of-order Stream Processing.* IEEE International Conference on Data Engineering (ICDE), 2018.

5. **Jonas Traub, Nikolaas Steenbergen, Philipp M Grulich, Tilmann Rabl, Volker Markl:** $I^2$*: Interactive Real-Time Visualization for Streaming Data.* International Conference on Extending Database Technology (EDBT), 2017.

**Research Talks.** Parts of the work on *Optimized On-Demand Data Streaming from Sensor Nodes* (Chapter 2) have also been presented at the 2nd BMBF Big Data All Hands Meeting (BDAHM) and the 2nd Smart Data Innovation Conference (SDIC) 2017 at KIT Karlsruhe (joint conferences), at the Stream Reasoning Workshop 2018 at the University of Zurich (UZH), and in several invited talks at international universities.

Parts of the work on stream discretization and window aggregation presented in Chapter 4 have also been presented at the FlinkForward Berlin conference 2018. The $I^2$ development environment presented in Chapter 5 was also presented at the FlinkForward Berlin conference 2017. These talks at developer conferences bridge the gap between research and practice and support the adoption of our contributions in industry.

**Open Source Contributions.** Our general and efficient window discretization and aggregation technique (Chapter 4) addresses an urgent need in industry [29, 170, 199] and is available as an open source framework which can be connected to diverse streaming engines including Apache Flink and Apache Beam. Our $I^2$ development environment (Chapter 5) comes as a ready-to-run Docker container and was implemented as an open source project based on Apache Flink [35] and Apache Zeppelin [12]:

- **General Stream Slicing with the Scotty Window Processor:**
  Project Website: `https://tu-berlin-dima.github.io/scotty-window-processor/`
  Open Source Repository: `https://github.com/TU-Berlin-DIMA/scotty-window-processor`

- **The $I^2$ Development Environment for Interactive Real-Time Visualization:**
  Project Website: `https://tu-berlin-dima.github.io/i2/`
  Open Source Repository: `https://github.com/TU-Berlin-DIMA/i2`
  Docker Hub: `https://hub.docker.com/r/tuberlindima/i2/`

Our sensor control software (Chapter 3) is the first to our knowledge, which provides guaranteed upper bounds for the time incoherence within sensor data tuples and continuously optimizes time coherence based on current network conditions and failures. In combination with our on-demand scheduler for sensor reads and data transmissions (Chapter 2), we provide a complete solution for efficient sensor data gathering and transmission in the IoT [181]. We plan to release our read scheduler and our sensor control software as an open source library, which will become part of the NebulaStream platform for application and data management in the IoT [206].

**Summary.** The contributions made in this thesis are highly relevant for emerging IoT databases which need to bridge the gap between data acquisition and data processing to solve scalability issues. Our examples show great potential with respect to resource savings, scalability, and sensor management. Our open source releases allow for integrating the system components presented in this thesis into novel IoT database systems as well as existing stream processing systems. Our research publications provide a basis for future research. For example, one can investigate optimal implementations of user-defined sampling functions, extend our failure handling mechanisms, or invent new benchmarks for demand-based data stream gathering, processing, and transmission.

## 1.5    Structure of the Thesis

**Chapter 1 - Introduction**

Chapter 1 gave an introduction to the thesis by presenting the thesis objectives and a high-level overview of our solution architecture. For each layer of our architecture, we outlined the research problems and our contributions. We closed the introduction with a description of the impact of the thesis contributions.

**Chapter 2 - Optimized On-Demand Data Streaming from Sensor Nodes**

Chapter 2 focuses on the sensor node layer. We address the problem of *oversampling on sensor nodes* and provide the *missing adaptivity* to sampling techniques. We introduce *user-defined sampling functions* to express data demands and optimize sensor read times to share sensor values and traffic among users and queries.

**Chapter 3 - Scalable Data Acquisition with Guaranteed Time Coherence**

Chapter 3 introduces a sensor control layer to orchestrate large numbers of sensor nodes. Besides scalability challenges, Chapter 3 addresses the problem of *time incoherence*. We introduce time coherence as data characteristic of sensor data tuples and provide synchronization independent coherence guarantees.

**Chapter 4 - Efficient Window Aggregation with General Stream Slicing**

Chapter 4 addresses window discretization and aggregation which is a major bottleneck of stream analysis systems. We prevent *repeated aggregate computation* by sharing partial aggregates among all users and queries. Our aggregation technique is more general than existing solutions and drastically improves throughput.

**Chapter 5 - Interactive Real-Time Visualization for Streaming Data**

Chapter 5 connects front-end applications and stream analysis systems. We present the $I^2$ development environment which addresses the problem of *visualization overload* and enables the *interactive exploration* of streaming data. $I^2$ eases the development and operation of live dashboard and corresponding pre-processing jobs.

**Chapter 6 - Additional Contributions**

Chapter 6 lists additional related research contributions of the author, which have been made while working on this thesis, but are not covered in other chapters.

**Chapter 7 - Conclusion**

Chapter 7 concludes the thesis and provides an outlook to future work.

# 2

# Optimized On-Demand Data Streaming from Sensor Nodes

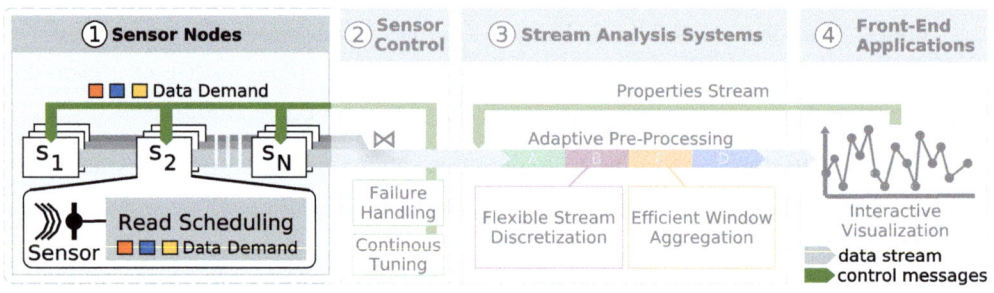

FIGURE 2.1: Scope of Chapter 2 - Read Scheduling on Sensor Nodes.

In this chapter, we focus on sensor nodes as foundation of our end-to-end architecture. We aim to make our sensor node system generally applicable. To this end, we introduce a read scheduler which works as source of sensor data streams: it reads (pulls) data from physical sensors and streams (pushes) that data to upstream processing pipelines. Any user, application, or sensor control systems can request live sensor data through our scheduler. Thus, we allow for sharing sensor nodes among many data consumers. Our scheduler multiplexes all requests and shares sensor reads and corresponding network traffic among all consumers to save costs. We present different examples where users and applications request data from sensor nodes directly. In Chapter 3, we will use the same read scheduler as part of our control layer that manages many sensor nodes.

## 2.1 Introduction

Billions of devices are equipped with sensors to supply data analysis applications with real-time data [193]. The resulting vast amount of data streams causes heavy network utilization and scalability challenges, which incur increased financial costs. Currently, sensor data analysis follows a monolithic architecture with a tight coupling of applications to sensors. However, the IoT works as a *sensor cloud* in which huge numbers of sensors are shared among huge numbers of applications. This requires us to break away from monolithic architectures and to introduce a new architecture that decouples sensor management from introducing new applications. In this chapter, we present how applications can express their data demands and how sensor nodes can produce tailored data streams according to these demands. Our solution addresses the problems of *over-sampling on sensor nodes* and *missing adaptivity*, which we introduced in Section 1.2.1.

Data requirements differ significantly among applications. For example, outlier detection requires high sampling frequencies and has low selectivity in local filters at the sensor node. The opposite is true for monitoring a long term trend in time series, which has a low sampling frequency and does not apply local filters. These varying requirements (i.e., the diversity of data demands) makes it challenging to prevent oversampling.

*Periodic sampling* reads and transfers data with a fixed frequency. This is insufficient due to *missing adaptivity*: adaptive sampling techniques dynamically adjust sampling rates depending on the variance within recent samples [59, 67, 71, 186]. With adaptive sampling, we retrieve detailed data (high sampling rate) from sensors which experience anomalies. However, most sensors do not experience anomalies at the moment and reduce their sampling rates. Thus, we can reduce sensor reads, data transmissions, and processing effort for the majority of sensors to save resources.

Adaptive sampling techniques provide good approximations of time series with significantly reduced average sampling rates compared to periodic sampling. However, adaptive sampling is impractical for other use-cases such as outlier or failure detection. There is no *one-for-all* sampling technique, which at the same time serves all queries and prevents oversampling. The naive approach to set up a smart sampling technique for each query independently is not satisfying either. It might avoid oversampling for one query, but it disregards commonalities between multiple queries, which from a global point of view, again causes *oversampling* and *redundant data transmissions*.

Current real-time analysis platforms do not take control of the production of their input streams [35, 177]. Instead, they rely on techniques such as load shedding [174] and back pressure handling [38], to avoid system crashes when data rates increase. Both techniques run centrally, after transferring the data from sensor nodes to a stream analysis system. Thus, they neither prevent oversampling nor redundant data transmissions.

Common sensor networks such as TinyDB [121] and Cougar [50] compile queries locally at a base station and then disseminate them to sensor nodes. Thereby, they focus on the optimization of a *single query*. Our architecture complements existing sensor networks by enabling the sharing of sensor reads and traffic costs among queries.

In this chapter, we introduce *on-demand streaming from sensor nodes*. While we make all data accessible, the amount of read and transferred data solely depends on the demand of executed queries instead of the amount of available data.

Our solution consists of two components: **First,** we solve the *oversampling problem* using *user-defined sampling functions (UDSFs)*. UDSFs allow for publishing the data demand of queries to data gathering components, which can then provide well orchestrated data streams. UDSFs are highly flexible, easy to implement, and keep the complexity of multi-query optimization transparent to the user. **Second,** we prevent *redundant transmissions* with an algorithm for *multi-query read scheduling*, which is executed at the sensor nodes. Our algorithm executes the minimum possible number of sensor reads only. Therefore, it shares sensor reads and traffic among queries and optimizes the times when sensor reads are performed. Summarizing, our contributions are as follows:

1. We introduce *user-defined sampling functions (UDSFs)* to overcome the *missing adaptivity* of periodic sampling and to avoid *oversampling*.

2. We contribute a *multi-query read scheduling algorithm*, which enables frequent read and traffic sharing among queries to avoid *redundant data transmissions*.

3. We further *optimize read times* based on given read time preferences while still executing only the *minimum number of reads* in total.

4. We experimentally validate our approach and show its effectiveness in a practical setting.

In the remainder of this chapter, we present a motivating example in Section 2.2 and explain backgrounds in Section 2.3. We show our architecture in Section 2.4 and introduce UDSFs in Section 2.5. Section 2.6 presents our scheduling algorithm. We present our theoretical analysis in Section 2.7 and our experimental evaluation in Section 2.8.

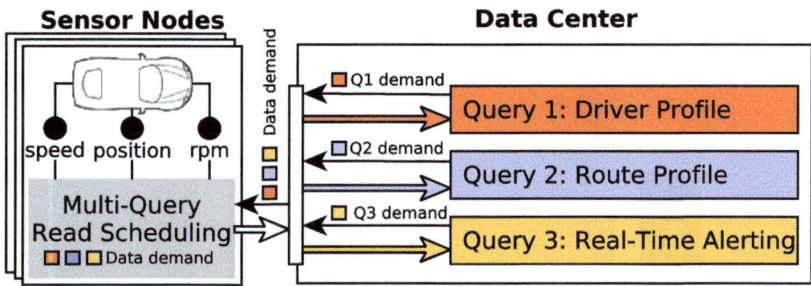

FIGURE 2.2: Multi-query read scheduling provides tailored data streams based on the data demand of queries.

## 2.2 A Motivating Example

We show our solution with an example in Figure 2.2. We use floating-car data[1] to provide alerts to drivers ahead of dangerous locations, which often cause heavy braking (e.g., tight curves or animal crossings). Similar assistance systems use floating car data for green light optimal speed control [143] and online traffic estimation [148].

Three queries are required in our example: Query 1 retrieves data to train a driver profile with a machine learning technique. Query 2 retrieves data to train a route profile. Query 3 combines route and driver profiles with current telemetry data to detect exceptional situations, which then leads to alerts.

Each query has a different data demand: Query 1 observes the aggressiveness of drivers (intensity of breaking and acceleration). Therefore, it adaptively increases sampling rates when accelerating or braking. Query 2 requires a sample at least every 20 meters to profile the road and, therefore, computes the next sensor read time as $t = \frac{20m}{\text{current speed}}$. Query 3 requires a sample at least every 0.3s.

We simulate our example with telemetry data from Formula 1 cars. Therefore, we replay sensor data from the fastest qualifying laps of 32 Formula 1 races in 2015 and 2016 with a 30Hz sampling rate. We utilize tolerances in sensor read times: Query 1 uses adaptive sampling with ±0.2s read time tolerance. Query 2 and 3 enforce minimum sampling rates, but allow higher rates.

Each query defines its data demand and read time tolerances in a UDSF. UDSFs empower domain experts to specify the data demand without specifying details of the

---

[1] *"The floating car data technology is a relatively new approach to collect traffic data. In contrast to usual approaches vehicles which float with the traffic stream are used as sensors to give information about the traffic states."* [184]

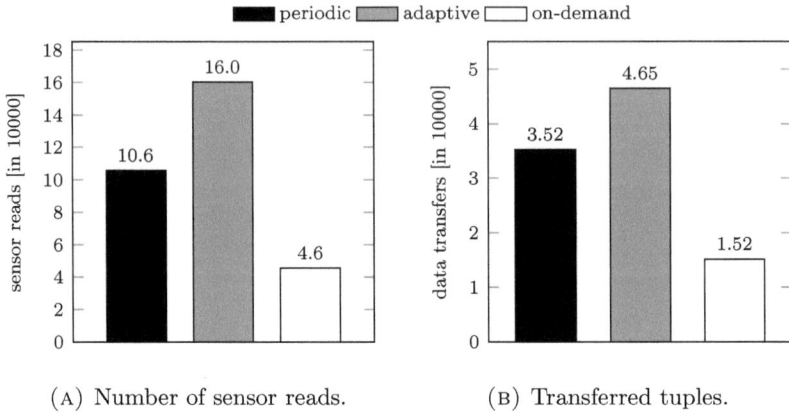

(A) Number of sensor reads.        (B) Transferred tuples.

FIGURE 2.3:  Sensor reads and transferred tuples for our introductory
use-case on Formula 1 data.

query execution. For example, we use domain knowledge to determine proper tolerance
intervals for read times. We found that ±0.2s read time tolerance for Query 1 provides
the best trade-off between result accuracy and savings achieved through read sharing.

We show the number of sensor reads and data transfers in Figure 2.3. *Periodic*
sampling falls back to the highest sampling rate which is requested by any UDSF at any
time. This results in more than 100 thousand sensor reads. *On-Demand* scheduling saves
57% in sensor reads compared to *periodic* sampling because it can adapt sampling rates at
runtime. *Adaptive* sampling can reduce sampling rates most of the time. However, when
executing queries independently, adaptivity does not make up for the missed opportunity
to share sensor reads among the queries. Respectively, *on-Demand* scheduling saves 72%
of the sensor reads compared to executing queries independently. In addition, on-demand
scheduling prevents thrashing when many queries require values from the same sensor
by sharing sensor values among queries.

We combine values from three sensors (speed, position, and rpm) in each tuple. Thus,
the number of transferred tuples is about one third of the number of sensor reads. The
increased tuple width has no significant effect on the transfer costs because a tuple still
fits in one network package. The payload data of the package (one to three values) is
small compared to the package header. The workload for initiating and acknowledging
the transfer of a package exceeds the workload for transferring the actual payload data
by far. This leads to significant savings in transfer costs when we reduce the number

of transferred tuples. In addition to combining three values in each tuple, we avoid transfers with adaptive filtering. We discuss adaptive filtering in detail in Section 2.5.5.

The reduction in data transmissions would cut charges for mobile network usage when monitoring a fleet of cars. Additionally, the reduced inbound traffic at a central analysis cluster prevents scale-out fees of cloud providers.

## 2.3 Background

Before we discuss *UDSFs* and our *multi-query read scheduling algorithm*, we provide an overview of sensor data transfer, adaptive sampling, and usage scenarios.

### 2.3.1 Pull- and Push-Based Data Transfer

A major difference between batch processing (analysis of data at rest) and stream processing (real-time analysis) is the way data transfers are initiated. MapReduce [49] systems and relational databases process previously stored data when they execute a query. Thus, they can pull data from disk as needed, for example, using the iterator model. In contrast, stream processing systems have no control over incoming streams, which can push data into the system at an arbitrary rate.

We combine push- and pull-based data transfer: on the one hand, we pull data from sensors[2] based on the data demand of queries. On the other hand, we asynchronously push data through the stream processing pipeline, which enables low latency processing.

*UDSFs* and our *read scheduling algorithm* are applicable wherever data is pulled from a source. This, for example, also holds for service APIs such as *Twitter Streaming* or *Google Cloud Prediction*. Avoiding oversampling on these APIs directly results in financial savings because charges apply per API call [73].

### 2.3.2 Adaptive Sampling

Adaptive sampling techniques such as AdaM [186], FAST [59], and L-SIP [67] reduce oversampling compared to periodic sampling. They reduce sampling rates on the fly whenever values evolve predictably or remain constant. At the same time, they increase sampling rates as required, to not exceed failure tolerances.

---

[2]We refer to physical sensors, such as photo cells or accelerometers, as *sensors*, and call the devices which host sensors *sensor nodes*.

─── *Definition: Periodic Sampling vs. Adaptive Sampling* ────────────

We adopt the definitions of *periodic sampling* and *adaptive sampling* from Trihinas et al. [186]: "For a metric stream M, *periodic sampling* is the process of triggering the collection mechanisms of a monitored source every $T$ time units. $T$ is a fixed interval, such that the $i$-th sample is collected at time $t_i = i \cdot T$ [...]

Adaptive sampling is the process of dynamically adjusting the sampling period $T_i$, based on some function, denoted as $\rho(M)$, containing information of the metric stream evolution (e.g. a moving average)." In our case, the *monitored source* is a sensor and $M$ is a stream of values collected (i.e., read) from that sensor.

─── *Formal Definition of the Adaptive Sampling Problem* ────────────

We adopt the formal definition of the adaptive sampling problem from Trihinas et al. [186]: Let $s_i(t_i, v_i)$ be the latest ($i$-th) sample read from a sensor with the timestamp $t_i$ (read time) and the value $v_i$. Let $T$ accept integer values (time units) in a range $[T_{min}, T_{max}] \subseteq \mathbb{Z}^+$ without loss of generality. We compare a metric stream $M$, consisting of periodic samples read every $T_{min}$ time units, with a stream $M'$ retrieved with adaptive sampling. We say that *dist* is the difference between $M$ and $M'$ according to some distance metric.

"The goal of adaptive sampling is to provide a sampling function $f(\cdot)$, capable of finding the maximum $T \in [T_{min}, T_{max}]$ to collect $s_{i+1}$, based on an estimation of the metric stream evolution $\rho(M)$, such that $M'$ differs from $M$ less than an imprecision value $\gamma$ ($dist<\gamma$) for the range $t \in [t_i, t_i + T]$. Thus, the problem is summarized with the following equation:

$$T^* = \underset{T}{\mathrm{argmax}}\{f(s, T, \rho(M), dist, \gamma) \mid dist < \gamma, T \in [T_{min}, T_{max}]\}" \text{ [186]}$$

Different use cases require different adaptive sampling techniques: for example, AdaM [186] is robust against abrupt value fluctuations and provides good approximations of time series. FAST [59], on the other hand, incorporates concepts of differential privacy for real-time aggregate monitoring. Our read scheduler allows for multiplexing different adaptive sampling algorithms in parallel on shared sensors to enable reduced average sampling rates. We implement AdaM and FAST as examples for adaptive sampling techniques. Both combine adaptive sampling with adaptive filtering. However, the algorithms differ fundamentally from each other: AdaM uses *Probabilistic Exponential Weighted Moving Averages* [37] for value estimations while FAST adopts a *Proportianal Integral Derivate* controller [130]. It is not required to understand the mathematical details of AdaM and FAST to follow the remainder of this thesis. However, we provide formal definitions of adaptive sampling, AdaM, and FAST on the next pages.

---

*A̲daptive M̲onitoring Framework (AdaM)* [186, 187]

AdaM provides an adaptive sampling algorithm which calculates $T_{i+1}$ with $O(1)$ time and space complexity. AdaM computes $T_{i+1}$ as follows:

$$T_{i+1} = \begin{cases} T_i + \lambda \cdot (1 + \frac{c_i - \gamma}{c_i}) & c_i \geq 1 - \gamma \\ T_{min} & \text{otherwise.} \end{cases}$$

$\lambda$ is a multiplication factor which may be set by users to adjust the aggressiveness of the adaptation. AdaM uses a Probabilistic Exponential Weighted Moving Average (PEWMA) [37] to compute a one-step ahead prediction for sensor values. $c_i$ denotes the confidence of this prediction. To compute $c_i$, AdaM first estimates a (moving) standard deviation ($\hat{\sigma}_i$) between predicted sensor values and actual sensor values. When reading a sensor value, AdaM computes $c_i = 1 - (|\hat{\sigma}_i - \sigma_i|)/\sigma_i$, which is the ratio between the failure of predicted standard deviation and the actual observed standard deviation. "The semantics behind the confidence are: *The more confident the algorithm is, the larger the outputted sampling period $T_{i+1}$ can be.*" [186]

---

<u>F</u>*iltering and <u>A</u>daptive <u>S</u>ampling for*
<u>D</u>*ifferentially Private <u>T</u>ime Series Monitoring (FAST)* [58, 59, 60, 61]

FAST includes an adaptive sampling component, which uses a *Proportional-Integral-Derivative (PID)* controller [9, 17, 18, 130] to adapt the sampling interval $T$. PID controllers are a common technique for feedback control in industry and research [57, 107, 197]. We now briefly explain a PID controller and show how it is used by FAST. We omit details about *differential privacy* in FAST to simplify the explanation and refer the reader to the original publication for a complete specification [58]. Some notations in the following description have been changed from the original ones to be consistent with our definitions of *adaptive sampling* and *AdaM* (see above).

A **PID controller** aims to achieve a desired result (e.g., a desired speed) by continuously adjusting a configuration (e.g., acceleration). The controller uses an error (e.g., the difference between desired and current speed) to calculate three terms: the *proportional (P)*, *integral (I)*, and *derivative (D)* term.

<u>P</u> is proportional to the current error. The larger the error, the larger the configuration change. <u>I</u> integrates over past values of the error. Thus, the longer an error persists, the larger the configuration change. <u>D</u> operates based on the change in the error. The smaller the change, the more dampening occurs to prevent overshooting.

**FAST** uses a *Kalmann Filter Prediction* procedure [94] to compute a prediction $(x_{i-1})$ of the metric evolution of $M$. After reading a new value, a *correction* mechanism updates $x_{i-1}$ to $x_i$. The error between $x_{i-1}$ and $x_i$ is calculated as follows:

$$E_i = |x_{i-1} - x_i| \ / \ x_i$$

The error $E_i$ is the input of the PID-Controller used by FAST:

$$\Delta_T = \underbrace{C_p E_i}_{\underline{P}roportional} + \underbrace{\frac{C_i}{k} \sum_{j=i-k}^{i} E_j}_{\underline{I}ntegral} + \underbrace{C_d \frac{E_i - E_{i-1}}{T_i}}_{\underline{D}erivative}$$

Thereby, $k$ is the number of previous error values which is considered in the integral term. $C_p$, $C_i$, and $C_d$ specify the weight of the proportional, integral, and derivative term. The result ($\Delta_T$) and two pre-configured interval adjustment parameters ($\theta$ and $\xi$) allow for computing $T_{i+1}$ as follows:

$$T_{i+1} = T_i + \theta(1 - e^{\frac{\Delta_T - \xi}{\xi}})$$

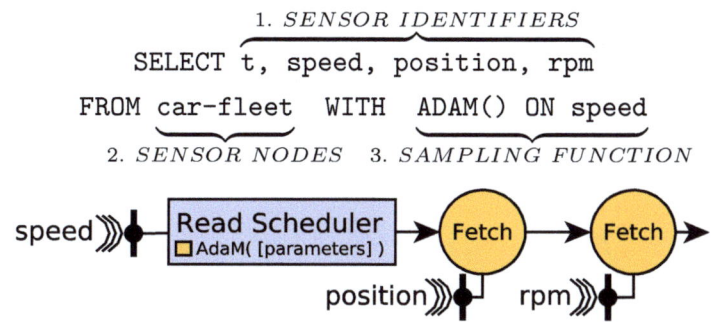

FIGURE 2.4: An example query with user-defined sampling and its corresponding processing pipeline.

### 2.3.3 The User's Perspective

It is important to highlight that the complexity of multi-query read scheduling is transparent to users. Users can still define streaming queries in declarative languages such as CQL [13] or SPL [81]. From the perspective of a user, a data stream consists of tuples $\langle t, v_1, v_2, ..., v_n \rangle$ where $t$ is the timestamp of a tuple and $v_1$ to $v_n$ are the values from all available sensors at time $t$.

#### 2.3.3.1 Data Acquisition from Sensor Nodes

We show an example query with its corresponding processing pipeline in Figure 2.4. The query acquires a data stream of tuples in the format $\langle t, v_1, v_2, ..., v_n \rangle$ as specified above. Based on this stream, one can compute a driver profile in accordance to our introductory example (Figure 2.2 on Page 17). We omit a more complex profiling algorithm for the sake of simplicity. The query consists of three parts:

1. Sensors are referenced by identifiers similar to column names in SQL.
2. Instead of tables, we refer to sensor nodes as data sources in the FROM clause.
3. We add a WITH clause to specify a UDSF and the sensor it is applied to.

The user specifies the data demand of the query by implementing a UDSF or choosing a pre-defined one. This empowers domain experts to express their data demand flexibly and also enables adaptive sampling techniques. We explain UDSFs in Section 2.5.

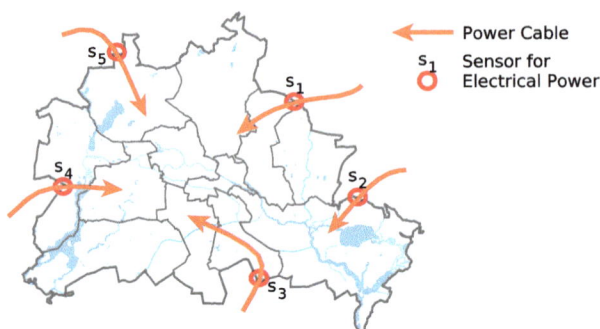

FIGURE 2.5: Example: Measuring the energy expenditure of Berlin.

The processing pipeline of the query starts with the read scheduler, which uses AdaM to sample the speed sensor. It then fetches the position and the revolutions per minute (rpm) in an ad-hoc fashion in order to construct the output tuples. This is regularly beneficial because we reduce sampling rates in comparison to periodic sampling with a constant rate. In this chapter, we focus on UDSFs and the functionality of the Read Scheduler to acquire values from a single sensor node.

### 2.3.3.2   Spatial and Temporal Aggregation

An aggregation is a combination of multiple values in a single summary. In our example query in Figure 2.4, we concatenate values from three sensors to one tuple, which is a *spatial aggregation*, i.e., a summary of values from different sources. We differentiate *spatial* and *temporal* aggregations. A *temporal* aggregation is a summary of values over time. For example, we can monitor the speed sensor with our query in Figure 2.4 and use a stream analysis system to compute the average speed for some time interval.

We now present an example for combining data acquisition with spatial and temporal aggregation. Figure 2.5 shows a map of Berlin. In this example, the power grid of Berlin is connected to Berlin's neighboring state Brandenburg with five major power cables. On each of these cables, a sensor monitors the electrical power in Watt (W). If we compute the sum of the values of all five sensors at some point in time, we get the combined electrical power at that time in Watt (spatial aggregation). If we monitor the electrical power over a course of time, we can derive the energy expenditure for that course of time in watt-hours (Wh) (temporal aggregation). The following declarative query combines spatial and temporal aggregation to compute an energy expenditure for each hour (one hour tumbling window):

$$\overbrace{\text{SELECT AVG}}^{\textit{Temporal Aggregation Function}}\underbrace{(v_1 + \cdots + v_5)}_{\textit{Spatial Aggregation}}\text{ FROM }\underbrace{s_1, \cdots, s_5}_{\textit{Sensor Nodes}}\text{ WITH }\underbrace{\text{PERIODIC(1s)}}_{\textit{Sampling Function}}\overbrace{\text{WINDOW 1h}}^{\textit{Temporal Window}}$$

Based on the query above, the system acquires and aggregates values as follows:

| $t$ | $v_1$ | $v_2$ | $\cdots$ | $v_5$ |
|---|---|---|---|---|
| 12:00:01 | 5kW | 5kW | $\cdots$ | 9kW |
| 12:00:02 | 3kW | 5kW | $\cdots$ | 8kW |
| $\vdots$ | $\vdots$ | $\vdots$ | $\ddots$ | $\vdots$ |
| 12:59:59 | 7kW | 5kW | $\cdots$ | 4kW |

$\xRightarrow[\text{aggregation}]{\text{spatial}}$

| $t$ | $\sum_{n=1}^{5} v_n$ |
|---|---|
| 12:00:01 | 26kW |
| 12:00:02 | 28kW |
| $\vdots$ | $\vdots$ |
| 12:59:59 | 24kW |

$\xRightarrow[\text{aggregation}]{\text{temporal}}$ 25kWh

One can observe that the system supports combining temporal and and spatial aggregations in a declarative query. It remains transparent to users if aggregations are performed on sensor nodes, in-network, or at a central analysis system. In Chapters 3 and 4, we discuss how the system actually performs aggregations: In Chapter 3, we introduce data acquisition pipelines which cover multiple sensors and can perform spatial aggregations. In Chapter 4, we optimize the performance of temporal aggregations, which are a typical bottleneck in stream analysis systems.

## 2.4 System Architecture

In this section, we present how *on-demand streaming from sensor nodes* eliminates unneccessary sensor reads and thus, data transmissions. In Figure 2.6a on Page 26, we illustrate how *on-demand streaming* integrates with streaming systems.

First, users submit their queries and their data demand (expressed by *UDSFs*) to a stream analysis cluster ①. We then propagate the UDSFs to the sensor nodes ②. To simplify the explanation in this chapter, we omit the the intermediate sensor control layer (Chapter 3) between stream analysis systems and sensor nodes. This layer uses the functionality of read scheduling on sensor nodes but does not require changes in the scheduling technique presented in this chapter. In general, any user, application, streaming system, control system, etc. can submit UDSFs to sensor nodes, which makes our technique generally applicable to diverse application scenarios.

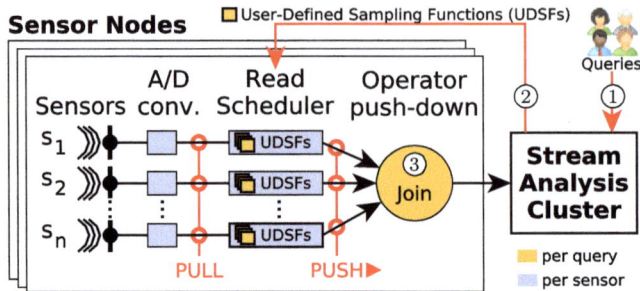

(A) Overall on-demand streaming architecture.

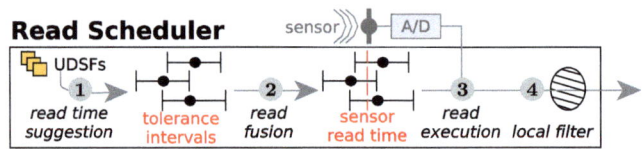

(B) Read scheduler internals.

FIGURE 2.6: On-demand streaming architecture.

For each sensor, we perform *read scheduling* in four phases (Figure 2.6b): *read time suggestion*, *read fusion*, *read execution*, and *local filtering*. First, during *read time suggestion* ①, each UDSF (provided with each query) proposes a read time with a tolerance interval. Second, during *read fusion* ②, we fuse proposed read times to a single sensor read, if the tolerance intervals overlap. Third, during *read execution* ③, we perform the actual read on the sensor. Finally, during *local filtering* ④, we determine if we need to transmit the obtained sensor value. We can, e.g., avoid transmitting values which are similar to previous ones or follow an expected trend.

*Read time suggestion* allows for *adaptive sampling* to avoid oversampling. This is especially important whenever charges apply per read (e.g., service API calls). *Read fusion* avoids redundant data transmissions and enables sensor read sharing among queries. It thereby reduces network charges. *Local filtering* further reduces data transmissions, which reduces the inbound traffic at the analysis cluster and prevents scalability issues.

**Complementary Techniques.** Our scheduler works complementary to the succeeding push-based processing pipeline (Figure 2.6a ③), which can consist of arbitrary stream transformations such as aggregations, filters, or stream joins [8, 45, 129]. It thereby goes hand-in-hand with techniques such as query fusion on sensor nodes [132, 200, 201], operator push-down, and *acquisitional query processing (ACQP)* [121]. The combination with ACQP is of special interest: we first apply read scheduling on a subset of sensors to avoid oversampling. We then further reduce the data with filters and aggregations. Finally, we fetch values from additional sensors for the remaining tuples only. We will discuss all mentioned techniques in more detail in Section 2.9.

**Alternative Architectures.** We study a setting were we execute read scheduling on sensor nodes. We tested our algorithms using Raspberry Pis and Android smart phones as sensor nodes and did not experience any performance problems. However, our read scheduler also works as a middleware layer which aggregates UDSFs (i.e. queries) at a more powerful machine close by the sensor nodes (i.e. a base station server or a router). Our read scheduler pulls values from sensors (i.e. it samples the sensor) on the fly based on the data demand expressed in UDSFs. This enables adaptive sampling but requires a low latency connection between the read scheduler and the sensor we sample.

## 2.5 User-Defined Sampling

Different applications may have contradicting sampling requirements. They may vary in sampling rates, may transfer different fractions of sensor values, and may have different requirements for read time precision and data freshness (maximum age of values arriving at the cluster).

*User-defined sampling functions (UDSFs)* allow for the precise definition of each query's data demand and facilitate *adaptive sampling* techniques. This makes them the basis for avoiding *oversampling*. They further model read time tolerances and preferences, which enables *read fusion* to solve the *redundant transmission problem*.

In the following section, we first discuss how we *enable read fusion* and *optimize sensor read times*. This leads to our model for the read times proposed by UDSFs (in short *read requests*). We then show how we can cover example applications with *UDSFs*. Finally, we introduce local filter functions to further reduce data transmissions.

### 2.5.1 Enabling Read and Traffic Sharing

Sampling techniques define exact times where values shall be read from sensors. The probability that we can fuse two requested reads (share sensor reads among queries) decreases with the read time precision and vice versa. In order to enable frequent

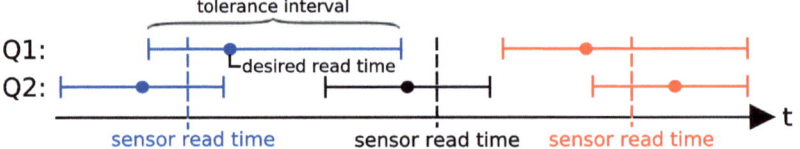

FIGURE 2.7: Example: Sharing sensor reads among two queries.

read fusion, applications have to specify their precision requirement for read times. We thus represent requested sensor reads (in short: *read requests*) as tolerance intervals instead of exact times. We share sensor reads as well as the corresponding traffic among queries whenever tolerance intervals overlap. For example, consider Figure 2.7: two queries periodically request sensor reads from the same sensor and we utilize read time tolerances to fuse requested reads.

For many use cases, a certain deviation from the desired read times (*read time slack*) is possible without harming the result quality. For example, consider a query which requires the current temperature every hour. This query does not require a nanosecond read time precision but can offer a tolerance, e.g., one minute. We found that sophisticated adaptive sampling techniques such as AdaM [186] and FAST [59] are robust against a certain slack in read times as we show in our experiments in Section 2.8.2.3.

## 2.5.2 Global Read Time Optimization

Our scheduling algorithm not only minimizes the number of sensor reads, it also optimizes the exact sensor read times. We provide semantics to model read time preferences by introducing penalty functions $(p(t))$. Each read request can define its individual penalty function to penalize read times within the tolerance interval which deviate from the desired (optimal) read time. Our optimizer minimizes the overall penalty when fusing read request of multiple queries to shared sensor reads.

For example, consider our introductory use case in Figure 2.2 on Page 17: Query 2 (Route Profile) requires a sample at least every 20 driven meters. Reading earlier is harmless and we can thus define our penalty function as $p(t) = 0$ (i.e., we do not apply any penalty for read time deviations). At the same time, we execute Query 1 (Driver Profile), which uses AdaM. In this case, read time slack might affect the result quality and thus we set $p(t) = t^2$. In general, we can set any penalty function that describes our

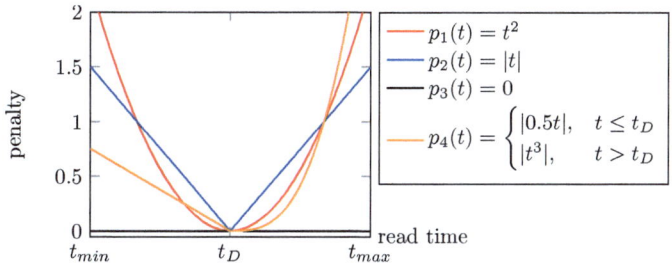

FIGURE 2.8: Examples for penalty functions.

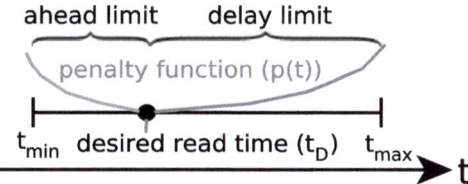

FIGURE 2.9: Read request with desired read time, tolerance interval, and
a convex penalty function.

read time preferences. In case of Query 1, we choose the quadratic function $t^2$ to avoid large deviations by penalizing them much more than smaller deviations.

In our example, the read time optimizer freely decides for a read time within the tolerance intervals of Query 2, because no penalty applies for deviating from the desired read time. At the same time, the optimizer minimizes the deviation from the desired read time for Query 1 to avoid the penalty of $t^2$.

Our optimizer minimizes the sum of the penalty functions for overlapping tolerance intervals. Thereby, it determines the next sensor read time. In order to enable the minimization at low computational costs, we require all penalty functions to be convex and to have their minimum at the desired read time ($t_D = 0$). We further shift penalty functions along the y-axis such that $p(t_D) = 0$. We show examples of supported penalty functions in Figure 2.8. Note that we can relax the definition of convex functions and allow functions which are non-differentiable at the desired read time $t_D$. We present the optimization process in detail in Section 2.6.

### 2.5.3  Modelling Read Requests

As a result of the considerations from the previous sections, we model *read requests* as illustrated in Figure 2.9 on Page 29:

- Each requested read is described by a tolerance interval $[t_{min}, t_{max}]$, which covers the desired read time $t_D$.

- The distance between $t_{min}$ and $t_D$ is the tolerance for reading ahead of $t_D$. Respectively, the distance from $t_D$ to $t_{max}$ is the tolerance to delay the read.

- Within each interval, read time preferences are modelled with a penalty function.

Our scheduling algorithm first minimizes the total number of executed sensor reads based on interval overlaps. This minimizes costs implied by sensor reads and data transmissions. It then optimizes the exact read times based on the given penalty functions. UDSFs can adjust read time tolerances and penalty functions for each read request.

### 2.5.4  User-Defined Sampling Functions

**Syntax.** Formula 2.1 shows the structure of a *user-defined sampling function (UDSF)*. Upon a sensor read, the function receives the current timestamp $t$ and the current sensor value $v$. In exchange, it returns a tuple $\langle t_{min}, t_D, t_{max}, p(t) \rangle$. The output tuple corresponds to our model for read requests and consists of the next desired read time $t_D$, the tolerance interval $[t_{min}, t_{max}]$, and the penalty function $p(t)$.

$$s : \langle t, v \rangle \rightarrow \langle t_{min}, t_D, t_{max}, p(t) \rangle$$

FORMULA 2.1: User-defined sampling function.

At any time, we only require the next read request from a sampling function. This allows for adapting sampling rates, read time tolerances, and penalty functions flexibly after each sensor read. We allow sampling functions to keep a state because many sampling techniques need to remember previous sensor values or variables. Sampling functions can access their own state and the state of associated local filter functions (Section 2.5.5).

**Examples.** The presented sampling function is easy to implement and facilitates various use-cases. Let us first consider our introductory example (Figure 2.2 on Page 17). Example 2.1 on Page 31 shows the sampling function serving Query 1 (Driver Profile). It also shows how the AdaM algorithm, as a representative for adaptive sampling functions, can be integrated in a UDSF. The call to the AdaM algorithm in Line 2 can be replaced with any other adaptive sampling algorithm. The shown implementation constantly applies a read time tolerance of $\pm 0.2s$ and a linear penalty function $p(t) = |t|$.

1: **upon sensor read** $\langle time, value \rangle$ **do**
2:      $t_D \leftarrow AdaM(time, value)$ // *get next read time*
3:      $t_{min} \leftarrow max(time, t_D - 0.2s)$ // *get ahead limit*
4:      $t_{max} \leftarrow t_D + 0.2s$ // *get delay limit*
5:      $p(t) \leftarrow abs(t - t_D)$ // *set penalty function*
6:      **return** $\langle t_{min}, t_D, t_{max}, p(t) \rangle$
7: **end**

EXAMPLE 2.1: AdaM with 0.2s read time tolerance.

One major advantage of user-defined sampling is the ability to adapt sampling rates driven by the values gathered before. Query 2 (Route Profile) from Figure 2.2 is an example for a case where we need an application specific data-driven sampling function: we require a value for at least every 20 meters driven. With periodic sampling, we would need to always assume the maximum speed of the car and set the time between two sensor reads to be $\frac{20m}{max(v)}$. However, cars seldom drive with their maximum speed and periodic sampling would cause *oversampling* during all the remaining time.

$$s_{20m} : \langle t, v \rangle \rightarrow \langle t + 1, t + \tfrac{20m}{v}, t + \tfrac{20m}{v}, 0 \rangle$$

EXAMPLE 2.2: Sample at least every 20 driven meter.

In contrast to periodic sampling, our user-defined function in Example 2.2 can calculate the next read time based on the current speed upon each sensor read. We further configured $t_{min}$ as the current timestamp plus 1, meaning that we subscribe to any sensor read, which will be executed before we passed 20m. Note that the added tolerance can only decrease the total number of executed sensor reads. The scheduler always prefers $t_D$ over any other time in $[t_{min}, t_{max}]$. The scheduler will only utilize the tolerance in case a sensor read must be executed anyways to serve another query.

$$s_{0.3s} : \langle t, v \rangle \rightarrow \langle t + 1, t + 0.3s, t + 0.3s, 0 \rangle$$

EXAMPLE 2.3: Read a value at least every 0.3s.

With Example 2.3, we address Query 3 from Figure 2.2. This query samples periodically with the same ahead limit as the previous example. This example emphasizes the compatibility of our approach with common periodic sampling. Our read scheduler seamlessly combines periodic sampling functions with more advanced sampling functions such as the ones in Example 2.1 and 2.2.

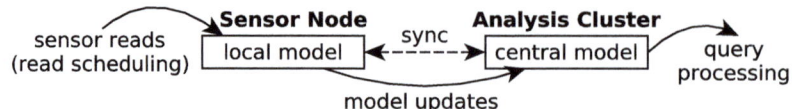

FIGURE 2.10: Model-driven data acquisition.

### 2.5.5 Local Filter Functions

$$f : \langle t, v \rangle \rightarrow \{true, false\}$$

FORMULA 2.2: Local filter function.

As an additional optimization, we couple our UDSFs with local filter functions (Formula 2.2). Local filtering allows for further reducing data transmissions. For example, we do not transfer sensor values if they remain constant or follow an expected trend. Similar to the sampling function, the filter function is called upon a sensor read with the current time and sensor value as parameters. It returns a boolean value, which indicates if the current measurement shall be transferred upstream. UDSFs and filter functions can communicate through a shared state.

*Model-driven data acquisition* (Figure 2.10) is an example for local filtering [52, 147]. This technique estimates sensor values using a model, which is based on previously gathered values (e.g., regression techniques or pattern learning). As shown in Example 2.4, the filter function compares sensor values with the model-based estimation. No data transmission is required if the difference lies within a failure tolerance, i.e., we save traffic if the central model is sufficiently precise.

```
1: upon sensor read ⟨time (t), value (v)⟩ do
2:     mv ← model.estimateValue(t)
3:     if abs(mv − v) > tolerance then
4:         model.update(t, v) // local model update
5:         return true // transfer value
6:     else
7:         return false // no transfer required
8:     end if
9: end
```

EXAMPLE 2.4: Local filter for model-driven data acquisition.

We refer the reader to the original works for detailed descriptions and throughout evaluations of the diverse adaptive filtering techniques available [42, 52, 89, 147, 186, 189].

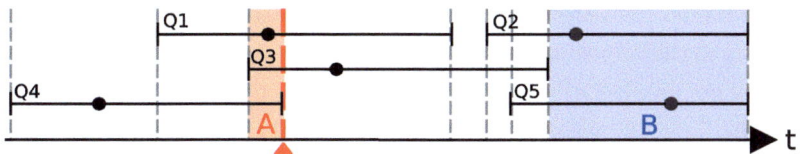

FIGURE 2.11: The latest possible time for the next read is the first interval end. Reading at this time minimizes the number of sensor reads.

## 2.6 Multi-Query Read Scheduling

Each query can define its own *UDSFs*. Accordingly, several different *UDSFs* can be present at a single sensor that is shared among queries. A naive approach would execute each UDSF separately and miss the opportunity to share sensor reads and data transmissions among them. We contribute an algorithm that exploits read time tolerances to share sensor values among multiple queries. Our multi-query read scheduling algorithm minimizes the number of sensor reads with respect to query needs. It further optimizes the exact read times with respect to the given penalty functions, while still performing the minimum number of sensor reads only.

### 2.6.1 Minimizing Sensor Reads

Our primary goal is to minimize the number of performed sensor reads. To that end, each *UDSF* suggests a read time in the form of a *read request* (Section 2.5.3). We then apply *read fusion* to combine *read request* with overlapping tolerance intervals. This maximizes read and traffic sharing among queries and minimizes sensor reads. Our algorithm is agnostic to the underlying algorithms of UDSFs. It solely operates based on the provided *read requests*.

**Guaranteed minimum of sensor reads.** We present a read scheduling algorithm, which guarantees to perform the minimum number of sensor reads only. Initially, during *read time suggestion*, all present UDSFs provide their next *read request*. We then minimize the number of sensor reads using *read fusion*. In Figure 2.11, we show an example for the *read fusion* phase, where five UDSFs provide their *read requests*. Given the read requests, we can determine the latest possible time for the next sensor read: it is the first end of any tolerance interval (red dashed line). Reading later would violate the read time tolerance of Q4 and is thus impossible. Reading earlier can only decrease the amount of fused read requests because only interval starts can lie before the first interval end. This leads to the important observation that *reading at the time of the first interval end minimizes the number of sensor reads.*

Once we perform the sensor read at the end of the Q4 interval, we can share the obtained value among three queries: Q1, Q3, and Q4. Our scheduling algorithm then acquires the next *read requests* from the *UDSFs* of Q1, Q3, and Q4. It keeps the intervals from Q2 and Q5 because they start in the future. Given all *read requests*, we repeat the described process to schedule the next read.

### 2.6.2 Optimizing Read Times

Our secondary goal is to optimize the deviation from desired read times, while still executing the minimum number of sensor reads only. Hence, we extend the *read fusion* phase of our algorithm with *read time optimization.*

**Preliminary Considerations.** We divide the time axis in non-overlapping time intervals, which we call *fragments.* Each start and each end of a tolerance interval is thereby considered as fragment separator. For example, consider Figure 2.11, where fragments are separated with dashed lines. The used fragmentation technique is known as stream slicing [36, 102, 111, 180, 179] and is widely used in streaming window aggregation.

The number of overlapping intervals - and thereby the read sharing potential - remains constant within fragments. This is the case because each start or end of a tolerance interval that changes the number of overlapping intervals, also marks the start of a new fragment. Thus, we perform the minimum number of sensor reads as long as we perform sensor reads in the last fragment before the first end of any tolerance interval. For example, consider the red shaded fragment in Figure 2.11.

**The Optimal Fragment.** As a result of our prior considerations, we aim to optimize the read time within the latest fragment before the first end of any tolerance interval. This guarantees executing the minimum amount of sensor reads, but reduces the deviations from the desired read times.

Algorithm 1 on Page 35 formalizes how we determine the optimal fragment in which we can optimize the exact read time. The optimal read time within the optimal fragment is the time that implies the smallest penalty (minimal sum of all penalty functions).

---

**Algorithm 1** Get the optimal fragment for the next read.

---

**Parameter:**

$rInt[\ ]$: Array of read requests $\langle t_{min}, t_D, t_{max}, p(t) \rangle$.

**Output:**

The optimal fragment for the next sensor read.

1: **function** GETOPTIMALFRAGMENT($rInt$)
2:     $t_{end} \leftarrow min(t_{max})$ **from** $rInt$
3:     $t_{start} \leftarrow max(t_{min})$ **from** $rInt$ **where** $t_{min} \leq t_{end}$
4:     **return** $[t_{start}, t_{end}]$
5: **end function**

---

**Algorithm 2** Read time optimization.

---

**Parameter:**

$rInt[\ ]$: Array of read requests $\langle t_{min}, t_D, t_{max}, p(t) \rangle$.

**Output:**

The optimized timestamp for the next sensor read.

1: **function** OPTIMIZEREADTIME($rInt$)
2:     $[t_{start}, t_{end}] \leftarrow$ GETOPTIMALFRAGMENT(rInt)
3:     $rInt \leftarrow$ ASSIGNINTERVALS($rInt$,$t_{start}$,$t_{end}$)
4:     **return** MINIMIZEPENALTY($rInt$,$t_{start}$,$t_{end}$)
5: **end function**

---

**Read Time Optimization.** We show the process of the read time optimization in Algorithm 2. We first call Algorithm 1 to get the optimal fragment. We then decide in Line 3 for which *read requests* we will use the next sensor value. This, for example, removes tolerance intervals which start after the selected optimal fragment (e.g., Q4 and Q5 in Figure 2.11). We finally minimize the penalty within the optimal fragment and return the read time. The penalty at any time is given by the sum of the penalty functions of all tolerance intervals being present at this time. Since each penalty function is convex, their sum $p_\Sigma(t)$ is also a convex function [151], which has a single minimum only. We can find this minimum (giving the optimal read time) with $O(log(\frac{l}{\Delta}))$ complexity, where $l$ is the length of the optimal fragment $[t_{start}, t_{end}]$ and $\Delta$ is the length of the confidence interval. We therefore initialize the confidence interval with $[t_{start}, t_{end}]$. We then calculate the derivative $p'_\Sigma(x)$ with x being the center of $[t_{start}, t_{end}]$. If $p'_\Sigma(x) = 0$, $x$ is the minimum. Otherwise, the sign of $p'_\Sigma(x)$ denotes if $x$ lies left or right of the minimum. If $x$ lies left, we assign $t_{start} \leftarrow x$, otherwise $t_{end} \leftarrow x$. While repeating the process, we half the confidence interval with each iteration until $t_{end} - t_{start} < \Delta$.

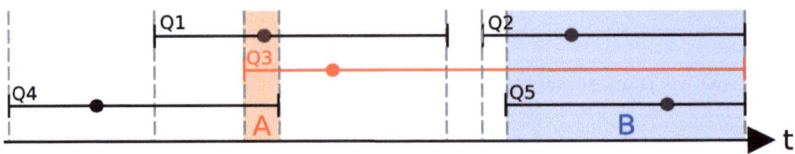

(A) Tolerance intervals possibly cover several read operations.

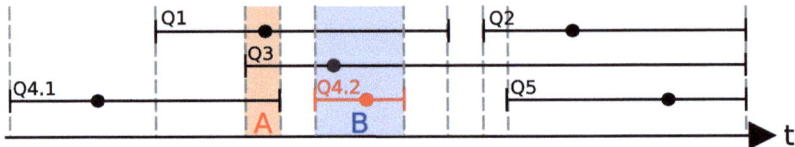

(B) New read requests may cause earlier read times.

FIGURE 2.12: Challenges in the assignment of read read requests to selected fragments in which we perform sensor reads.

**Assigning Read Requests to Fragments.** In order to optimize read times, we need to assign *read requests* to the optimal fragment in which we perform the next sensor read (Line 3 in Algorithm 2). The read time optimization within the optimal fragment is then based on the penalty functions of the assigned read requests only.

So far, we just considered the first upcoming read, but not the succeeding ones. In the remainder of the chapter, we call the optimal fragment for the next sensor read **A**, and the latest possible fragment for the second sensor read **B**.

Assigning read requests to fragments is not always straight forward. We show the trivial case in Figure 2.11. Each tolerance interval covers only one selected optimal fragment. Accordingly, we assign read requests either to the first read (Fragment A) or the second read (Fragment B). This example changes in Figure 2.12a. The Q3 tolerance interval now covers both, the first selected fragment (A) and the second selected fragment (B). In case we assign Q3 to Fragment A, it will not affect the read time optimization for Fragment B and vice versa.

We present the assignment process, including the non-trivial cases, in Algorithm 3 on Page 37. The algorithm first determines the latest possible fragment for the second read, which is marked blue in Figures 2.11 and 2.12a. Therefore, our algorithm defines $rInt'$ as an array of all read requests, which cannot be assigned to A (Line 2). It then calls Algorithm 1 as subroutine with $rInt'$ as parameter to determine fragment B (Line 3).

---

**Algorithm 3** Assign read requests to selected fragments.

---

**Parameters:**

   $rInt[\ ]$: Array of read requests $\langle t_{min}, t_D, t_{max}, p(t) \rangle$.

   $[t_{start}, t_{end}]$: The optimal interval for the next read.

**Output:**

   $rInt[\ ]$: Read requests assigned to the next read.

 1: **function** ASSIGNINTERVALS($rInt, t_{start}, t_{end}$)

 2:    $rInt' \leftarrow$ **all** $r \in rInt$ **where** $r.t_{min} > t_{end}$

 3:    $[t'_{start}, t'_{end}] \leftarrow$ GETOPTIMALFRAGMENT(rInt')

 4:    **for each** $r \in rInt$

 5:        **if** $[t_{start}, t_{end}] \not\subseteq r$ **then** remove $r$ from $rInt$

 6:        **else if** $[t'_{start}, t'_{end}] \not\subseteq r$ **then** keep $r$ in rInt

 7:        **else if** $t_{end} > r.t_D$ **then** keep $r$ in rInt

 8:        **else if** $t'_{start} < r.t_D$ **then** remove $r$ from rInt

 9:        **else if** $r.p(t'_{end}) < r.p(t_{end})$ **then**

10:           remove $r$ from $rInt$ (Figure 2.13a)

11:        **else if** $r.p(t_{start}) < r.p(t'_{start})$ **then**

12:           keep $r$ in rInt (Figure 2.13b)

13:        **else** remove $r$ from $rInt$ (Figure 2.13c)

14:        **end if**

15:    **end for each**

16:    **return** $rInt$

17: **end function**

---

Definition: Let $r$ be a *read requests* in the form $\langle t_{min}, t_D, t_{max}, p(t) \rangle$ and $i$ be an interval $[t_{start}, t_{end}]$. We then say that $r \subseteq i$ if $[r.t_{min}, r.t_{max}] \subseteq i$.

---

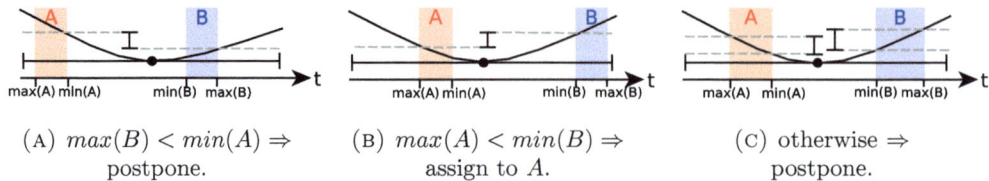

(A) $max(B) < min(A) \Rightarrow$ postpone.

(B) $max(A) < min(B) \Rightarrow$ assign to $A$.

(C) otherwise $\Rightarrow$ postpone.

FIGURE 2.13: Deciding for a fragment in case a tolerance interval overlaps with several sensor read times.

In the special case that all read requests can be assigned to A, $rInt'$ is empty in Algorithm 3. B is thus undefined and we assign all read requests to A. In the regular case, where we can compute A and B, we distinguish among seven cases to decide if we assign a tolerance interval to Fragment A. Intervals which are not assigned to A will get assigned to other fragments upon the optimization of subsequent read times.

**Case 1: No overlap with A.** We cannot assign tolerance intervals to A, which do not overlap with A (Line 5). This would violate the read time tolerance.

**Case 2: No overlap with B.** We assign tolerance intervals to A, which do not overlap with B (Line 6). This ensures that such tolerance intervals cannot cause additional sensor reads before B. This retains the guarantee to execute the minimum number of sensor reads only.

**Case 3: $t_D$ before end of A.** We assign tolerance intervals to A, which have their desired read time before the end of A (Line 7). This is sure to be optimal because the penalty can only increase towards B in this case.

**Case 4: $t_D$ after start of B.** We do not assign tolerance intervals to A, which have their desired read time after the start of B (Line 8), because the penalty decreases towards B.

The remaining cases are shown in Figure 2.13. Both, A and B, overlap with the tolerance interval. A must be before the desired read time, and B after the desired read time.

Fragment B is the latest possible time for the second read. However, it is important to highlight that B is subject to change: after the first read is performed, all *UDSFs*, whose read requests were assigned to A, provide their next read requests. The corresponding new tolerance intervals possibly end before B, which moves B closer to A.

For example, consider Figure 2.12b on Page 36. The tolerance interval Q4.2 appears after A and causes B to shift towards A. Due to our limited knowledge about the second read time - we only know that it wont be later than B - we cannot guarantee that our assignment is optimal. Nonetheless, we propose a best effort approach based on the minimum and maximum values of the penalty in A and B:

**Case 5: $max(B) < min(A)$.** We do not assign tolerance intervals to A for which the penalty in B is always smaller than the penalty in A (Line 9/Figure 2.13a). In this case, it is guaranteed that there will be another read after A with reduced penalty.

**Case 6: $max(A) < min(B)$.** We assign tolerance intervals to A in case the penalty is always smaller in A than in B (Line 11/Figure 2.13b). This decision is not guaranteed to be optimal because B could possibly shift closer to A. However, A is regularly quite close to the desired read time when this condition holds true.

**Case 7: *otherwise*.** We do not assign tolerance intervals to A in case there is an overlap in the penalties of A and B (Line 13/Figure 2.13c). The penalty in B can still reduce when B moves towards A. In case it does not, we can arrive at the same penalty in B as we could in A.

We now have all pieces at hand, which we require for our overall scheduling algorithm: *(i)* we can select optimal fragments in which we perform sensor reads, *(ii)* we can smartly assign read requests to the optimal fragments, and *(iii)* we can minimize the penalty for the next sensor read time.

## 2.6.3 The Overall Scheduling Algorithm

The overall read scheduling algorithm (Algorithm 4 on Page 40) operates based on the *UDSFs* present at a sensor. It is called upon each sensor read and returns the time of the next sensor read. It further applies the local filter functions and initiates the transfer of the sensor values as needed.

At start-up time, we perform one initial sensor read and pass it as parameter to all *UDSFs* to obtain their first read requests. This initializes the *rInt* array with read requests from all *UDSFs*. When we add a new *UDSF*, the scheduler requests the next read request from the new *UDSF* with the previous sensor value as parameter. We omit this initialization process in Algorithm 4.

Each subsequent sensor read is processed in four steps:

---

**Algorithm 4** The overall scheduling algorithm.

---
**State:**

   $udsf[\ ]$: Array of *user-defined sampling functions.*
   $rInt[\ ]$: Array with next read requests from all
         *UDSFs* in the form $\langle t_{min}, t_D, t_{max}, p(t) \rangle$.

**Output:**

   The timestamp of the next sensor read.

1: **upon sensor read** $\langle t, v \rangle$ **do**
2:    $[t_{start}, t_{end}] \leftarrow$ GETOPTIMALFRAGMENT(rInt)
3:    $rInt_{now} \leftarrow$ ASSIGNINTERVALS(rInt,$t_{start}$,$t_{end}$)
4:    **for** $i$ **from** 0 **to** $udsf.size - 1$ **do**
5:       **if** $rInt[i] \in rInt_{now}$ **then**
6:          *// Apply local filter of udsf[i]*
7:          **if** $udsf[i].f(t,v)$ **then**
8:             subscribe $udsf[i]$ to current read $\langle t, v \rangle$
9:          **end if**
10:          *// next read request for udsf[i]*
11:          $rInt[i] \leftarrow udsf[i].s(t,v)$
12:       **end if**
13:    **end for**
14:    transmit current read $\langle t, v \rangle$ to subscribers
15:    **return** OPTIMIZEREADTIME(rInt)
16: **end**

---

1. In Line 2 and 3, we assign read requests to the current sensor read using Algorithms 1 and 3 (see Page 37).

2. For each read request, which is assigned to the current sensor read, we apply the local filter of the corresponding *UDSF* (Line 5). In case the value passes the filter, we subscribe the *UDSF* to the upcoming data transmission (Line 8). In any case, we acquire the next read request and store it in the *rInt* array (Line 11).

3. We initiate the data transmission of the current sensor value to all subscribers (Line 14). This happens through an asynchronous function call to not delay the computation of the next read time.

4. Finally, we call OPTIMIZEREADTIME($rInt$) (Algorithm 2 presented on Page 35) and return the time for the next sensor read.

Note that the calls to

- GETOPTIMALFRAGMENT($rInt$) and

- ASSIGNINTERVALS($rInt$,$t_{start}$,$t_{end}$)

within Algorithm 2 are redundant to the calls in the first step (Line 2 and 3) of Algorithm 4. An efficient implementation would keep the assignment as state to prevent doubled computation. We omit this optimization to simplify the exposition.

## 2.7 Analytical Evaluation

In this section, we provide an analytical evaluation of *on-demand streaming* and show how the fraction of prevented sensor reads depends on key properties of UDSFs. The goal of this section is to provide a theoretical understanding of the impact of sensor read sharing on the number of required sensor reads and data transmissions. The formulas presented in this section allow for estimating the savings achieved by *on-demand streaming* before deploying sensor nodes. Moreover, one can use our formulas to estimate the network traffic produced by a sensor node based on UDSF characteristics.

### 2.7.1 Key Properties of Sampling Functions

*UDSFs* have two key properties: *(i)* the average read frequency ($\lambda_i$) and *(ii)* the average tolerance interval length ($l_i$). In the following, we analyze the fraction of the prevented sensor reads with respect to these properties. Several *UDSFs* can be present at the same sensor. We derive the key properties $\lambda_{total}$ and $l_{total}$ for the ensemble of all $n$ *UDSFs* from the individual key properties $\lambda_1...\lambda_n$ and $l_1...l_n$ as follows:

FORMULA 2.3: The combined read frequency.
$$\lambda_{total} = \sum_{i=1}^{n} \lambda_i \text{ (the sum of all } \lambda\text{)}$$

FORMULA 2.4: The combined tolerance interval length.
$$l_{total} = \frac{\sum_{i=1}^{n} \lambda_i l_i}{\lambda_{total}} \text{ (the } \lambda\text{-weighted average of all } l\text{)}$$

## 2.7.2 Distribution of Tolerance Intervals

We model the start times of tolerance intervals with a *poisson point process* with the event rate $\lambda_{total}$. Poisson processes [46, 96] are widely used in statistics to model independent random events such as the starts of phone calls [31]. The starts of tolerance intervals are comparable to these use cases. They may occur at any time, have peak times, and periods of low utilization.

---

*Definition: Poisson Point Process and Exponential Distribution* [31, 46, 96]

We use a stationary Poisson Point Process to model the start of tolerance intervals of read requests. A stationary Poisson Point Process has a constant parameter, in our case $\lambda_{total}$, which is called *event rate* [96]. In our case, the *event rate* specifies the average number of starting tolerance intervals (Poisson Points) per unit of time.

"Consider two real numbers $a$ and $b$, where $a \leq b$, and which may represent points in time. Denote by $N(a, b]$ the random number of points of a homogeneous Poisson point process existing with values greater than $a$ but less than or equal to $b$. If the points form or belong to a homogeneous Poisson process with parameter $\lambda > 0$, then the probability of $n$ points existing in the above interval $(a, b]$ is given by:

$$P\{N(a,b] = n\} = \frac{[\lambda(b-a)]^n}{n!} e^{-\lambda(b-a)} \text{" [96]}$$

The times between two consecutive events (in our case interval starts) are exponentially distributed with a mean inter-event time of $1/\lambda$. The *exponential distribution* is described by the formula $f_\lambda(x) = \lambda e^{-\lambda x}$ for $x \geq 0$ (Figure 2.14).

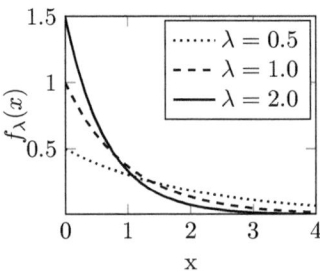

FIGURE 2.14: Plot of the Exponential Distribution with mean $1/\lambda$.

The plot in Figure 2.14 shows that short times between sensor reads (small $x$) are considered frequent, and that large times between sensor reads (large $x$) are rare.

---

average read interval length (l)

| λ | 0.01 | 0.02 | 0.03 | 0.04 | 0.05 | 0.06 | 0.07 | 0.08 | 0.09 | 0.1 | 0.11 | 0.12 | 0.13 | 0.14 | 0.15 | 0.16 | 0.17 | 0.18 | 0.19 | 0.2 |
|---|------|------|------|------|------|------|------|------|------|-----|------|------|------|------|------|------|------|------|------|-----|
| 1 | 1 | 2 | 3 | 4 | 5 | 5 | 6 | 7 | 8 | 9 | 10 | 11 | 11 | 12 | 13 | 14 | 14 | 15 | 16 | 17 |
| 2 | 2 | 3 | 5 | 7 | 9 | 10 | 12 | 13 | 15 | 16 | 18 | 19 | 20 | 22 | 24 | 24 | 25 | 26 | 27 | 28 |
| 3 | 3 | 5 | 8 | 10 | 13 | 15 | 17 | 19 | 21 | 23 | 24 | 26 | 27 | 29 | 30 | 31 | 32 | 33 | 35 | 36 |
| 4 | 3 | 7 | 10 | 13 | 16 | 19 | 21 | 24 | 26 | 28 | 29 | 31 | 33 | 34 | 36 | 37 | 38 | 39 | 40 | 41 |
| 5 | 4 | 8 | 12 | 16 | 19 | 22 | 25 | 28 | 30 | 32 | 34 | 35 | 37 | 38 | 40 | 41 | 42 | 44 | 45 | 46 |
| 6 | 5 | 10 | 15 | 19 | 22 | 26 | 28 | 31 | 33 | 35 | 37 | 39 | 41 | 42 | 44 | 45 | 46 | 47 | 48 | 49 |
| 7 | 5 | 11 | 16 | 21 | 25 | 28 | 31 | 34 | 36 | 38 | 40 | 42 | 44 | 45 | 46 | 48 | 49 | 50 | 51 | 52 |
| 8 | 6 | 13 | 18 | 23 | 27 | 31 | 34 | 37 | 39 | 41 | 43 | 45 | 46 | 48 | 49 | 50 | 51 | 52 | 53 | 54 |
| 9 | 7 | 15 | 20 | 25 | 30 | 33 | 36 | 39 | 41 | 43 | 45 | 47 | 48 | 51 | 52 | 54 | 54 | 55 | 56 | 56 |
| 10 | 7 | 15 | 22 | 27 | 32 | 35 | 38 | 41 | 43 | 45 | 47 | 49 | 50 | 52 | 53 | 54 | 55 | 56 | 57 | 58 |
| 11 | 8 | 17 | 24 | 29 | 34 | 37 | 40 | 43 | 45 | 47 | 49 | 51 | 52 | 54 | 55 | 56 | 57 | 58 | 59 | 60 |
| 12 | 9 | 18 | 25 | 31 | 35 | 39 | 42 | 44 | 47 | 49 | 51 | 52 | 54 | 55 | 56 | 57 | 59 | 59 | 60 | 61 |
| 13 | 10 | 19 | 27 | 32 | 36 | 40 | 43 | 46 | 48 | 50 | 52 | 54 | 55 | 57 | 58 | 59 | 60 | 61 | 62 | 62 |
| 14 | 11 | 21 | 28 | 34 | 38 | 42 | 45 | 47 | 50 | 52 | 54 | 55 | 56 | 58 | 59 | 60 | 61 | 62 | 63 | 64 |
| 15 | 11 | 22 | 29 | 35 | 39 | 43 | 46 | 49 | 51 | 53 | 55 | 56 | 58 | 59 | 60 | 61 | 62 | 63 | 64 | 65 |
| 16 | 12 | 23 | 31 | 36 | 41 | 44 | 48 | 50 | 52 | 54 | 56 | 58 | 59 | 60 | 61 | 62 | 63 | 64 | 65 | 66 |
| 17 | 12 | 24 | 32 | 37 | 42 | 46 | 48 | 51 | 53 | 55 | 57 | 58 | 60 | 61 | 63 | 63 | 64 | 65 | 66 | 66 |
| 18 | 13 | 25 | 32 | 38 | 43 | 47 | 50 | 52 | 55 | 56 | 58 | 59 | 61 | 62 | 64 | 64 | 65 | 66 | 67 | 67 |
| 19 | 14 | 26 | 33 | 40 | 44 | 48 | 51 | 53 | 55 | 57 | 59 | 60 | 62 | 63 | 64 | 65 | 66 | 67 | 67 | 68 |
| 20 | 14 | 27 | 35 | 41 | 45 | 49 | 52 | 54 | 56 | 58 | 60 | 61 | 62 | 64 | 65 | 66 | 66 | 67 | 68 | 69 |
| 21 | 15 | 28 | 36 | 41 | 46 | 49 | 52 | 55 | 57 | 59 | 60 | 62 | 63 | 64 | 65 | 66 | 67 | 68 | 69 | 69 |
| 22 | 16 | 28 | 37 | 43 | 47 | 51 | 53 | 56 | 58 | 60 | 61 | 62 | 64 | 65 | 66 | 67 | 68 | 69 | 69 | 70 |
| 23 | 16 | 29 | 37 | 44 | 48 | 51 | 54 | 57 | 59 | 61 | 62 | 63 | 64 | 66 | 67 | 68 | 68 | 69 | 70 | 71 |
| 24 | 17 | 29 | 39 | 44 | 49 | 52 | 55 | 58 | 59 | 61 | 63 | 64 | 65 | 66 | 67 | 68 | 69 | 70 | 70 | 71 |
| 25 | 17 | 31 | 39 | 45 | 49 | 53 | 56 | 58 | 60 | 62 | 63 | 65 | 66 | 67 | 68 | 69 | 70 | 70 | 71 | 72 |
| 26 | 18 | 31 | 40 | 46 | 50 | 54 | 56 | 59 | 61 | 62 | 64 | 65 | 66 | 67 | 68 | 69 | 70 | 71 | 72 | 72 |
| 27 | 20 | 33 | 40 | 46 | 51 | 54 | 57 | 59 | 61 | 63 | 64 | 66 | 67 | 68 | 69 | 70 | 71 | 71 | 72 | 73 |
| 28 | 19 | 33 | 42 | 48 | 52 | 55 | 58 | 60 | 62 | 64 | 65 | 66 | 67 | 68 | 69 | 70 | 71 | 72 | 72 | 73 |
| 29 | 20 | 34 | 42 | 48 | 52 | 55 | 58 | 60 | 63 | 64 | 66 | 67 | 68 | 69 | 70 | 71 | 72 | 72 | 73 | 74 |
| 30 | 21 | 35 | 43 | 49 | 53 | 56 | 59 | 61 | 63 | 65 | 66 | 67 | 68 | 69 | 70 | 71 | 72 | 73 | 73 | 74 |

(vertical axis label: average read frequency ($\lambda$))

TABLE 2.1: Fraction of prevented sensor reads [in %] compared to an execution without sensor read sharing. The savings increase when $\lambda$ or $l$ increase. The time unit is irrelevant as long as it is the same for $\lambda$ and $l$.

The distribution of the lengths of tolerance intervals is most realistically described by an exponential distribution with the mean $l_{lotal}$. This is because the exponential distribution assumes short intervals to occur most frequently. The probability for longer intervals decreases exponentially with the interval length. Accordingly, we expect small read time tolerances frequently and long read time tolerances rarely. Thus, most users will define small tolerance intervals and only a few users will define large tolerances.

From now on, we write $l$ for $l_{lotal}$ and $\lambda$ for $\lambda_{lotal}$ to simplify the presentation.

## 2.7.3 The Fraction of Prevented Sensor Reads

In Table 2.1, we compare *on-demand streaming* with a naive approach, which does not apply sensor read sharing. The fraction of prevented sensor reads depends on the key properties $\lambda$ and $l$ of *UDSFs*. The savings increase rapidly when either sampling rates ($\lambda$) or interval length ($l$) increase. Note that one can expand Table 2.1 with additional rows and columns easily. Thus, the key observation is that savings increase towards 100% when $\lambda$ or $l$ increase, and decrease when $\lambda$ or $l$ decrease.

┌─ *Definition: Birth and Death Process* [97] ───────────────────────────

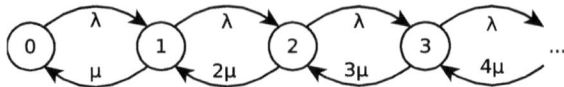

FIGURE 2.15: Tolerance intervals in a birth and death process.

A *Birth and Death Process* models the growth and/or regression of a population. The *state* of the process corresponds to the size of the population. For example, the number of living humans or, in our case, to the number of started but not yet ended intervals. States are connected with *transition rates* which may depend on the state. For example, if there are four living humans (state $i = 4$), each pair of humans has two children (birth rate $2i/2$), and humans live 90 years, then $\lambda = \frac{\text{birth rate}}{\text{time}} = \frac{(2\cdot4)/2}{90\text{years}}$.

   Figure 2.15 shows the Birth and Death Process for tolerance intervals. Our *interval starts* follow a *poisson process* with the *event rate* $\lambda$. Thus, the *transition rate* from any state $i$ to the state $i + 1$ is $\lambda$. The mean length of tolerance intervals is $l$ and lengths are exponentially distributed. This leads to the *event rate* of $\mu = 1/l$ for the mortality of one interval. Accordingly, the *transition rate* from any state $i$ to the state $i - 1$ (i.e., the mortality for $i$ open intervals) is $i\mu = i/l$.

   We describe births (interval starts), mortality (interval ends), and the population (open intervals) as functions of the time called $b(t)$, $m(t)$, and $o(t)$ respectively [97].

In order to calculate the savings shown in Table 2.1, we model the begin and end of tolerance intervals in a birth and death process (see definition above). Based on this process, we can compute the number of started and ended intervals recursively with the step width $\Delta_t$ as follows:

FORMULA 2.5: Initialization - no interval started or ended.
$$b(0) = m(0) = o(0) = 0$$

FORMULA 2.6: Number of started intervals up to time $t$.
$$b(t) = \lambda t$$

FORMULA 2.7: Number of ended intervals up to time $t + \Delta_t$.
$$m(t + \Delta_t) = m(t) + o(t)\mu\Delta_t$$

FORMULA 2.8: State at time $t + \Delta_t$ (open intervals).
$$o(t + \Delta_t) = \lambda t - m(t)$$

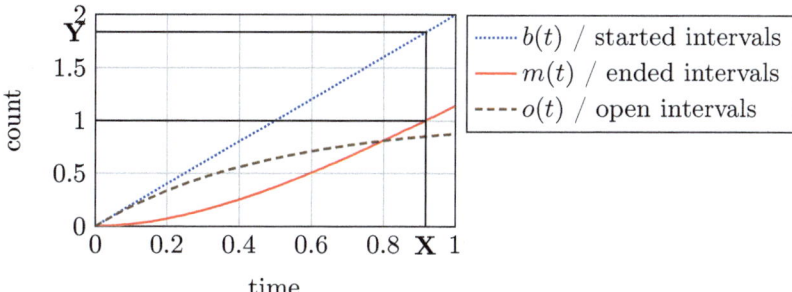

FIGURE 2.16: Expected values for the number of started, ended, and open intervals for $\lambda = 2$ and $l = 0.5$.

We show a plot of these functions for $\lambda = 2$ and $l = 0.5$ in Figure 2.16. Since the transition rate $\lambda$ remains constant, we can observe that $b(t)$ is linear. The transition rate for ending intervals increases with the number of open intervals causing $m(t)$ to first grow exponentially and then asymptotically reach the slope of $b(t)$. Because $o(t) = b(t) - m(t)$, it increases asymptotically towards a constant value.

The values $X$ and $Y$ are especially important in Figure 2.16: $X$ is the expected time until the first interval ends. $Y$ is the expected number of started intervals up to time $X$. According to our read scheduling algorithm (Section 2.6.1), we execute a sensor read as soon as the first tolerance interval ends (time $X$). We then assign the obtained value to all intervals, which started up to this time. Hence, $Y$ is the number of intervals which can regularly share a sensor read. The fraction of prevented sensor reads is thus $1 - 1/Y$.

---

*Definition: The Erlang B Formula* [31, 171]

The Erlang B Formula calculates the blocking probability for requests (e.g., phone calls) which are issued to a shared system (e.g., a call center) that can handle at most $N$ requests in parallel. In our example, the blocking probability is the chance that a call to the call center cannot be answered because all lines are busy.

Each request has a length (e.g., the duration of the phone call). Requests are issued following a poisson process with event rate $\lambda$. The mean length of a request is $l$ and lengths are exponentially distributed (see definitions in Section 2.7.2). $A = \lambda l$ is the resulting system load in the Erlang unit (Erl). The Erlang B formula calculates the blocking probability as follows:

$$P_{\text{blocking}}(A, N) = \frac{\frac{A^N}{N!}}{\sum_{i=0}^{N} \frac{A^i}{i!}}$$

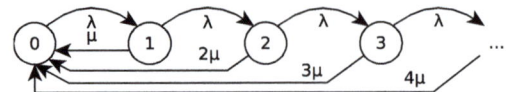

FIGURE 2.17: Tolerance intervals in a birth and death process considering earlier interval ends in case of shared sensor reads.

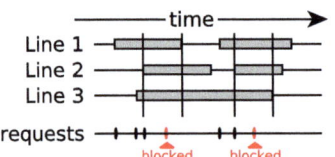

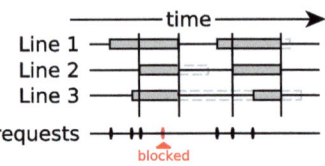

(A) Result with Erlang B (Figure 2.15).   (B) Result with read sharing (Figure 2.17).

FIGURE 2.18: Comparison of birth and death processes with example requests issued to a systems with $N = 3$ parallel lines.

### 2.7.4 Differentiation from the Erlang B Formula

The Erlang B Formula [31] (defined above) is widely used in queuing theory to calculate the blocking probability for phone calls in a system with a maximum of $N$ parallel calls. Phone calls are modelled as intervals starting in a poisson process and having exponentially distributed lengths. Intuitively, this is similar to our scenario where tolerance intervals start in a poisson process and have exponentially distributed lengths.

Despite these similarities, we cannot use Erlang B to calculate the fraction of presented sensor reads, because Erlang B assumes an equilibrium between starting and ending calls [171]. In contrast to this, we perform a sensor read as soon as the first interval ends and thereby address all intervals which began up to this time. We thus implicitly end all intervals and reset the state to 0, which results in the birth and death process shown in Figure 2.17. Accordingly, our algorithm never reaches an equilibrium between tolerance interval begins and ends. Instead, it repeats a growing phase after each sensor read. As a result, the blocking probability given by the Erlang B formula is much larger than fraction of prevented sensor reads.

Figure 2.18 compares the birth and death process of the Erlang B formula (Figure 2.15) with the one including earlier interval ends due to shared sensor reads (Figure 2.17). We can observe that the same requests lead to different outcomes: In Figure 2.18a, the end of one interval has no effect on other intervals, i.e., the end of one phone call does no affect other calls. In Figure 2.18b, the end of one interval causes a sensor read which addresses all read requests and thereby ends all intervals.

## 2.8 Experimental Evaluation

In this section, we evaluate on-demand streaming from sensor nodes on real-world sensor data. We present our experimental setup, show our results, and close with a discussion.

### 2.8.1 Experimental Setup

**Data.** We replay recorded sensor data from two datasets: First, the *Formula 1* telemetry data which we introduced in our introductory use-case in Section 2.2. Second, sensor data from a *football* match which was provided with the DEBS'13 Grand Challenge [133]. We monitor the speed of the ball, which is tracked with a 2000Hz sampling rate and μm/s precision.

**Workloads.** Our experiments use three query sets:

*Introductory use-case:* We presented an initial evaluation of our introductory use case in Section 2.2. We use AdaM as adaptive sampling technique in combination with the UDSF from Example 2.2 and periodic sampling.

*Random UDSFs:* We use queries with random UDSFs to study the scalability of our solution to large numbers of concurrent queries and users. In our experiments, one UDSF corresponds to one query. Thus, the number of UDSFs and the number of queries are the same. In general, queries can define multiple UDSFs to request data from several sensors. Our scheduling algorithm solely operates based on the UDSFs and is agnostic to all other query properties. As in our analytical evaluation (Section 2.7), each UDSF reads in a poisson process and applies exponentially distributed read time tolerances. We defined poisson processes and exponential distributions in Section 2.7.2 on Page 42.

*AdaM and FAST:* We execute AdaM and FAST individually to examine their robustness against read time slack (see definitions in Section 2.3.2 on Page 19). This verifies that read time tolerances do not harm the result quality of adaptive sampling techniques.

### 2.8.2 Detailed Experiments

We analyzed the number of sensor reads and transferred tuples for our introductory use-case in Section 2.2. In the following section, we show that our solution also scales to larger query sets. Therefore, we compare our on-demand data streaming approach with

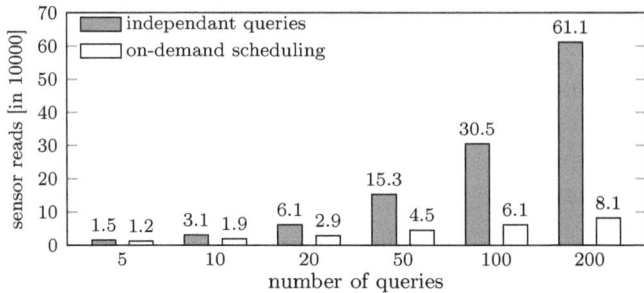

FIGURE 2.19: Number of sensor reads and data transmissions for an increasing the number of queries. (random UDSFs; ∅sampling rate 1Hz per UDSF; ∅tolerance ±0.04*s*).

an independent execution of multiple queries. Then, we evaluate the achievements of our read time optimizer. Finally, we investigate the impact of read time slack on different sampling strategies.

### 2.8.2.1  Shared Sensor Reads and Traffic

**Scaling the Query Set.** *On-demand* scheduling scales to larger query sets. We increase the number of queries up to 200 in Figure 2.19. Increasing the number of queries is equivalent to increasing the sampling frequency of queries: our read scheduler solely operates based on submitted read requests. Thus, the number of read request makes the difference rather than the number of queries.

*Periodic* sampling is virtually impossible in this experiment: UDSFs read in a Poisson process, which simulates heavy peaks in sampling rates. Periodic sampling would fall back to the maximum sampling rate, which is in the order of $10^9$Hz. Hence, we compare an independent query execution with our on-demand streaming approach.

For the *independent execution of queries*, the number of sensor reads and data transmissions increases linearly with the number of queries. This is because each read request causes a sensor read and a transmission.

*On-demand scheduling* can fuse read requests whenever their tolerance intervals overlap. The probability for such overlaps increases with the number of read requests. Thus, read and traffic sharing becomes more frequent with larger query sets. We increase the number of queries by factor 40. However, the number of reads increases by less than factor 7, saving 87% in reads and transfers.

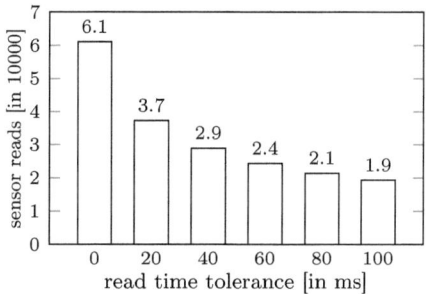

FIGURE 2.20: Sensor reads/transfers for for an increasing read time tolerance. (20 queries, i.e., 20 random UDSFs, $\varnothing$sampling rate 1Hz/UDSF).

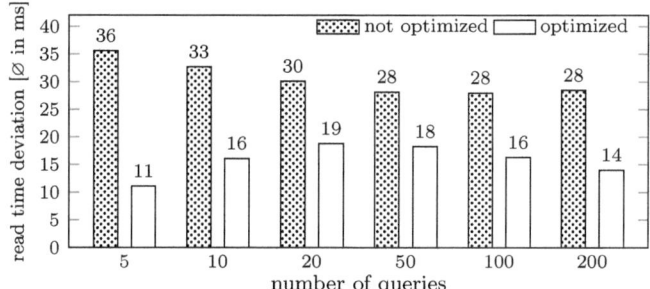

FIGURE 2.21: Impact of read time optimization on read time deviations for an increasing number of queries. (random UDSFs; $\varnothing$sampling rate 1Hz per UDSF; $\varnothing$tolerance $\pm 0.04s$).

**Increasing Tolerances.** Another way to increase the probability for read fusion is to increase read time tolerances. We analyze this effect in Figure 2.20. We therefore fix the number of queries to 20. The number of sensor reads decays exponentially when the tolerance increases. This observation is in accordance with the theoretical coincidence probability of random events with exponentially distributed lengths described by Erlang et al. [31].

### 2.8.2.2 Read Time Optimization

We now evaluate the deviation from desired read times in our experiments. Our read time optimizer never increases the amount of sensor reads or transfers. However, it reduces the mean deviation from desired read times by up to 69% in our experiment with larger query sets (Figure 2.21).

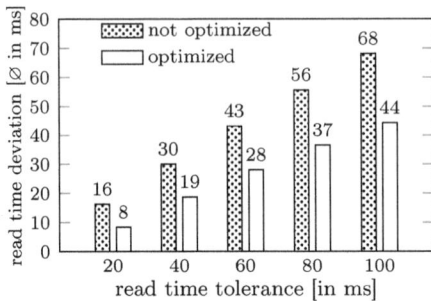

FIGURE 2.22: Read time optimization with increasing read time tolerance. (20 queries, i.e., 20 random UDSFs, ∅sampling rate 1Hz per UDSF).

We observe two contradicting effects in Figure 2.21: On the one hand, more read
requests increase read time deviations. The probability of read sharing increases and
we utilize tolerances to fuse reads. This effect dominates up to 20 concurrent queries.
On the other hand, more read requests decrease read time deviations: It becomes more
probable that multiple sensor reads take place within the tolerance interval of a read
request. In such cases, the optimizer selects the sensor read which implies the smallest
read time deviation. This effect dominates for 50 or more concurrent queries.

In Figure 2.22, we study how an increasing read time tolerance affects the optimization. The read time deviation increases with the read time tolerance, because we use
additional tolerances primarily to reduce sensor reads and data transmissions. Thus, the
selected fragments, in which we perform the optimization, deviate more from the desired
read times of read request.

**Query Prioritization.** Each UDSF can define its individual penalty function to
model read time preferences within tolerance intervals. We use this feature to prioritize
selected UDSFs when optimizing read times. For example, prioritized UDSFs may pe-
nalize read time deviations with $p(t) = t^2$, while non-prioritized UDSFs set $p(t) = |t|$.
We analyze the impact of such a prioritization in Figure 2.23 on Page 51. Prioritization
reduces read time deviations considerably for the prioritized UDSFs. This effect declines
when the fraction of prioritized UDSFs increases. When many UDSFs are prioritized,
sensor reads are often shared among prioritized UDSFs which repeals the prioritization.
The read time deviation for non-prioritized UDSFs increases with the fraction of prioritized UDSFs. The same holds for the overall mean deviation. Hence, we recommend to
prioritize small subsets of UDSFs only.

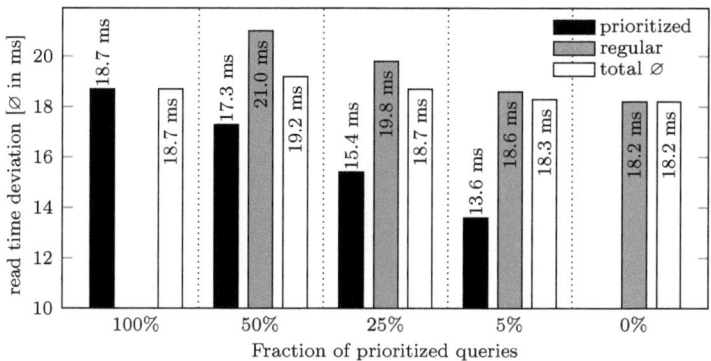

FIGURE 2.23: Query prioritization with penalty functions.
(20 queries; ∅sampling rate 1Hz/query; ∅tolerance ±0.04s).

Prioritizing all queries (100%) leads to a mean read time deviation of 18.7ms. Prioritizing no query (0%) reduces the mean read time deviation to 18.2ms. This is because $p(t) = |t|$ (not prioritized) grows linearly when the read time deviation increases. This minimizes the overall sum of read time deviations and, thereby, the mean read time deviation. In contrast, $p(t) = t^2$ (prioritized) grows quadratically and focuses on avoiding high deviations rather than minimizing the mean deviation.

We consider the example from Figure 2.23 as being a gentle prioritization. We can of course apply more strict differentiations between UDSFs by increasing the differences between penalty functions. For example, by multiplying the functions or by increasing the power. Our introductory use-case is an extreme yet realistic example for UDSF prioritization: the AdaM UDSF tolerates read time slack, but with rather high penalty of $p(t) = t^2$. Other queries forbid any read time delay, but are fine with reading earlier. The penalty for reading ahead of the desired read time is thus zero. Accordingly, we optimize read times solely on behalf of AdaM, resulting in a mean deviation in the order of nanoseconds (Figure 2.24 on Page 52).

### 2.8.2.3 The Effect of Read Time Slack

Our experiments show that read time tolerances lead to fewer sensor reads and transferred tuples. Hence, we advocate read time tolerances for adaptive sampling techniques. We now analyze how read time deviations affect AdaM and FAST, our representatives of

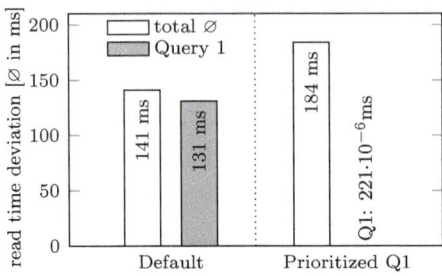

FIGURE 2.24: Read time optimization on behalf of a single query in our
introductory use-case.

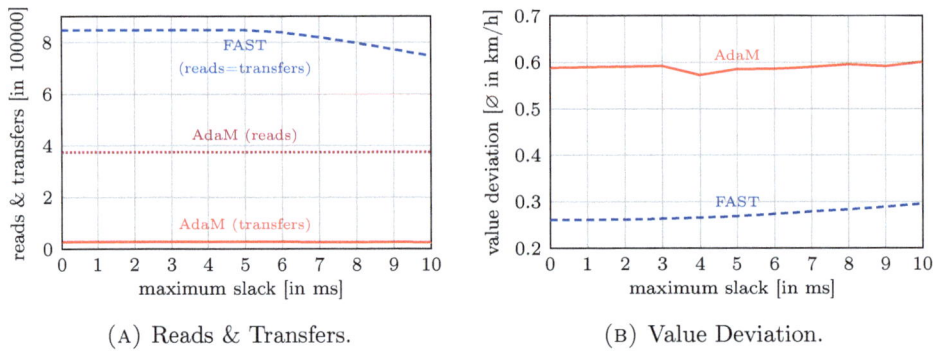

(A) Reads & Transfers.                  (B) Value Deviation.

FIGURE 2.25: AdaM and FAST on football data with read time slack.

adaptive sampling techniques. Therefore, we affect sensor reads by uniformly distributed random slacks. In this section, we monitor the speed of the ball during a football match.

We shows the number of sensor reads and transfers for different read time slacks in Figure 2.25a. Both, AdaM and FAST, are robust against slack: the number of sensor reads and transfers remains almost constant for slacks up to ±5ms. Larger slacks reduce sensor reads for FAST, because read time delays can be larger than the average read frequency. The adaptive filter of AdaM massively reduces data transfers as it avoids sending consecutive similar measures when the football is on the ground or airborne.

The mean deviation between the obtained speed graph and the underlying DEBS'13 raw data increases slightly with the slack (Figure 2.25b). However, we consider both techniques as robust because they retain a mean deviation of less than 0.6 km/h on the volatile speed of a football.

### 2.8.3 Discussion

On-demand streaming from sensor nodes reduces the number of sensor reads and the amount of transferred data by 57% in our introductory use-case and by up to 87% with larger query sets (i.e. more read requests per time). In comparison, periodic sampling leads to extremely high sampling rates, because it falls back to the maximum sampling rate required at any time. Adaptive sampling reduces sensor reads for a single query, but falls short in combining multiple different data demands. On demand sampling unites adaptive sampling with the multiplexing of data demands, which explains the savings.

In our experiments, the read time optimizer reduces the mean deviation from desired read times by up to 69%. Our optimizer never increases the number of sensor reads or the amount of transferred data. We allows for prioritizing queries by penalizing read time deviations. We show two examples with gentle and strong prioritizations.

We require read time tolerances to enable frequent read and traffic sharing among queries. Our experiments show that AdaM and FAST, as examples for adaptive sampling techniques, are robust against read time slack. This verifies that read time tolerances are applicable to adaptive sampling techniques.

## 2.9 Related Work

The problem of oversampling has been studied from various angles. However, we observed that there is no *one-fits-all* solution: either algorithms are limited to specific use-cases [59, 147], miss adaptivity [121, 176], or do not consider shared sensors [166, 186]. In the following section, we discuss how *UDSFs* and *multi-query read scheduling* incorporate, extend, and aid existing oversampling reduction techniques. We then present related work from the field of sensor networks regarding multi-query optimization and sensor read scheduling.

**Reduced Oversampling.** TinyDB [121] introduces the concept of acquisitional query processing (ACQP) to control when and how often to sample. It arranges database operators together with fetch operators (sensor reads) in a common processing pipeline. Operators with low selectivity, such as filters or aggregations, can thus reduce (filter out) data tuples before succeeding fetch operations and thereby prevent sensor reads. However, TinyDB only allows for periodic sampling algorithms at the source of a processing pipeline. This still leads to oversampling because it prevents adaptive sampling [59, 67, 186]. Our UDSFs overcome this limitation. Our sensor read scheduler further complements TinyDB with the ability for read and traffic sharing.

Model-driven data acquisition is another way to reduce the number of sensor reads [42, 52, 89, 147, 189]. The key idea is to train a model with historical sensor values, which then serves as primary source for stream analysis systems to answer queries (Figure 2.10 on Page 32). Sensor nodes transmit sensor values only if the model-based prediction of sensor values does not provide a sufficient precision, which saves network traffic. One can implement model-driven data acquisition as UDSF as we have shown in Section 2.5.5. The proposed algorithms neither mention nor hinder read sharing among queries.

An orthogonal approach to reduce oversampling is the joint optimization of data acquisition and delivery [166]. This method trades-off data transfer costs (slow transfer, low cost) against sampling costs (high frequency, high cost) while providing data freshness guarantees. Our work complements this approach because the data freshness benefits from read and traffic sharing among queries.

**Multi Query Optimization.** Several works propose to optimize the query execution across queries and users in sensor networks. Li et al. [115] apply data sharing among queries through the fusion of aggregate queries, utility-driven compression, and global transmission scheduling. Two techniques, called *Dynamic* and *aMST* [202], provide spatial resource sharing in addition to time sharing in a mobile sensor network. However, these publications do not consider sensor read scheduling and can be applied supplementary to our scheduling algorithm.

Xiang et al. [200, 201] as well as Mueller and Alonso [132] optimize a batch of queries as a whole to eliminate redundancies and fuse similar operations. They set the sampling rate of sensors to be the greatest common divisor of the sampling rates from all queries. In contrast to our work, both approaches rely on periodic sampling to compute the required greatest common divisor.

**Scheduling Algorithms.** Tavakoli et al. [176] also utilize read time tolerances for sensor read scheduling. They model overlaps of tolerance intervals in an online evolving interval-cover graph which they use to determine read times. In contrast to our solution, their approach is limited to periodic sampling and does not not optimize exact read times.

Fang et al. [62] and CATS [208] address the issue of sampling continuous intervals (e.g. video and audio recording). They explore tolerances in the placement of recording intervals to maximize interval overlaps. We consider the challenge to maximize interval overlap as orthogonal to the optimization of exact sensor read times. Further scheduling algorithms from the field of sensor networks study transmission scheduling [25, 56, 131,

185]. They switch between sleep times and transmission periods in order to save energy, but do not cover sensor read scheduling or read sharing among queries.

**In summary**, our *UDSFs* and *multi-query read scheduling* form a common framework to incorporate the presented oversampling reduction techniques. *UDSFs* work as general abstraction for sampling functions. *Multi-query read scheduling* transparently multiplexes *UDSFs* on shared sensors, leading to a global cost optimization.

## 2.10   Conclusion

We have introduced user-defined sampling functions (UDSFs) as well as a multi-query scheduling algorithm for sensor reads. These are powerful means to solve the problem of *oversampling*: USDFs enable diverse adaptive sampling techniques and allow for defining the data demand of each query. Our multi-query scheduling algorithm multiplexes UDSFs and utilizes read time tolerances to minimize sensor reads with respect to query needs. Thereby, the complexity of multi-query scheduling is transparent to the user.

Our experimental evaluations show savings of 87% in sensor reads and data transfers for an example with real-world sensor data. In addition, our read time optimizer reduces the deviation from desired read times by up to 69% in our experiments. We further allow for prioritizing queries in a flexible way. Overall, on-demand data streaming from sensor nodes leads to significantly reduced sampling rates and corresponding savings in communication costs without sacrificing data quality.

Our solution prevents a tight coupling between sensor nodes and data consumers. Any consumer can request data streams from sensors by submitting UDSFs while sensor nodes are agnostic to specifics of the requesting systems. This makes it easy to share sensor nodes among diverse consumers such as existing sensor network middleware [1], in-network database systems [119, 121], and visualization applications [183]. In the following chapter, we integrate our read scheduler in our sensor control layer.

# 3

# Scalable Data Acquisition with Guaranteed Time Coherence

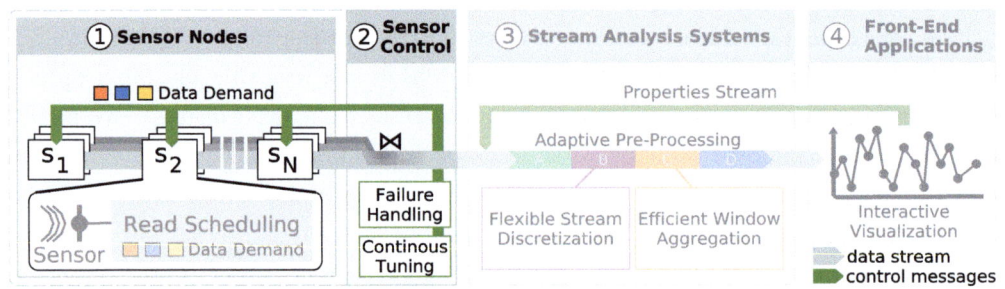

FIGURE 3.1: Scope of Chapter 3 - The Sensor Control Layer.

In this chapter, we focus on the sensor control layer, which orchestrates large numbers of sensor nodes. Thereby, we address scalability issues as well as the problem of time incoherence. Our system automatically arranges sensor nodes in pipelines to distribute computation effort and to prevent central bottlenecks at stream analysis systems. Thereby, our system adapts automatically to failures and changing network conditions to maintain configurable latency limits and coherence requirements. We explore concepts and algorithms to quantify and optimize the time coherence of data tuples. For each tuple, we provide a guaranteed time coherence that is independent of clock synchronization among sensor nodes. This prevents time-correlation errors in applications not detectable by current approaches and quantifies the result precision.

## 3.1   Introduction

Stream analysis systems have access to a growing number of data streams from sensor nodes in the IoT [193]. Analytical applications correlate these data streams to facilitate fast event detection and respective reactions. Typically, sensor measurements consist of a timestamp $t$ and a value $v$. Stream analysis systems [35, 177, 205] and time series databases [20, 190] join measurements from different sensors to tuples in the form $\langle t, v_1, \ldots, v_n \rangle$ (see Section 2.3.3). Applications assume that these tuples represent a concise snapshot of all values (i.e., measurements) taken at time $t$. In this chapter, we show that this assumption does not hold in the IoT and that tuples are affected by an unknown *time incoherency*. We then present a solution which addresses the problem of *time incoherence* as well as *scalability challenges* introduced in Section 1.2.2.

In the IoT, many different users and organizations operate diverse sensor nodes such as smart phones, weather stations, smart watches, and connected cars [108]. The precision of system clocks on these devices depends on various aspects including time synchronization, clock drift, security vulnerabilities, and intended manipulation:

- Most devices synchronize their clocks through the Network Time Protocol (NTP) [124, 125, 126], which has known security issues [55, 192]: The first two versions of NTP did not provide authentication methods [124]. Version three introduced an authentication based on pre-shared keys that are exchanged offline [125]. For example, the *NIST Authenticated NTP Service* ships keys via postal mail [64]. Version four provides an authentication method based on public keys [126]. However, this method is rarely used and vulnerable to brute force attacks as it uses small 32-bit seeds [55]. In practice, most sensor nodes do not use NTP authentication and are vulnerable to spoofing attacks [196].

- Many applications give an incentive to deliberately manipulate the system time [192]. For example, a parcel service can delay clocks on handset scanners to hide late deliveries and a software user can delay clocks to hide the expiration of a license.

- Each device requires an oscillator to track the progress of time. Many sensor nodes use cheap quartz crystals for that purpose, which have widespread clock drifts depending on the temperature [146].

We conclude that timestamps require an input validation [153, 192] and propose a solution which allows for *scalable data gathering with guaranteed time coherence*.

Imprecise timestamps can cause application failures such as wrong correlations, missed event detections, and false predictions. Therefore, it is crucial for applications to quantify the imprecision of timestamps and to provide time coherence guarantees for sensor data tuples. For example, think about a traffic control system: a camera provides photos of license plates and multiple other sensors measure speeds, weights, and safety distances of vehicles. When joining photos with sensor measures, it is crucial to ensure time coherence to identify the right mappings between license plates and measures. Our sensor control layer optimizes time coherence and provides coherence guarantees.

With the rise of the IoT, we aim to join measurements from thousands of sensors with coherence guarantees. Therefore, we are facing the performance limits of central stream joins performed in stream analysis systems. The number and volume of data streams a server can process is bounded by network bandwidth, parallel connection limits, memory requirements, and CPU power. Systems which utilize edge computing capabilities can overcome these performance limitations by avoiding central computation and transmission bottlenecks. Our sensor control layer addresses scalability issues by utilizing edge computing capabilities, and, at the same time, guarantees time coherence.

We present SENSE, our sensor control system which gathers time coherent data tuples from distributed sensors. SENSE combines *central stream joins* with a new architecture based on *sensing loops*. This ensures scalability to thousands of sensor nodes.

SENSE is *not* meant for replacing time synchronization. Advances in time synchronization [106, 163, 165] reduce clock deviations and directly lead to an improved estimated coherence in SENSE. The estimated coherence is the difference between sensor read times assuming correct clock synchronization among clocks of sensor nodes.

However, we take into account that sophisticated techniques for time synchronization have not yet seen widespread adoption in the IoT and that timestamps may be manipulated. To this end, we allow for specifying an incoherence limit for tuples which is maintained by the system even if node clocks are not synchronized at all.

For each tuple, SENSE provides a guaranteed time coherence which is the maximum difference between sensor read times, independent of clock synchronization. Coherence estimates and guarantees then work as key data characteristic in applications and quantify the result precision. We further introduce algorithms which optimize the resource utilization under latency and time coherence constraints. Finally, we add fault-tolerance mechanisms to make our solution robust against sensor and network failures.

Overall, this chapter makes the following contributions:

1. We present an architecture for acquiring values from large numbers of sensors with guaranteed time coherence and low latency (Section 3.4).

2. We introduce time coherence as a fundamental data characteristic of sensor data tuples (Section 3.5).

3. We optimize the coherence of result tuples and provide coherence guarantees which are independent of clock synchronization among sensor nodes (Section 3.6).

4. We pre-schedule sensor reads for future requests (Section 3.7) and provide fault-tolerance mechanisms for sensor and network failures (Section 3.8).

5. We experimentally evaluate our solution and show that it scales to thousands of sensors, provides low latencies, and operates efficiently (Section 3.9).

In the remainder of this chapter, we present an application example in Section 3.2 and discuss sources of incoherence in Section 3.3. We then present our contributions and experiments in Sections 3.4-3.9. Finally, we discuss related work in Section 3.10 and conclude in Section 3.11.

## 3.2 Application Example: Precision of Multilateration

In this section, we introduce time coherence failures and show how the coherence measures of SENSE prevent these failures in an example application.

**Application Example.** We demonstrate SENSE in a multilateration application. Multilateration is a common technique to locate the source of a signal by measuring the times when the signal arrives at three or more sensors. Common applications of multilateration are finding the epicenter of an earthquake, locating positions of lightnings in thunderstorms, or locating aircrafts.

The delta among the arrival times of a signal at different sensors exposes the delta in the distances between the signal source and sensors. From these distances, multilateration applications compute the position of the signal source (e.g., an aircraft or a lightning). We visualize our example in Figure 3.2 on Page 60. We use three sensors (blue crosses) to locate the source of thunder (i.e., the positions of lightnings) in a thunderstorm. The signal disseminates from its source (black point) with sonic speed which

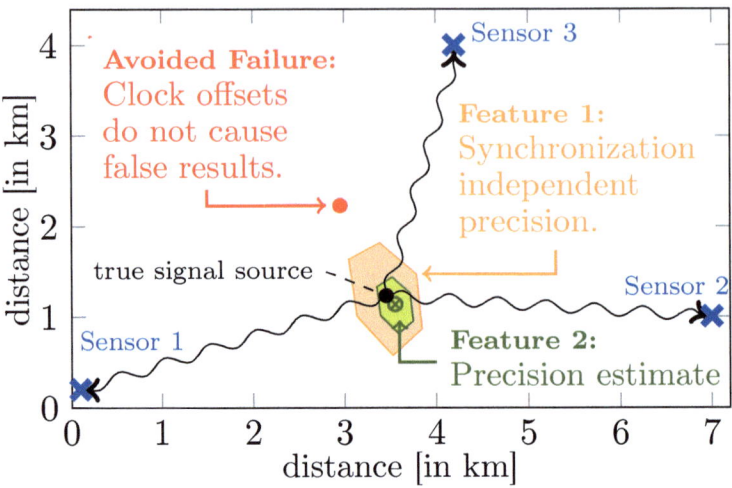

FIGURE 3.2: Multilateration example.

is about $343\frac{m}{s}$ ($1236\frac{km}{h}$; 767mph). We know the positions of sensors and compute the positions of lightnings. We will revisit our example in Section 3.6.7 and provide more details about our calculations. These details are not required to follow the example, but demonstrate how applications can use coherence measures we introduce in this chapter.

**Possible Failures.** Offsets among sensor node clocks add an observation error to the arrival times of a signal, which results in false locations. For example, the red point in Figure 3.2 (labeled as *Avoided Failure*) shows the computed lightning location which results from Sensor 2 being two seconds behind Sensor 1 and Sensor 3 being two seconds ahead of Sensor 1. Existing techniques simply assume that sensors report correct arrival times. Thus, they neither detect, quantify, nor prevent this error.

**Feature 1 - Synchronization Independent Precision.** In SENSE, users can specify a precision requirement which is *independent of clock synchronization* among sensor nodes. This precision requirement is reflected in an upper limit for coherence guarantees called $C_{g_{max}}$. For example, the orange area in Figure 3.2 (labeled as *Feature 1*) depicts the precision for $C_{g_{max}}$=2 seconds. With $C_{g_{max}}$=2 seconds, SENSE will locate the signal in the orange area even if sensor node clocks have arbitrary offsets. Thus, SENSE would avoid the failure in Figure 3.2 and locate the signal source in the orange area instead.

**Feature 2 - Precision Estimate.** The coherence estimate ($C_e$) allows for computing the area in which we expect the signal source assuming perfect synchronization among sensor node clocks (green area in Figure 3.2, labeled as *Feature 2*). In our example, sensors have a read time precision of $\pm0.5$ seconds, which is reflected in $C_e$. The result is a slight deviation in the location of the signal source (green point $\otimes$). The strength of our solution is the ability to quantify possible deviations (green area, labeled as *Feature 2*) instead of returning calculated locations only.

In summary, our coherence measures enhance applications by avoiding failures, by providing precision guarantees which are independent of clock synchronization, and by quantifying precision estimates.

## 3.3 Sources of Incoherence

There exist many reasons for deviations among sensor node clocks which impact time coherence. In this section, we highlight important observations with respect to these sources of incoherence. These observations lead to system requirements which motivate design decisions in SENSE.

**Clock Drift.** In Figure 3.3 on Page 62, we visualize clock drifts of three different clock types: (A) Raspberry Pi system clocks, which use the processor frequency as reference [26], (B) Real time hardware clocks, which have an integrated quartz crystal and cost about 14$ per unit [136], and (C) high precision clocks, which cost about 23$ per unit [142]. We provide supplementary technical information for all clocks and our simulation in the info box below the figure on Page 62.

We make three observation in Figure 3.3:

**1) Cheap clocks are heavily affected by clock drift.**
Regular system clocks on Raspberry Pis, which are widely used as sensor nodes, drift up to $\pm0.14$s/hour (3.36s/day). Remembering our example in Section 3.2, this drift causes major errors in the result after just a few hours uptime without clock synchronization. However, failing synchronization is a frequently reported issue on devices such as Raspberry Pis [135, 210], which should not cause failures in upstream analysis systems.

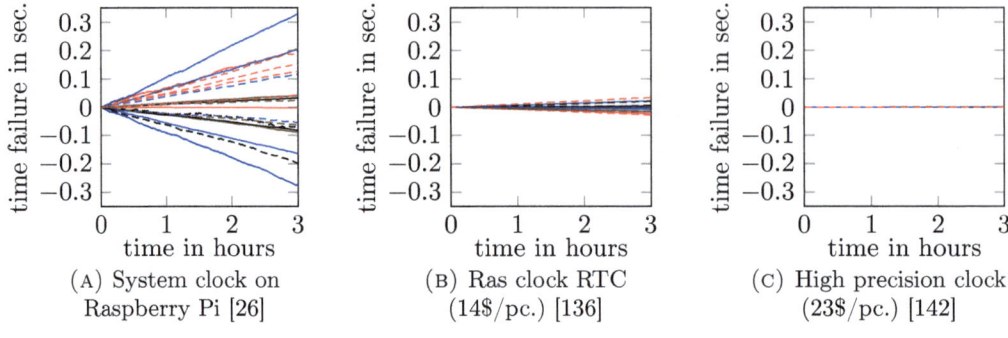

(A) System clock on Raspberry Pi [26]

(B) Ras clock RTC (14$/pc.) [136]

(C) High precision clock (23$/pc.) [142]

FIGURE 3.3: Clock drifts of 20 simulated clock instances for three different clock types assuming perfectly synchronized clocks on startup.

*Technical Details on Figure 3.3*

| Clock | PPM | Price | Frequency |
|---|---|---|---|
| Raspberry Pi System Clock [26] | 40 | free | 1 MHz |
| PCF2127 Real Time Clock [136] | 3 | 14$ | 32.768 kHz |
| 449-LFTVXO076344CUTT [142] | 0.1 | 23$ | 19.2 MHz |

TABLE 3.1: Specifications of different clocks at 30°C

In Figure 3.3, we present the clock drifts of different clocks. The figure shows the clock drifts of the selected clocks at 30°C. Table 3.1 summarizes the clock specifications of the selected clocks. The *parts per million* (PPM) provide an upper bound to the amount of additional or missed oscillations. For example, the Raspberry Pi system clock has a frequency of 1MHz (i.e. $10^6$ oscillations per second) and drifts with 40PPM. Thus, it drifts by $\pm 40/10^6$ seconds per second which is a drift of $\pm 0.144$ seconds per hour.

We obtained the data for Figure 3.3 by simulating the clock on the level of its oscillator. The expected amount of missed oscillations of a specific clock is assumed to be uniformly distributed within the ranges the manufacturer provided. This value – in the following referred to as $p$ – is sampled once per clock instance. The oscillator is modelled as a Bernoulli process. Thus, each time a timestamp $t_{i+1}$ is requested from a clock instance, we sample a Binomial distribution with probability $1 + p$ and the amount of trials equal to the time that passed since the last request $(t_{i+1} - t_i)$ in seconds multiplied by the clock model's frequency.

In addition, many devices do not have an own oscillator and depend on external oscillations which could possibly fail, such as the oscillation of the electricity grid. For example, in March 2018 thousands of devices, including electric meters and inverters of solar plants, accumulated more than 6 minutes delay, due to a conflict between Kosovo and Serbia about who is responsible for providing additional energy [175]. This caused the oscillation to stay below the desired 50Hz for more than a month [32, 123]. Hence, a conflict between two countries affected clocks everywhere in Europe. Although the power grid was brought back to its regular frequency [69], one still finds wrong timestamps in the logs of many smart meters and solar plants. This example shows that clocks may malfunction for surprising and unexpected reasons. In this chapter, we present a solution which makes systems robust against clock synchronization failures and clock drifts.

**2) Sensor nodes with precise clocks are expensive.**
We want to correlate data from thousands of sensors in the IoT [193]. These sensors are regularly hosted on cheap devices (sensor nodes) such as micro controllers, Arduinos, or Raspberry Pis. A precise clock alone costs 14$ or more, whereas a whole Raspberry Pi costs about 35$ (without a precise clock). Thus, large numbers of sensor nodes can hardly be upgraded with precise clocks due to the high price.

**3) Cheap clocks measure short time spans precisely.**
Even cheap clocks can measure short time spans precisely. We call the timeframe between the current time and the read time of a sensor value *age of the value*. Clock drift is the only factor which pollutes the measured ages of values. For example, the Raspberry Pi system clock drifts at most 0.006s/min. We regularly request values from sensors which are only a few seconds old and, thus, we can use the age of values as a reliable and precise measure.

**Clock Synchronization.** Sensor nodes limit the impact of clock drifts with repeated clock synchronization. NTPv4 is one of the most common synchronizations protocols and claims to be precise within *a few tens of milliseconds* [126]. However, when it comes to large numbers of sensors, there is no precise synchronization among all of them:

**1) The precision depends on the network.**
NTPv4 specifies its precision for *fast local area networks* [126]. Other networks may have larger latencies or more volatile transmission times which leads to more frequent and less reliable re-synchronization. Especially devices connected via mobile networks may experience precision issues.

**2) Not all devices have synchronized clocks.**

Many low-cost sensor nodes do not synchronize their clocks at all. For example, many micro controllers just start their clocks when powered on, only providing a simple up-time counter instead of a real clock. Since we regularly require the age of values instead of read times, our solution integrates sensors without synchronized clocks seamlessly.

**Resulting System Requirements.** We conclude that SENSE shall quantify the uncertainty about times provided by sensor nodes with coherence measures. SENSE shall provide synchronization independent coherence guarantees, and limit incoherence with time coherence optimization.

## 3.4 SENSE Architecture

In this section, we define coherence measures and introduce the SENSE architecture. We define coherence measures in Section 3.4.1, introduce our *general network and node setup* in Section 3.4.2, present the *global architecture* which covers the connection and interaction among distributed sensor nodes in Section 3.4.3, and describe the *internal architecture*, i.e., the software components of sensor nodes, in Section 3.4.4.

### 3.4.1 Definition of Coherence Measures

**Coherence of a Tuple / $C_{real}$:** Let a tuple contain the values $v_1, ..., v_N$ from $N$ sensors and let $t_1, ..., t_N$ be the times when $v_1, ..., v_N$ were measured. The coherence of a tuple is the timeframe between $\min(t_1, \ldots, t_N)$ and $\max(t_1, \ldots, t_N)$ in which $v_1, ..., v_N$ were measured. Tuple coherence is a key indicator to detect incoherent tuples and to prevent false analysis results. Ideally, all values of a tuple would be measured at the same time, which would result in the optimal coherence 0.

**Coherence Estimate of a Tuple / $C_e$:** We use the term *estimate* for the computed coherence ($C_e$) to emphasize the uncertainty about its correctness. $C_e$ equals $C_{real}$ if there is no offset among sensor node clocks. In practice $t_1, \ldots, t_N$ are obtained from different sensor node clocks and may be affected by clock drift. Thus, the computed coherence estimate $C_e$ of a tuple may diverge from the real coherence.

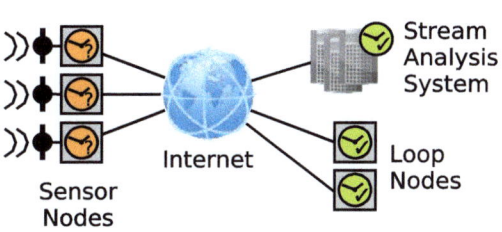 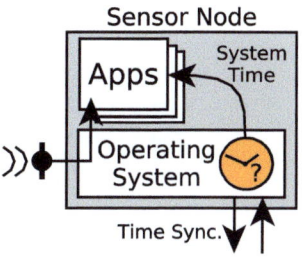

(A) Network connections and locations of clocks.    (B) Sensor node architecture.

FIGURE 3.4: General network and node setup in the IoT.

**Coherence Guarantee of a Tuple** / $C_g$: The coherence guarantee of a tuple is a timeframe which is guaranteed to be larger or equal than the real coherence of the tuple ($C_g \geq C_{real}$). We use the term *guarantee* to emphasize that $C_{real}$ is guaranteed to be smaller or equal than $C_g$ even if there are arbitrary offsets among sensor node clocks. The guarantee $C_g$ ensures that time coherence is bounded.

**Read Time Deviation** / $\Delta_t$: Each sensor data tuple has a timestamp $t$ which is the desired read time (i.e., request time) for values contained in the tuple. $\Delta_t$ is the maximum deviation between the desired read time $t$ and any actual read time $t_i$ of a value $v_i$ contained in the tuple. For example, if we request a tuple with $t=5$ and sensor provide values read at $t_1=4$ and $t_2=7$, then $\Delta_t=\max(\mathrm{abs}(5-4), \mathrm{abs}(5-7))=2$.

### 3.4.2 General Network and Node Setup

In this section, we discuss our assumptions with respect to network connections, communication protocols, geographic proximity, processing capabilities, and reliable clocks.

Our general setup covers key components of different IoT architectures [66, 103] (Figure 3.4a). Typically, sensor nodes communicate through the internet and/or local networks via standard TCP/IP protocols [65]. They may use additional protocols and message brokers to manage their communication such as MQTT [168] or ZeroMQ [80]. We require acknowledgements of receipt, but do not make any additional assumptions with respect to communication protocols or connection types (e.g., WiFi, LTE, or cable).

We differentiate trusted (⊘) and untrusted (⊘) clocks. For *trusted clocks*, we control time synchronization and can validate that the time is correct (i.e., properly set with known precision). For *untrusted clocks*, we cannot enforce correctness.

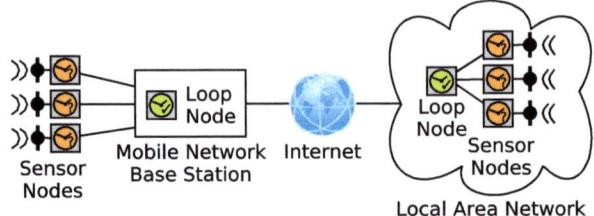

FIGURE 3.5: Exploiting local proximity of loop nodes and sensor nodes.

We operate a small number of nodes with trusted clocks which we call *Loop Nodes*. Loop nodes are servers which control the data acquisition from sensor nodes (to be discussed in Section 3.4.3). Since the number of loop nodes is small, we can afford to equip them with high precision clocks and make sure that trusted clocks are in sync.

The majority of devices are sensor nodes with untrusted clocks. Common sensor nodes are smart phones (e.g., Android or iOS systems) and small computers (e.g., Arduinos and Raspberry Pis), which are operated by diverse users and organizations. Since we do not control the clocks on these devices, we cannot enforce their correctness.

Figure 3.4b shows a sketch of the software architecture of sensor nodes. They consist of an operating system and an application layer. The operating systems allows for accessing sensors through driver modules [72] and maintains the system clock. The application layer (user space) hosts applications which access sensors and system time through the operating system. On sensor nodes, SENSE runs on the application layer – either as an application on its own, or as a library integrated in a host application such as a smart phone app. Ideally, sensor nodes can schedule sensor reads, have sufficient memory to buffer recent sensor values, and can retrieve these values upon request. Most sensor nodes fulfill these requirements. However, we discuss in Section 3.4.4 how we integrate sensor nodes which do not have sufficient memory and processing capabilities.

SENSE exploits geographic proximity if it leads to fast network connections among sensor nodes and loop nodes. Figure 3.5 shows two examples of a desirable proximity. On the left, a loop node is collocated with the base station of a mobile network and manages connected sensor nodes. On the right, a loop node and sensor nodes are collocated in the same local area network. Both setups lead to low latency and low jitter[1], which improves coherence guarantees. Despite these benefits, SENSE does not require local proximity and adapts to the observed latency, time coherence, and jitter.

---

[1]Network jitter is the variance of transmission times in a network.

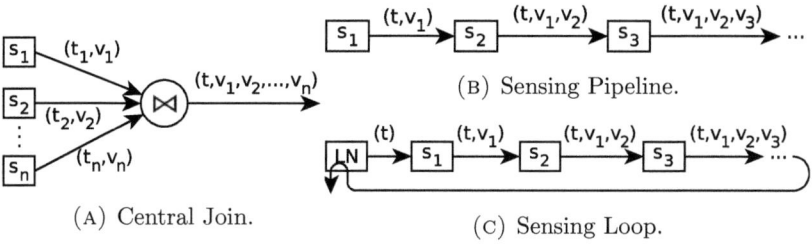

(A) Central Join.

(B) Sensing Pipeline.

(C) Sensing Loop.

FIGURE 3.6: Topologies for sensor data acquisition.

### 3.4.3 Global Architecture

Two common topologies for sensor data acquisition are *Central Joins* (Figure 3.6a) and *Sensing Pipelines* (Figure 3.6b). First, we discuss advantages, disadvantages, and limitations of these topologies. Then, we introduce *Sensing Loops* (Figure 3.6c) to overcome the limitations observed before.

In a **central join** topology, each sensor streams pairs of timestamps $(t)$ and values $(v)$ to a central server which joins time-value-pairs from all sensors. Examples are smart phone apps which report values to a server and stream joins in systems such as Apache Flink [35] and Spark [205]. The main advantage of this solution is its low latency. The latency is low, because sensors transmit their values directly to the central server. However, there are two major disadvantages in a central join topology: 1. The join cannot provide any guarantee for the time coherence of result tuples because it relies on the correctness of the timestamps transmitted from sensor nodes. 2. The solution does not scale to large numbers of sensors because of a limited number of concurrent network connections and an increasing join complexity. Especially in case of sensor failures, one cannot know if values are lost or late. Waiting for late tuples which never arrive increases the latency considerably.

In a **sensing pipeline**, one node initiates a request and passes it to the succeeding node in the pipeline. Each node in the pipeline adds a value from its sensor and forwards the tuple to the next sensor until the tuple contains all values. Example applications are Sensor Networks [6, 50, 121, 194]. Users submit queries to the network which collects data from sensors - possibly performs in-network computation [119, 154] - and finally returns result tuples to the user. The advantage of sensing pipelines is that they overcome scalability limitations of central servers which receive result tuples. Since the result tuple is produced in-network, there is only one connection to the receiver instead of a large

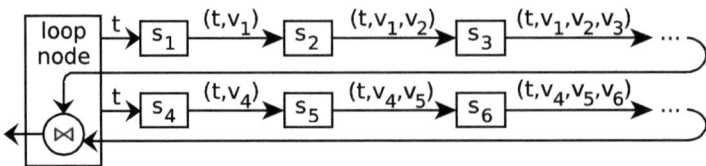

FIGURE 3.7: Example of an architecture combination.

number of concurrent connection from individual sensors. Moreover, there is no need to perform a join centrally, which reduces complexity.

Although sensing pipelines overcome scalability limitations on the receiver side, we still face scalability issues with large numbers of sensors. Since each transmission hop between sensor nodes introduces additional latency, the time between measuring a value and receiving the value at a central server increases considerably. Similar to central joins, it is impossible to ensure time coherence, because we still rely on separate sensor node clocks. We overcome the limitations of Central Joins and Sensing Pipelines by extending Sensing Pipelines to *Sensing Loops* and by combining *Sensing Loops with Central Joins*:

**Sensing loops** (Figure 3.6c) extend *Sensing Pipelines* with an additional *Loop Node* (LN). The loop node initiates requests by sending a request timestamp to the first sensor node in the pipeline. Once the request passes the pipeline, the last sensor node returns the result tuple to the loop node.

**Enabling Coherence Guarantees.** Sensing Loops enable coherence guarantees because sensor data tuples pass by the same clock (the loop node clock) twice. Thus, the loop node remembers the time a request was sent (loop start time $l_s$) and observes the time when it receives the result tuple (loop end time $l_e$). If all sensors read ad-hoc upon request (i.e., retrieve the current sensor value when they receive an input tuple), we can guarantee that the coherence of the tuple is smaller than the loop duration ($C_g = l_e - l_s$). This guarantee does not take any sensor node clock into consideration, which makes it independent of clock synchronization among sensor nodes. We extend this idea in the remainder of this chapter with read scheduling approaches going beyond ad-hoc reads. Thereby, we utilize our read scheduler which we presented in Chapter 2.

**Scaling to Large Numbers of Sensors.** The scalability issue of long sensing pipelines results from long latencies in too long pipelines. The scalability issue of central joins

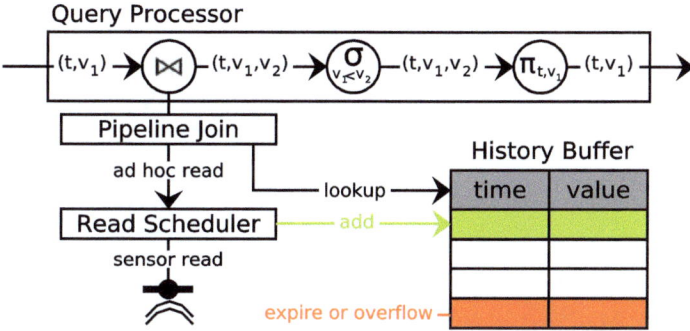

FIGURE 3.8: Overview of sensor node internals.

results from too many parallel network connections and an increasing computation effort for large numbers of sensors. We combine both solutions in Figure 3.7 to overcome scalability limitations. We automatically split and merge sensing loops depending on latency and coherence requirements, as well as observed network conditions. The loop node then centrally joins the results of all sensing loops.

For example, a sensing loop can collect values from 100 sensor nodes with less than three seconds latency. The loop node can join results returned by 100 loops with less than a second latency. In combination, we can provide a time coherent snapshot from 10000 sensors with less than four seconds latency and a coherence guarantee below three seconds. In the remainder of this chapter, we show we can further optimize coherence.

### 3.4.4  Internal Architecture

In the following paragraphs, we describe different components of the sensor node application. We show an overview of all these components in Figure 3.8.

**Query Processor.**  Our query processor is a stream processor, which adopts a tuple-at-a-time processing model similar to common streaming systems such as Apache Flink and Apache Storm. Each tuple passes through a processing pipeline, which includes gathering sensor values (pipeline join), as well as data manipulations (e.g., selections, projections, or spatial aggregations) [121].

We introduced spatial aggregations in Section 2.3.3.2 on Page 24. If a sensor node is part of a processing pipeline which computes a spatial aggregate, it can perform an incremental aggregation step to add its sensor value to the spatial aggregate. We show

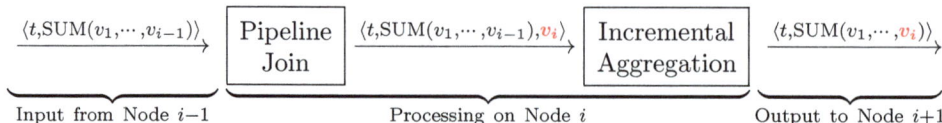

FIGURE 3.9: Incremental spatial aggregation in sensor node pipelines.

an example in Figure 3.9: The $i$-th sensor node in a processing pipelines receives an aggregate of values from nodes one to $i-1$. Node $i$ then fetches a value for time $t$ with a pipeline join (to be discussed). This value is added to the aggregate with an incremental aggregation step before the node transmits the result tuple to its succeeding node $i+1$.

In this chapter, we focus on the time coherence of result tuples with respect to sensor read times and, thus, we focus on data gathering operations instead of aggregations. However, our solution supports spatial aggregation as shown above.

**Pipeline Join.**   Our pipeline join is a sophisticated replacement of a simple ad-hoc sensor read. Instead of reading sensor values ad-hoc when processing a tuple, we join input tuples with a recent sensor measurement. For each tuple, each sensor node selects the best value from its history buffer with respect to coherence measures.

**Read Scheduler.**   The read scheduler is an active component which performs sensor reads and adds the resulting values and read timestamps to the buffer of the sensor node. The read scheduler also performs requested ad-hoc reads. We use a read scheduler which was introduced in Chapter 2 [178]. This scheduler supports reading periodically, scheduling sensor reads at specific times, reading ad-hoc, and adaptive sampling techniques such as AdaM [186], FAST [59], and L-SIP [67] (defined in Section 2.3.2). Adaptive sampling techniques can reduce the number of required sensor reads, which saves energy. We discuss the scheduling approaches which are relevant for this chapter in Section 3.7.

**History Buffer.**   The history buffer of a sensor node stores read times and sensor measurements. The read scheduler adds entries to the buffer. The history buffer handles the expiration of buffer entries. Entries expire regularly after a certain time or after they were joined with a tuple. In case of failures, there may be buffer overflows which are also handled by the history buffer. We discuss our expiration and overflow mechanisms in detail in Section 3.8.2.

**Sensor Node Limitations.** We are aware that sensor nodes exist that cannot support all components described above. We ensure that our solutions can seamlessly integrate such nodes. If a sensor node cannot run a sophisticated read scheduler, we read values from sensors periodically, which is commonly supported by sensor nodes (Section 3.7). If a sensor node has a buffer that is too small, we address buffer overflows with an overflow mechanism (Section 3.8.2). If a sensor node cannot process custom operations going beyond sensor reads, we will not assign additional operators to the node [121]. We will also not assign operators to a node which has insufficient computational power. We did not experience any performance issues due to pipeline joins. The pipeline join requires a lookup in the history buffer to find the value with the closest timestamp. This memory lookup has a time complexity of $O(log(N))$ where $N$ is the size of the buffer. In our experiments on Raspberry Pis, we observed that the join requires much less computation effort than performing sensor reads and networking tasks.

## 3.5   Coherence Guarantees and Coherence Estimates

In this section, we discuss how SENSE calculates coherence guarantees $(C_g)$ and coherence estimates $(C_e)$ for tuples. We illustrate our discussion with diagrams which are inspired by UML sequence diagrams. In these diagrams, time processes from top to bottom, and columns separate locations (i.e., sensor nodes) at which actions take place.

### 3.5.1   Coherence Guarantees

In contrast to sensing pipelines and central joins, sensing loops can provide a coherence guarantee which is independent of clock synchronization among sensor node clocks. The loop node observes the coherence guarantee for each sensor data tuple which passes the loop. We compute the coherence guarantee at the loop node with Formula 3.1. We name the start time of a tuple passing through the loop $l_s$ and the end time $l_e$. When performing a pipeline join, each sensor $s_i$ provides the age $\alpha_i$ of its value $v_i$ used for the join. Thus, $\alpha_i$ is the age of $v_i$ at the join time at $s_i$. Be reminded that the age $\alpha_i$ is highly precise for recent measurements even with the cheapest clocks (Section 3.3).

$$C_g = (l_e - \min(\alpha_1, \ldots, \alpha_N)) - (l_s - \max(\alpha_1, \ldots, \alpha_N)) \qquad (3.1)$$

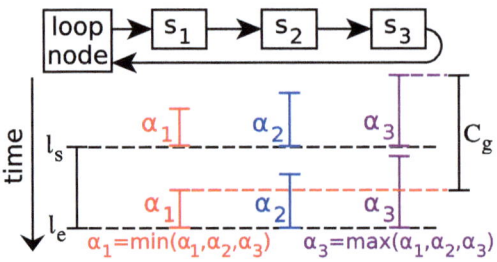

FIGURE 3.10: Illustration of the coherence guarantee $C_g$.

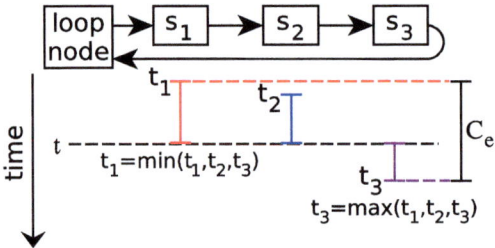

FIGURE 3.11: Illustration of the coherence estimate $C_e$.

Figure 3.10 illustrates the observation of the coherence guarantee. We know that all pipeline joins are performed between $l_s$ and $l_e$. Thus, the latest possible read time of a value in the tuple is $l_e - \min(\alpha_1, \alpha_2, \alpha_3)$, which is $l_e - \alpha_1$ in our example. The earliest possible read time of a value in the tuple is $l_s - \max(\alpha_1, \alpha_2, \alpha_3)$, which is $l_e - \alpha_3$ in our example. The coherence guarantee is the timeframe between the earliest and the latest possible read time calculated in Formula 3.1.

### 3.5.2 Coherence Estimate

We calculate $C_e$ at the loop node with Formula 3.2. Figure 3.11 illustrates the calculation. Each sensor node $s_i$ provides the read time $t_i$ of its value $v_i$ used for the sensor data tuple. We take the latest read time of any value (according to sensor node clocks) which is $\max(t_1, \ldots, t_n)$ and subtract the earliest read time of any value which is $\min(t_1, \ldots, t_n)$.

$$C_e = \max(t_1, \ldots, t_n) - \min(t_1, \ldots, t_n) \tag{3.2}$$

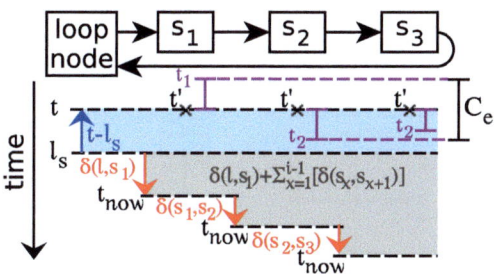

FIGURE 3.12: $C_e$ without clock synchronization.

Formula 3.2 calculates $C_e$ under the assumption that sensor node clocks are synchronized correctly. Thus, it provides an estimate which disregards clock deviations. Alternatively, we can calculate $C_e$ independent of clock synchronization if we know or estimate data transmission latencies instead. $C_e$ may be more precise based on transmission latencies than based on clock synchronization. For example, if transmission times are constant (hardware buses), well predictable (dedicated connection), or negligible (fibre optics).

Figure 3.12 illustrates how we compute $C_e$ based on transmission and processing latencies among sensor nodes. Let $\delta(s_a, s_b)$ be the transmission and processing latency between two sensors $s_a$ and $s_b$, and let $\delta(l, s_a)$ be the transmission and processing latency between the loop node and a sensor $s_a$. Let $t_{now}$ be the current time according to the unsynchronized sensor clock. Then the desired read time $t'$ according to the unsynchronized sensor clock is given by Formula 3.3. We perform the pipeline join based on the calculated $t'$ - ignoring the desired read time $t$ contained in the tuple. Thus, we make the join independent of time synchronization.

$$t' = t_{now} + (t - l_s) - (\delta(l, s_1) + \delta(s_1, s_2) + \cdots + \delta(s_{i-1}, s_i))$$

$$t' = t_{now} + (t - l_s) - (\delta(l, s_1) + \sum_{x=1}^{i-1} \delta(s_x, s_{x+1})) \tag{3.3}$$

As a result of the join, we receive $v_i$ and $t'_i$. $t'_i$ is the read time of $v_i$ according to the unsynchronized clock at $s_i$. We compute $t_i$ from $t'_i$ based on the shift between $t$ and $t'$ with the formula $t_i = t'_i + (t - t')$. Finally, we can compute $C_e$ from $t_i, \ldots, t_N$ as before with Formula 3.2.

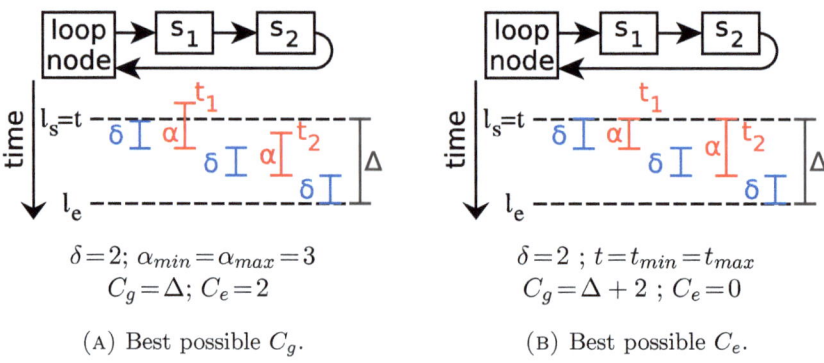

$$\delta=2;\ \alpha_{min}=\alpha_{max}=3$$
$$C_g=\Delta;\ C_e=2$$

(A) Best possible $C_g$.

$$\delta=2\ ;\ t=t_{min}=t_{max}$$
$$C_g=\Delta+2\ ;\ C_e=0$$

(B) Best possible $C_e$.

FIGURE 3.13: The tradeoff between $C_e$ and $C_g$.

### 3.5.3 Coherence Tradeoff ($C_e$-$C_g$-Tradeoff)

We compute a coherence guarantee ($C_g$) and a coherence estimate ($C_e$) for each tuple. There exists a tradeoff between the best possible $C_g$ and the best possible $C_e$ of a tuple. We show this tradeoff in Figure 3.13. In our example, we specify the mean hop time $\delta=2$ and acquire values from $N=2$ nodes. In Figure 3.13a, we show the optimal read times with respect to $C_g$. $C_g$ is optimal if $\alpha_{min}=\alpha_{max}$. However, if $\alpha_{min}=\alpha_{max}$ (i.e., if all ages are identical), then $t_1, \ldots, t_N$ deviate from the request time $t$ which increases $C_e$. In Figure 3.13b, we set $t=t_{min}=t_{max}$ which is the optimum with respect to $C_e$. In exchange, $\alpha_{max} - \alpha_{min}$ is 2 which increases $C_g$ respectively.

Typically, users want to specify a precision requirement which translates to an upper limit for $C_g$ which we call $C_{gmax}$. At the same time, users want to receive a result which is as precise as possible. Usually, a smaller $C_e$ improves the result quality assuming that sensor nodes try to provide correct timestamps for their values. In the next section, we describe how we tradeoff between $C_g$ and $C_e$ automatically such that we minimize $C_e$ ensuring $C_g \leq C_{gmax}$.

## 3.6 Optimizing Time Coherence

In this section, we present how we optimize the coherence estimate while enforcing an upper bound for the coherence guarantee. First we present an overview of the solution, then we present the algorithms and formulas used at loop nodes and sensor nodes. Finally, we present an example calculation which demonstrates our algorithms and formulas.

### 3.6.1    Solution Overview

We automatically adjust two parameters ($\alpha$ and $\mu$) to trade off between the best coherence guarantee and the best coherence estimate. The loop node computes the coherence guarantee ($C_g$), the coherence estimate ($C_e$), and the roundtrip time ($\Delta$) for each tuple which passes through the sensing loop. Using these values ($C_g$, $C_e$, and $\Delta$), the loop node continuously tunes $\alpha$ and $\mu$ and disseminates updates to all sensor nodes in the loop. We attach $\alpha$ and $\mu$ to regular sensor data tuples to prevent additional messages.

When a sensor node receives a tuple (i.e., a sensor data request), it adds a value from its buffer based on the current values of $\alpha$ and $\mu$ (pipeline join). Let $t$ be the desired timestamp of the tuple and $t_{now}$ be the current time according to the sensor node clock. To achieve an optimal $C_g$, we would select a value read at $t_{now}$-$\alpha$. To achieve an optimal $C_e$, we would select a value read at $t$. Thus, we select a value which was read between $t_{now}$-$\alpha$ and $t$. The current value of $\mu$ specifies which value between $t_{now}$-$\alpha$ and $t$ we select. In the next sections, we discuss how sensor nodes select values from buffers based on $\alpha$ and $\mu$ and how loop nodes tune $\alpha$ and $\mu$.

### 3.6.2    Sensor Node Algorithm

We now discuss how sensor nodes, which are part of a sensing loop, join input tuples (i.e., sensor data requests) with sensor values from their buffers. A sensor node, which is the $i$-th node in the loop, receives tuples in the folloring format:

$$\langle t, \alpha, \mu, \alpha_{min}, \alpha_{max}, t_{min}, t_{max}, v_1, \ldots, v_{i-1} \rangle$$

The node joins each tuple with a value $\langle t_i, v_i \rangle$ from its local sensor stored in the history buffer. The resulting output tuple has the following format:

$$\langle t, \alpha, \mu, \alpha_{min}, \alpha_{max}, t_{min}, t_{max}, v_1, \ldots, v_i \rangle.$$

$\alpha_{min}$ and $\alpha_{max}$ are the minimum and maximum age of any value ($v_1, \ldots, v_N$) at the join time at the respective sensor node. $t_{min}$ and $t_{max}$ are the minimum and maximum timestamps $t_i$ of any value ($v_1, \ldots, v_N$) according to sensor node clocks.

We define the following optimization function which selects the best available value $v_i$ from the sensor node buffer:

$$\mathrm{opt}(t, t_{now}, \mu, \alpha) = \underset{t_i \in \mathrm{Buffer}}{\mathrm{argmin}} [\underbrace{\mathrm{abs}(t_i - t)}_{\text{cost of } C_e} + \underbrace{(t_{now} - t_i - \alpha)^2 \cdot \mu}_{\text{cost of } C_g}] \tag{3.4}$$

This optimization function expresses the tradeoff between $C_e$ (first part) and $C_g$ (second part). The first part increases linearly for worse $C_e$. The second part has a higher order to emphasize its weight strongly when approaching an upper bound for $C_g$. The parameter $\mu \in \mathbb{R}^+$ weights the second part to adapt the tradeoff against the first part.

### 3.6.3   Loop Node Algorithm

We now discuss how we tune $\mu$ and $\alpha$ on loop nodes. In addition to our notations defined before, our formulas and algorithms in this section use the following variables. A full list with all notations can be found on Page 162.

$\delta$ : Mean hop time between sensor nodes.

$N$: Number of sensor nodes in a sensing loop.

$D_{max}$: Desired upperbound for $C_g$ (max. incoherence).

$t_l$ : The last time $\mu$ and $\alpha$ have been updated.

$p$ : Variable which indicates if $D_{max}$ was met ($C_g < D_{max}$).

$s$ : Step width exponent (scales step width for $\mu$ updates).

$w$ : Step width for $\mu$ updates.

Before we discuss how we select $\alpha$ and $\mu$, we define $D_{max}$. $D_{max}$ is a system internal variable which specifies the optimization goal for $C_g$. In SENSE, users set an upper bound $C_{g_{max}}$ for $C_g$, which the system tries to maintain for all tuples. Each tuple has its individual coherence guarantee $C_g$, which may vary among tuples due to changing network conditions, processing delays on sensor nodes, or failures. All these effects are reflected in the roundtrip time $\Delta$.

We monitor the standard deviation $\sigma$ of $\Delta$ and set $D_{max}$ such that a configurable fraction of tuples has $C_g \leq C_{g_{max}}$. Per default, we set $D_{max} = C_{g_{max}} - 3\sigma$. Assuming that values of $\Delta$ are normally distributed, $C_g \leq C_{g_{max}}$ holds for 99.85% of our result tuples according to the 68–95–99.7 rule [144]. Monitoring $\sigma$ has the negligible overhead of storing three floating point values.

We show the overall algorithm that tunes $\alpha$ and $\mu$, calculates $C_e$ and $C_g$, and emits result tuples in Algorithm 5 on Page 77. This algorithm processes each sensor data tuple which returns to the loop node after passing the sensing loop.

First, we compute the round trip time $\Delta$ for the tuple we process in Line 1. In Lines 2 and 3, we compute $C_g$ and $C_e$ as discussed before. We then emit the result tuple, including $C_g$ and $C_e$ in Line 4. The remainder of the algorithm updates $\alpha$ and $\mu$. We update $\alpha$ and $\mu$ as soon as we observe the effect of previous updates. In Line 5, we

---

**Algorithm 5** Optimization of $\alpha$ and $\mu$ at the loopnode.

---

**State:** $l_s$,$N$,$t_l$,$s$,$\mu$,$p$
**Parameters:** Tuple: $\langle t, \alpha_{min}, \alpha_{max}, t_{min}, t_{max}, v_1, \ldots, v_N \rangle$

| | | |
|---|---|---|
| 1: | $\Delta \leftarrow l_s - \text{time}()$ | ◁ compute roundtrip time |
| 2: | $C_g \leftarrow \Delta + \alpha_{max} - \alpha_{min}$ | ◁ compute coherence guarantee |
| 3: | $C_e \leftarrow t_{max} - t_{min}$ | ◁ compute coherence estimate |
| 4: | $\text{emit}(t, C_g, C_e, v_1, \ldots, v_N)$ | ◁ emit result tuple |
| 5: | **if** $l_s \geq t_l$ **then** | ◁ did earlier updates take affect? |
| 6: | $\quad \alpha \leftarrow \Delta/2$ | ◁ compute $\alpha$ without shift |
| 7: | $\quad s \leftarrow s + (p == \text{sign}(D_{max} - C_g) \ ? \ 1 : -1)$ | ◁ calculate step width exponent |
| 8: | $\quad w \leftarrow 2^s$ | ◁ set step width for $\mu$ |
| 9: | $\quad \mu \leftarrow \mu \ / \ (2\, \text{sign}\,(D_{max} - C_g)\, w\mu + 1)$ | ◁ calculate new $\mu$ |
| 10: | $\quad$ **if** $p == \text{sign}(D_{max} - C_g)$ **then** | |
| 11: | $\quad\quad p \leftarrow \text{sign}(D_{max} - C_g)$ | ◁ remember direction |
| 12: | $\quad$ **else** | |
| 13: | $\quad\quad p \leftarrow 0$ | ◁ half step size if direction changed |
| 14: | $\quad$ **end if** | |
| 15: | **end if** | |

---

check if the last $\alpha$ and $\mu$ update took affect for the tuple we process. For example, if we request a sensor data tuple every 0.2s and the roundtrip time is 1s, this condition will be true for every fifth tuple.

**Selecting $\alpha$.** The optimum for the coherence guarantee is the roundtrip time $\Delta$ of a tuple. This optimum ($C_g = \Delta$) is achieved if all sensor nodes provide values with equal ages $\alpha_i$ according to their local clocks at the join time $t_{now}^{(i)}$. In general, an arbitrary age $\alpha_i$ leads to an optimal $C_g$ as long as the age is the same on all sensor nodes. However, different $\alpha$ values imply smaller or larger read time deviations $\Delta_t$. An optimal $\alpha$ implies the minimum mean squared deviation between $t$ and $t_1, \ldots, t_N$ (optimal $\Delta_t$). Our algorithm calculates the optimal $\alpha$ in Line 6 using Formula 3.5. We derive Formula 3.5 mathematically in Section 3.6.8 and provide an example in the following paragraph.

$$\alpha = \frac{\delta(N+1)}{2} + (l_s - t) = \frac{\Delta}{2} + (l_s - t) \tag{3.5}$$

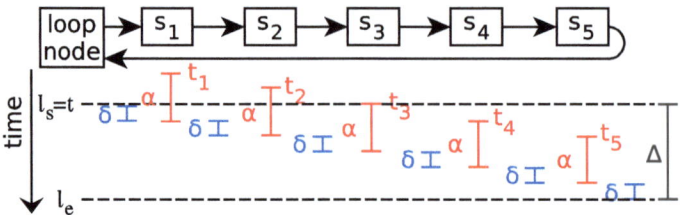

FIGURE 3.14: Selecting the optimal $\alpha=3$ for $\delta=1$ and $N=5$.

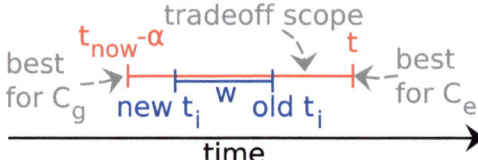

FIGURE 3.15: The step width $w$ in the tradeoff scope.

In Figure 3.14, we show an example with $N=5$ nodes and a mean hop time of $\delta=1$, which leads to $\alpha=3$. We observe that half of the nodes select values read before $t$ and the other half selects values read after $t$. This minimizes the mean squared error (i.e., difference) between $t$ and $t_1, \ldots, t_N$. Note that we set the request time $t$ equal to the loop start time $l_s$ in our example. Differences between $t$ and $l_s$ would be added to $\alpha$ (rear part of Formula 3.5) which leads to the same mean squared error. We also calculate alpha without the shift between $t$ and $l_s$ in Line 6 of Algorithm 5. We add shifts $(l_s - t)$ to $\alpha$ whenever we send out a tuple from the loop node.

**Selecting $\mu$.** As discussed in Section 3.6.2, sensor nodes select a value read between $t_{now}$-$\alpha$ (optimal $C_g$) and $t$ (optimal $C_e$) depending on $\mu$. Figure 3.15 illustrates this tradeoff scope. Before we select $\mu$, we calculate the update step width $w$ with respect to the tradeoff scope. Ideally, our result tuples have the best possible $C_e$ while not exceeding the desired upper bound for $C_g$ which we computed as $D_{max}$ (see above).

*Update Step Width:* First, we compute the exponent $s$ of the step with in Line 7 of Algorithm 5. We then compute the step width $w=2^s$ in Line 8. In order to set the exponent $s$, we introduce an additional state variable $p$ which can have three stages depending on the previous run of the algorithm:

$$1 \text{ if } C_g > D_{max}, \quad -1 \text{ if } C_g < D_{max}, \quad \text{or} \quad 0 \text{ if } C_g = D_{max}.$$

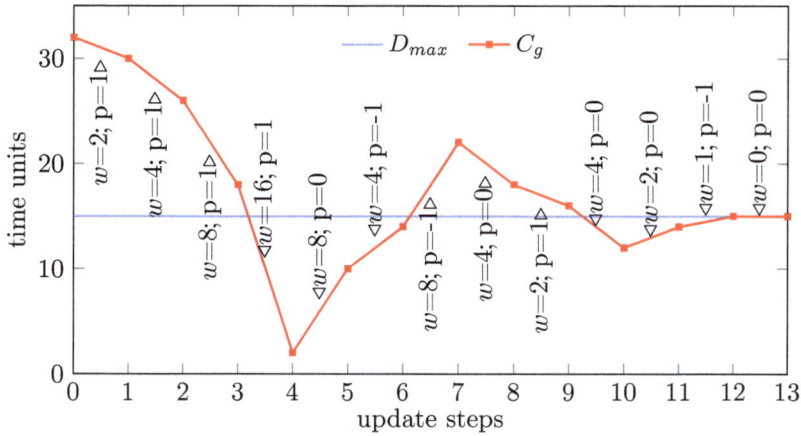

FIGURE 3.16: Convergence of $C_g$ to $D_{max}$ with corresponding $w$ and $p$.

We set $p = 0$ if $C_g > D_{max}$ changes to $C_g < D_{max}$ or vice versa. We use $p$ to control when we decrement or increment the exponent $s$ of the step width $w$ (double or half $w$).

Figure 3.16 shows an example where $C_g$ converges to $D_{max}$. For each step, we show $w$ and $p$ next to the curve separated with semicolon. As long as $C_g$ approaches $D_{max}$, we increment $s$ (i.e., double $w$) in each step (up to Step 4). This ensures that we reach $D_{max}$ fast. As soon as we jump over the $D_{max}$ border, we change the direction, decrement $s$ (i.e., half $w$), and set $p = 0$ (Step 5). Setting $p = 0$ ensures that we decrement $s$ again for the next step (Step 6). We always decrement $s$ twice after changing the direction. This ensures that we converge towards $D_{max}$. In our example, we reach $C_g = D_{max}$ after 13 steps.

*Update $\mu$:* We derive a formula for updating $\mu$ such that changing $w$ changes the analytic optimum for $t_i$ by $w$ on sensor nodes (blue bar in Figure 3.15).

$$\mu \leftarrow \frac{\mu}{2 \operatorname{sign}(D_{max} - C_g) w \mu + 1} \tag{3.6}$$

We update $\mu$ according to the desired step width $w$ with Formula 3.6 (Line 9 in Algorithm 5). We derive this formula analytically in Section 3.6.8. We transfer the parameter $\mu$ to sensor nodes instead of sending $w$ directly because we gain important flexibility. By computing the optimal read time on the sensor node based on $\mu$, we can consider additional information in the optimization such as the timestamps available in the buffer and selected values of previous nodes. This information is not available before the loop starts. We explain these additional optimizations in Section 3.6.6. Moreover, we can weight deviations in $w$ flexibly on sensor nodes. For example, we penalize deviations in the direction of $C_e$ with a higher order function than deviations in the direction of $C_g$.

**Initialization of $\alpha$ and $\mu$.** We first acquire one tuple from sensors nodes with ad-hoc reads and, thereby, obtain $\Delta$, which we use to initialize $\alpha$ (Formula 3.5). To initialize $\mu$, we estimate $t_{now}^{(i)}$ at any node $i$ based on $\delta$ (see calculation of $\alpha$). We then set the first value of $\mu$ such that the coherence guarantee is just met in case $\delta$ does not change. We derive the respective initialization formula in Section 3.6.8.

### 3.6.4  Example Calculation

We provide an example calculation in Figure 3.17 on Page 81 which demonstrates how we tune $\alpha$ and $\mu$. In this example, we optimize $\alpha$ and $\mu$ in a loop with two sensor nodes.

The loop node receives a result tuple (id 0) and computes the coherence guarantee of the tuple (red line). We observe that $C_g > D_{max}$. The loop node now computes $p$, $\alpha$, $s$, $w$, and $\mu$ with the formulas presented in the previous sections. At $t = 135$, the loop node sends a request (id 1) to Node 1, which selects a value from its buffer according to Formula 3.4 presented in Section 3.6.2. Then, Node 1 forwards the tuple to Node 2 with updated $\alpha_{min}$ and $t_{min}$. Analogue to Node 1, Node 2 selects a value from its buffer and adjusts $\alpha_{max}$ and $t_{max}$. Node 2 returns the result tuple to the loop node where we compute $C_g$ and $C_e$. We observe that $C_e$ increased and $C_g$ reduces compared to the previous tuple. We now achieved $C_g \leq D_{max}$ as intended.

### 3.6.5  Splitting and Merging Sensing Loops

If we either exceed $D_{max}$ or do not satisfy our latency requirements, the loopnode splits the set of sensor nodes into multiple sensing loops. The maximum number of sensing loops is specified according to the loop node performance.

We split sensing loops such that the roundtrip times of loops equal each other. This isolates stragglers and therefore increases the global performance of the system. The pipelines with the smallest roundtrip time are considered for a merge whenever the combined roundtrip time is expected to fulfill the latency and the coherence requirement.

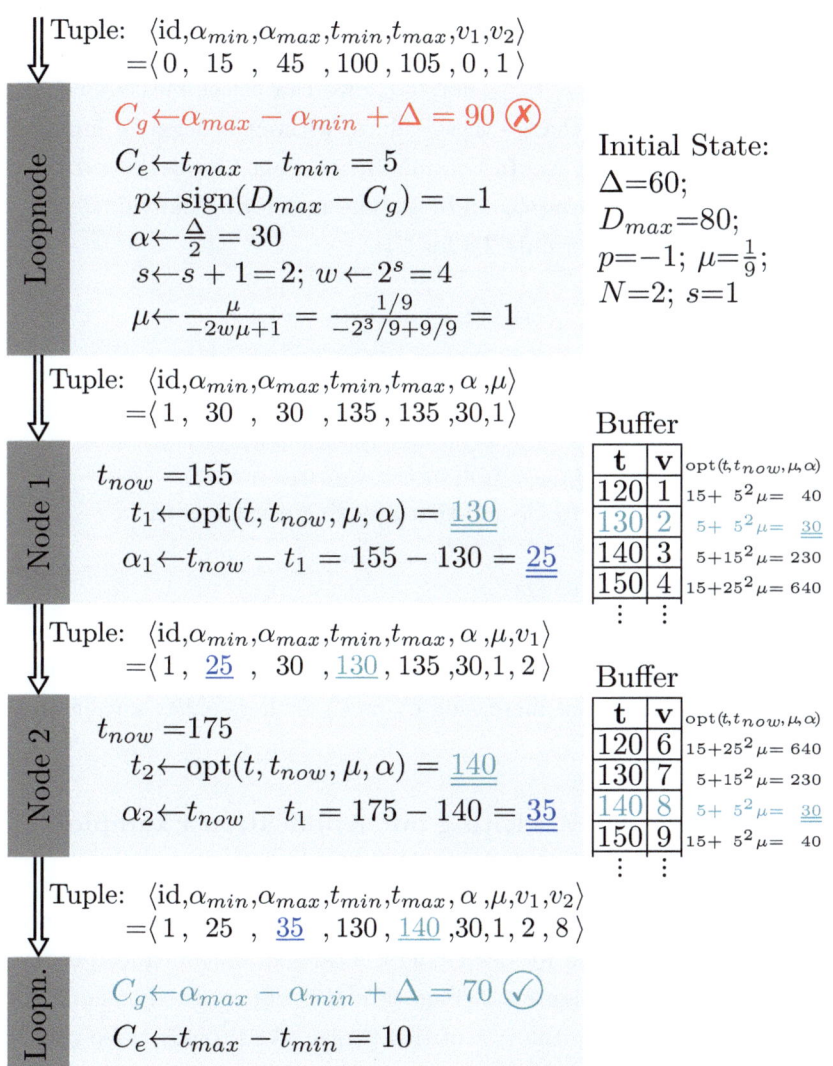

FIGURE 3.17: Example calculation: One optimization iteration for $\alpha$ and $\mu$ in a sensing loop with two nodes.

### 3.6.6 Additional Optimizations

We apply an additional optimization on sensor nodes which utilizes our knowledge about read times on previous nodes in the loop. More precisely, at any sensor node, we know the current values of $\alpha_{min}$, $\alpha_{max}$, $t_{min}$, and $t_{max}$. Since $C_e$ and $C_g$ do not change, if we change neither $\alpha_{min}$, $\alpha_{max}$, $t_{min}$, nor $t_{max}$, we can select measurements from the history buffer, which do not change these values, without a negative impact on $C_e$ or $C_g$. This allows for improving $\Delta_t$. In Formula 3.4 on Page 75, we showed the combined cost function for deviations from $C_e$ and $C_g$. The underlying individual cost functions are Formula 3.7 for $C_e$ and Formula 3.8 for $C_g$:

$$\text{cost}_{C_e}(t, t_i) = \text{abs}(t_i - t) \tag{3.7}$$

$$\text{cost}_{C_g}(t_{now}, t_i, \alpha) = (t_{now} - t_i - \alpha)^2 \tag{3.8}$$

We extend these cost functions to express that selecting a value with
$$t_{now} - t_i = \alpha_i \in [\alpha_{min}, \alpha_{max}]$$
implies no costs with respect to $C_g$ and that selecting a value with
$$t_i \in [t_{min}, t_{max}]$$
implies no costs with respect to $C_e$.

This optimization allows for utilizing failures of previous nodes to select a value which is as close as possible to $t$ if this does neither increase $C_e$ nor $C_g$. Moreover, the extended cost functions prevent increasing $C_e$ or $C_g$ if there exists a value in the buffer which does not increase $C_e$ or $C_g$.

### 3.6.7 Multilateration: Revisiting our Application Example

In Section 3.2, we provided an application example which quantifies the precision of a multilateration using our coherence measures $C_e$ and $C_g$. We now have all formulas and techniques at hand which allow for describing the calculation which lead to the example provided in Section 3.2 and Figure 3.2 (Page 60). It is not required to understand these calculations in order to follow the rest of this thesis. We provide these calculations as an example for applications developers who want to utilize coherence measures.

We first define the positions of sensors as
$$s_1(100, 200), \quad s_2(7000, 1000), \quad \text{and} \quad s_3(4200, 4000).$$
The real location of the signal source in our example is $\quad S(3456, 1234) = (x, y)$.

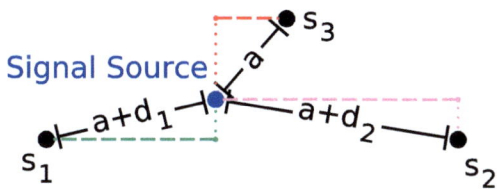

FIGURE 3.18: Sketch of the distances between the
signal source and the sensors.

We measure the arrival times of the signal at our three sensors. $t_1$, $t_2$, and $t_3$ are
the times when the signal arrives at $s_1$, $s_2$, and $s_3$. The signal arrives first at the closest
sensor which is $s_3$. Then, the signal arrives $t_1 - t_3$ later at $s_1$ and $t_2 - t_3$ later at $s_2$.
We can convert these time frames to distances by multiplying them with the signal
dissemination speed. In our example this is sonic speed which is 343m/s. We name
the resulting distances $d_1$ and $d_2$. In addition we name the unknown distance between
$s_3$ and the signal source $a$. Figure 3.18 provides a sketch of the distances between the
signal source and the sensors. With the Pythagorean Theorem, we derive the Equation
System 3.9:

$$a^2 = (4200 - \mathrm{x})^2 + (4000 - \mathrm{y})^2$$
$$(a + d_1)^2 = (100 - \mathrm{x})^2 + (200 - \mathrm{y})^2 \qquad (3.9)$$
$$(a + d_2)^2 = (7000 - \mathrm{x})^2 + (1000 - \mathrm{y})^2$$

With perfectly synchronized sensor node clocks, we measure $d_1 \approx 647.37$ and $d_2 \approx$
687.40. We can now solve the equation system for $a$, $x$, and $y$ to receive the position of
the signal source $x = 3456$, $y = 1234$, and $a = 2864.31$. Any localization failure can be
computed by adjusting $d_1$ and $d_2$ with respect to wrongly measured signal arrival times.

The coherence guarantee $C_g$ quantifies the uncertainty about the precision of signal
arrival times. Given $l_s$, $l_e$, $\alpha_{min}$, and $\alpha_{max}$, we can compute a time period in which the
signal arrived at a sensor. The earliest possible arrival time of the signal is $l_s - \alpha_{max}$.
The latest possible arrival time is $l_e - \alpha_{min}$. The time frame between the earliest and
the latest possible time is $C_g$. To get the guaranteed location precision (orange area
in Figure 3.2 on Page 60), we calculate the earliest and latest possible arrival times for
all three sensors. We then calculate six localizations of the signal source which result

from combinations of earliest and latest possible arrival times. These are all combinations excluding the two combinations which include all earliest and all latest arrival times. The resulting positions are the corners of the guaranteed detection area. One can observe that changing any detection time from its minimum to its maximum results in a linear movement of the computed location from one corner to another corner of the guarantee area. Thus, the real location of the signal source must be inside this area.

We compute the area of the precision estimate analogue to the area of the precision guarantee with $t_{min}$ being the earliest arrival time and $t_{max}$ being the latest arrival time.

### 3.6.8 Mathematical Details

In this section, we provide mathematical details on our formulas for $\alpha$ and $\mu$. We mathematically derive the update rules for $\alpha$ and $\mu$ as well as the initialization rule for $\mu$. It is not required to understand the mathematical details presented in this section in order to follow the remainder of this thesis. However, we include these details to enable future research and to allow for improving and extending our formulas.

#### 3.6.8.1 Derivation of the $\alpha$-Formula

In this section, we mathematically derive Formula 3.5, which computes the optimal $\alpha$ on the loop node. Our goal is to find the value for $\alpha$ which implies the minimum mean squared error between the request time $t$ of a tuple and the read times $(t_1, \ldots, t_N)$ of values $(v_1, \ldots, v_N)$ contained in the tuple.

Formula 3.10 computes the mean squared error which depends on $\alpha$ and the join times $t_{now}^{(1)}, \ldots, t_{now}^{(N)}$ on sensor nodes.

$$\text{ERR}(\alpha, t_{now}^{(1)}, \ldots, t_{now}^{(N)}) = \frac{1}{N} \sum_{i=1}^{N} \left( t - (t_{now}^{(i)} - \alpha) \right)^2 \qquad (3.10)$$

We select $\text{argmin}(\text{ERR}(\alpha, t_{now}^{(1)}, \ldots, t_{now}^{(N)}))$ as $\alpha$ to minimize the error. Because the actual join times at sensor nodes are unknown at the loop node, we replace them with estimated join times $(\mathbb{E}(t_{now}^{(1)}), \ldots, \mathbb{E}(t_{now}^{(N)}))$ in Formula 3.11. The expected value of $t_{now}^{(i)}$ is $l_s + \delta i$ because node $i$ receives the tuple $i$ hops after the loop start time $l_s$. The mean hop time is $\delta = \Delta/(N+1)$ and we know $\Delta$ from previous tuples.

$$\text{ERR}\left(\alpha, \mathbb{E}\left(t_{now}^{(1)}\right), \ldots, \mathbb{E}\left(t_{now}^{(N)}\right)\right) = \frac{1}{N} \sum_{i=1}^{N} (t - (l_s + \delta i - \alpha))^2 \qquad (3.11)$$

We now define Formula 3.12 and insert it into Formula 3.11 which results in Formula 3.13.

$$\alpha = x + (l_s - t) \tag{3.12}$$

$$\text{ERR}\left(\alpha, \mathbb{E}\left(t_{now}^{(1)}\right), \ldots, \mathbb{E}\left(t_{now}^{(N)}\right)\right) = \frac{1}{N}\sum_{i=1}^{N}(x - \delta i)^2 \tag{3.13}$$

We observe in Formula 3.14 that the second derivative of Formula 3.13 with respect to $x$ is positive. Thus, the minimum of the function $\text{ERR}\left(\alpha, t_{now}^{(1)}, \ldots, t_{now}^{(N)}\right)$ can be found at the simple zero of the first derivative with respect to $x$.

$$\frac{\partial^2}{\partial^2 x}\text{ERR}\left(\alpha, t_{now}^{(1)}, \ldots, t_{now}^{(N)}\right) = 2 > 0 \tag{3.14}$$

$$\begin{aligned}\frac{\partial}{\partial x}&\text{ERR}\left(\alpha, \mathbb{E}\left(t_{now}^{(1)}\right), \ldots, \mathbb{E}\left(t_{now}^{(N)}\right)\right)\\ &= 2Nx - 2\delta\sum_{i=1}^{N}i = 2Nx - \delta N(N+1)\end{aligned} \tag{3.15}$$

We now set Formula 3.15 equal to 0 and solve the equation for x which leads to Formula 3.16. Inserting Formula 3.12 for $x$ leads to Formula 3.17 for the optimal $\alpha$.

$$x = \frac{\delta(N+1)}{2} = \frac{\Delta}{2} \tag{3.16}$$

$$\alpha = \frac{\delta(N+1)}{2} + (l_s - t) = \frac{\Delta}{2} + (l_s - t) \tag{3.17}$$

### 3.6.8.2 Derivation of the $\mu$-Formula

In this section, we derive an update rule for $\mu$, intending to change the coherence guarantee of the next tuple by $u$. The direction of the change is determined by $\text{sign}(D_{max} - C_g)$. $u$ directly translates to the step width $w$ introduced in Section 3.6.2 ($2w = u$). We assume that $\Delta$ remains unchanged. We aim to derive a function *update* that satisfies the Condition 3.18.

$$\mu_{new} = \text{update}\,(\mu, u) \qquad \text{s.th.} \tag{3.18}$$

$$C_g\,(\mu_{\text{new}}) = C_g\,(\mu) + u$$

In the remainder of this section, we first derive the optimal timestamp $t_{i;opt}$ to be selected at an arbitrary node $i$ as a function of $\mu$. We observe that the desired change $u$ in $C_g$

depends solely on the change in the distance between the largest and smallest age selected at a node. We thus express $t_{i;opt}$ as the optimal age $\alpha_{i;opt}$ and compute the change $u$ relative to an update in $\mu$. Finally, we discuss the relationship between $u$ and $w$ which leads to Formula 3.6 for the update of $\mu$.

Let $i \in \{1, \dots, N\}$ be an arbitrary but fixed node identifier. We aim to find the minimum of Cost Function 3.19.

$$\text{cost}_{\mu, \alpha, t_{now}^{(i)}, t} (t_i) = \text{abs}(t_i - t) + \left(t_{now}^{(i)} - t_i - \alpha\right)^2 \mu \qquad (3.19)$$

Function 3.19 is convex because it is the sum of two convex functions [151]. It has exactly one global minimum for a fixed $\mu$. However, Function 3.19 is non-differentiable at $t_i = t$. Therefore we must consider $t_i = t$ as a candidate for the global minimum in addition to two candidates $t_{i;1}$ and $t_{i;2}$ for the domains $A_1 := (-\infty, t)$ and $A_2 := (t, \infty)$. The global minimum is located at the candidate which implies the smallest cost.

We compute $t_{i;1}$ and $t_{i;2}$ in Formula 3.22 which we determine based on the derivations of our cost function given in Formula 3.20 and 3.21.

$$\frac{\partial}{\partial t_i} \text{cost} (\cdot) = \text{sign} (t_i - t) + 2\mu \left(t_i - (t_{now}^{(i)} - \alpha)\right)$$

$$= \pm 1 \qquad + 2\mu \left(t_i - (t_{now}^{(i)} - \alpha)\right) \qquad (3.20)$$

$$\frac{\partial^2}{\partial^2 t_i} \text{cost} (\cdot) = 2\mu > 0 \qquad (3.21)$$

$$\frac{\partial}{\partial t_i} \text{cost}\big|_{A_{1,2}} = 0 \Leftrightarrow t_{i;1,2} = \frac{\mp 1}{2\mu} + t_{now}^{(i)} - \alpha \qquad (3.22)$$

Plugging the values $t_{i;1,2}$ in the cost function reveals that the function's optimum lies between the optimum for the coherence guarantee $t_{now}^{(i)} - \alpha$ and the request timestamp $t$. To condense the notation, we define the difference between $t$ and $t_{now}^{(i)} - \alpha$ as $r$ in Equation 3.23.

$$r_i := t - \left(t_{now}^{(i)} - \alpha\right) \qquad (3.23)$$

The evaluated cost function at each of the two candidates $t_{i;1,2}$ is given by Equation 3.24.

$$\text{cost}\,(t_{i;1,2}) = \text{abs}\left(\frac{\mp 1 + 2\mu r_i}{2\mu}\right) + \frac{1}{4\mu} \tag{3.24}$$

Considering which of the values $t_{i;1}$ or $t_{i;2}$ has lower cost we receive Equivalence 3.25.

$$\text{cost}\,(t_{i;1}) \gtrless \text{cost}\,(t_{i;1}) \Leftrightarrow \underset{t_{i;c} \in \{t_{i;1}, t_{i;2}\}}{\text{argmin}}\,(\text{cost}(t_{i;c})) \gtrless t \Leftrightarrow 0 \gtrless r_i \tag{3.25}$$

Using Equivalence 3.25 the selected candidate $t_{i;c}$ out of $t_{i;1,2}$ is given by Formula 3.26.

$$t_{i;c} = \frac{\text{sign}(r_i)}{2\mu} + t_{now}^{(i)} - \alpha \tag{3.26}$$

It remains to determine for which values of $\mu$ the minimum of the cost function is located at $t_{i;c}$ and for which values of $\mu$ it is located at $t$. Therefore, we compare the evaluated cost function at $t_{i;c}$ and $t$ in Equivalence 3.27.

$$\text{cost}(t) = r_i^2 \cdot \mu$$
$$\text{cost}(t_{i;c}) = \frac{-1 + 2\mu \, \text{abs}(r_i)}{2\mu} + \frac{1}{4\mu}$$
$$\text{cost}\,(t_{i;c}) \le \text{cost}(t) \Leftrightarrow \mu \ge \frac{1}{2\,\text{abs}(r_i)} \tag{3.27}$$

We can now write the optimal value of $t_i$ as a function of $\mu$ in Definition 3.28. Definition 3.29 specifies the corresponding optimal age at node $i$.

$$t_{i;\text{opt}}\,(\mu) := \begin{cases} \frac{\text{sign}(r_i)}{2\mu} + t_{now}^{(i)} - \alpha & \mu \ge \frac{1}{2\,\text{abs}(r_i)} \\ t & \text{otherwise.} \end{cases} \tag{3.28}$$

$$\alpha_{i;\text{opt}}\,(\mu) := \begin{cases} \frac{-\text{sign}(r_i)}{2\mu} + \alpha & \mu \ge \frac{1}{2\,\text{abs}(r_i)} \\ t_{now} - t & \text{otherwise.} \end{cases} \tag{3.29}$$

The difference between all selected $\alpha_i$ values is equal to

$$\frac{1}{2\mu} + \alpha - \left(\frac{-1}{2\mu} + \alpha\right) = \frac{1}{\mu}.$$

This leads to Formula 3.30 for the coherence guarantee $C_g$.

$$C_g = \min\left(\Delta + \frac{1}{\mu}, 2\Delta\right) \tag{3.30}$$

If $\mu > \frac{1}{r_1}$, we achieve the desired change of $u$ in $C_g$ by updating $\mu$ according to Formula 3.31. Otherwise, the old value of $\mu$ is already optimal.

$$\frac{1}{\mu_{new}} = \frac{1}{\mu} + u \Leftrightarrow \mu_{new} = \frac{\mu}{1 + \mu u} \tag{3.31}$$

By now we derived the $\mu$ update rule depending on $u$. We now discuss the relation between $u$ and $w$ and derive the $\mu$ update rule depending on $w$ in Equation 3.32. In case $D_{max}$ was met, we target to improve the coherence estimate $C_e$ for the next tuple at the cost of increasing $C_g$ closer to $D_{max}$. Otherwise, $C_g$ needs to be reduced. Thus, the direction of the $\mu$ update is given by $\text{sign}(D_{max} - C_g)$. The optimal age $\alpha_{i;opt}$ needs to be reduced or increased depending on the position $i$ in the pipeline. Whether we need to increase or decrease the age $\alpha_{i;opt}$ is determined by $\text{sign}(r_i)$ in the first line of Equation 3.32. In the general update rule, which is independent of $i$, $\text{sign}(r_i)$ cancels out (Line 2 in Equation 3.32).

$$\alpha_{i;opt}\left(\mu_{new}\right) = \alpha_{i;opt}\left(\mu\right) + \text{sign}(r_i)\,\text{sign}(D_{max} - C_g)w$$
$$\Leftrightarrow \frac{1}{\mu_{new}} = \frac{1}{\mu} - 2\,\text{sign}(D_{max} - C_g)w$$
$$\Leftrightarrow \mu_{new} = \frac{\mu}{2\,\text{sign}(D_{max} - C_g)w\mu + 1} \tag{3.32}$$

Comparing Equation 3.31 with Equation 3.32 yields that $u=2w$. Line 3 of Equation 3.32 is the final general $\mu$ update rule.

### 3.6.8.3 Derivation of the $\mu$-Initialization rule

Even though the method of selecting the update step width $w$ is very efficient and ensures fast convergence, it is reasonable to initialize $\mu$ taking into consideration the targeted $C_g$-$C_e$-tradeoff. In the Section 3.6.8.2, we derived $C_g = \Delta + \frac{1}{\mu}$ in Equation 3.30 for $\mu > \frac{1}{r_1}$. After estimating the round trip time $\Delta$, we can use $D_{max}$ for initializing $\mu$ to optimize the coherence estimate while maintaining the upper bound of the guarantee.

We aim to set $C_g = D_{max} - \Delta$ which is achieved by initializing $\mu$ with Equation 3.33.

$$\mu = \frac{1}{D_{max} - 2\Delta} \tag{3.33}$$

## 3.7 Scheduling Sensor Reads

SENSE uses three alternative techniques for scheduling sensor reads on sensor nodes to fill history buffers.

**Ad-hoc.** Reading ad-hoc is the simplest solution for scheduling sensor reads. Whenever a tuple arrives at the sensor node, we read a value from the sensor and add that value to the tuple.

Ad-hoc reading has three advantages:

1. no scheduler needs to run,

2. we require no buffer to store sensor values, and

3. we achieve an optimal coherence guarantee $C_g$ because the age $\alpha$ is 0 for all values.

In exchange, we face three disadvantages:

1. the coherence estimates $C_e$ are larger and we cannot optimize them.

2. We can only request current data but no stored values for earlier timestamps which increases the read time deviation $\Delta_t$.

**Periodic.** Scheduling sensor reads periodically (e.g., every 20ms) is the most common approach for sensor data acquisition. We gather values from sensors at a fixed frequency and store them in the history buffer.

Periodic scheduling has three advantages:

1. it is supported by almost all sensors,

2. it allows for optimizing coherence estimates and guarantees when selecting values from the sensor node buffer, and

3. we can access historic data from the buffer.

At the same time, there are three disadvantages:

1. the coherence guarantee reduces compared to reading ad-hoc because the age $\alpha$ differs among values from different nodes,

2. we require history buffers and need to handle buffer overflows, and

3. we potentially read sensor values which we never use for any tuple.

**Schedule Next Read.** SENSE pre-schedules the next sensor read if possible. Given the time of the next request, a sensor node can read a value exactly at the optimal time and store only that value in its history buffer. Many algorithms which request sensor reads can provide their next request time up front which enables pre-scheduling. Examples are adaptive sampling techniques such as Adam [186], FAST [59], and L-SIP [67] as well as on-demand scheduling techniques [178].

Scheduling the next read has four advantages:

1. we read required values only,

2. we only need small buffers at sensor nodes and buffer overflows are unlikely,

3. we can achieve the best results for coherence estimates because we can schedule sensor reads precisely, and

4. we can still access past data points from sensor node buffers.

There are two disadvantages:

1. the coherence guarantee reduces compared to reading ad-hoc because the age $\alpha$ differs among values, and

2. we need to transmit the time of the next request to sensor nodes to enable pre-scheduling.

## 3.8   Failure Handling

We now discuss fault-tolerance mechanisms for link outages, node outages, and buffer overflows. We first introduce fallback nodes and then explain buffer overflow handling.

### 3.8.1  Introducing Fallback Nodes

We introduce fallback nodes to address link outages, node outages, and buffer overflows. A fallback node replaces sensor nodes in case of failures and may be hosted redundantly on several servers, sensor nodes, or loop nodes.

If a sensor node cannot reach its succeeding node in the loop (i.e., missing TCP acknowledgement), it sends output tuples to the fallback node instead. The fallback node then tries to reach the next available node in the loop and forwards the tuple to that available node skipping nodes which are unavailable at the moment. We remember unreachable nodes at the loop node and check periodically if they are back online. These checks are performed asynchronously and do not delay processing tuples. At first, the fallback node tries to compensate for missing values with a cached value from the un-reachable node. If this fails, it tries to compensate for missing values with measures from an alternative sensor nearby. If no alternative sensor or cached value is available the fallback node adds a null value. In all cases, the loop node receives a final result tuple which it can forward directly. This is an advantage compared to central join topologies, which cannot know if missing values are lost, late, or if the respective sensors are down.

### 3.8.2  Managing Buffer Overflows

Buffer Overflows on sensor nodes are another issue which we address with fallback nodes. For example, a history buffer can overflow if a node does not receive requests for an unusual long time and, thus, cannot prune sensor values. In general, buffer overflows are most probable at the last node in the loop, because the last node has the longest delay before it receives a request from the loop node.

If a sensor node cannot store additional values in its buffer but expects requests which require additional values, it sends the oldest values to the fall back node and overwrites them with new values. If a sensor node cannot reach any fallback node but needs to overwrite buffered values, succeeding tuples which require overwritten data will fall back to the oldest value in the history buffer. When a sensor node receives a tuple which requires values sent to the fallback node, it forwards the tuple to the fallback node which will add the respective values to the tuple and then forward the tuple to succeeding nodes in the loop.

In Algorithm 6 on Page 92, we show how we manage buffered values on sensor nodes. Our buffer is a ring buffer, `pos` is the next write position, and $W_{join}$ and $W_{send}$ are two watermarks which keep track of processed tuples and values sent to the fallback node.

---

**Algorithm 6** Buffer management on sensor nodes.

---

**State:** pos,$W_{join}$,$W_{send}$,buffer

  1: **function** JOINTUPLE(inputTuple)
  2:      **if** inputTuple.t $< W_{join}$ **then**
  3:         Forward input tuple to fallback node.
  4:      **else**
  5:         Select best $v_i$ from buffer with Formula 3.4.
  6:         Send result tuple to the next node.
  7:      **end if**
  8:      $W_{send} \leftarrow \min(t_{now} - \alpha, t)$
  9: **end function**
10: **function** READVALUE( )
11:      **if** buffer[pos].t $> W_{send}$ **then**
12:         Send buffer[pos] to fallback node.
13:         $W_{join} \leftarrow$ (buffer[pos].t + buffer[pos-1].t)/2
14:      **end if**
15:      buffer[pos] $\leftarrow$ sensor.read()
16:      pos $\leftarrow$ pos + 1
17: **end function**

---

When we receive a tuple, we usually join it with a value from the sensor node buffer in the JOINTUPLE function. The watermark $W_{join}$ is a timestamp which indicates which values have been sent to the fallback node. If the request time $t$ of a tuple is smaller than $W_{join}$, the required sensor value has been sent to the fallback node (Line 3). Otherwise, the required value is available in the sensor node buffer (Line 5). We finally set $W_{send}$ to remember that we processed all requests up to the request time $t$ of the processed tuple (Line 8). We calculate $W_{send}$ such that we can overwrite values in the buffer which have timestamps smaller than $W_{send}$ without sending them to the fallback node.

In the function READVALUE, we add a new sensor value to the buffer, which overwrites an old value in the buffer. In Line 11, we check if we need to send the value we overwrite to the fallback node. This is the case, if we expect requests which potentially require the value we overwrite. If we send a value to the fallback node, we set $W_{join}$ accordingly in Line 13. $W_{join}$ specifies which requests are sent to the fallback node and which requests are processed locally. If the optimal read time for a request is closer to the value we sent to the fallback node, we also send the request to the fallback node. Otherwise, we process the request locally.

## 3.9  Evaluation

We first present our experimental setup. Then, we evaluate the automatic time coherence optimization of SENSE, followed by an analysis of throughput, latency, and CPU utilization. Finally, we evaluate SENSE for a large-scale parameter space to show its general applicability.

### 3.9.1  Experiment Setup

Our sensor nodes are network connected devices which implement the algorithms presented in this chapter. We use the NS-3 network simulator [150] to simulate network delays, jitter, and transmission failures for up to 1000 sensor nodes to evaluate our technique. We transmit 64bit timestamps with nanosecond precision and 64bit values as payload. Note that the type of acquired sensor data does not affect the outcome of our experiments because our algorithms do not process the acquired sensor values.

In Section 3.9.3, we evaluate throughput, latency, and CPU-load. We run these experiments on one core of an Intel Core i7-7600U CPU with 2.80GHz and 4MB cache on a computer with 15GB main memory. We monitor the CPU usage with *getrusage* [122] and show sustained throughput [95]. Other experiments evaluate the adaptivity of our approach with respect to changing network conditions and the optimization of the $C_e$-$C_g$-tradeoff. The results of these experiments depend on the simulated conditions, but they are independent of the underlying hardware on which we run the simulation.

### 3.9.2  Optimizing Time Coherence

In this experiment, we evaluate the time coherence optimization introduced in Section 3.6. Recall that the user-defined incoherence limit $C_{g_{max}}$ is transformed to a system internal threshold $D_{max}$, which adapts to network conditions. We analyze two scenarios: In Scenario Ⓐ, we decrease $D_{max}$ (better guarantee, worse estimate). In Scenario Ⓑ, we increase $D_{max}$ (worse guarantee, better estimate). In our experiment, we analyze the following aspects: 1. The adaptivity with respect to changing coherence requirements. 2. The optimization of the $C_e$-$C_g$-tradeoff with respect to $D_{max}$. 3. The functionality of loop splits and merges. 4. Different approaches for scheduling sensor reads.

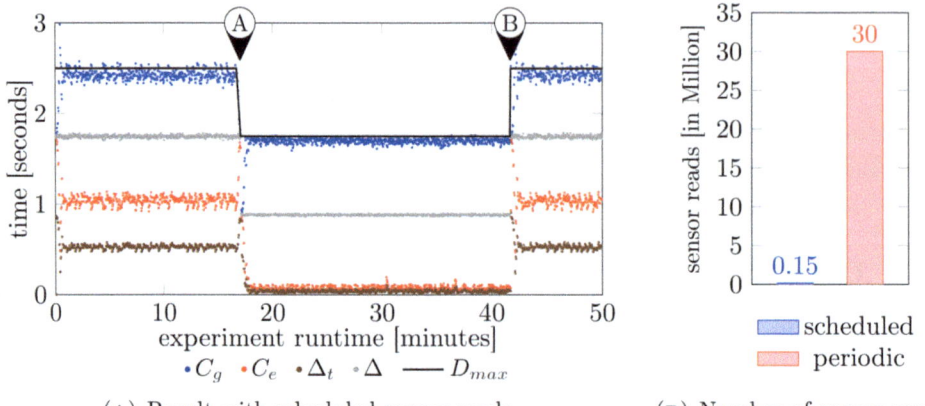

(A) Result with scheduled sensor reads.    (B) Number of sensor reads.

FIGURE 3.19: Evolution of coherence guarantees and estimates for changing incoherence limits ($D_{max}$).

**Setup.** We show the results for data transmissions via LTE [141, 150]. We also tested Wifi and LAN connections that exhibited less volatile transmission times leading to better results than LTE. We simulate a sensing loop with 200 sensor nodes.

**Scenario A: Decreasing $D_{max}$.** In Figure 3.19a at time Ⓐ, we change the system internal threshold $D_{max}$ such that $D_{max}$ is below the roundtrip time $\Delta$, which forces SENSE to adapt by splitting the sensing loop.

The gray dots in Figure 3.19a show the roundtrip times $\Delta$ of tuples in the sensing loop. As explained in Section 3.5, the minimum value for $C_g$ is $\Delta$. Since we reduce $D_{max}$ slightly below $\Delta$ in our experiment, SENSE correctly detects that we cannot achieve $C_g \leq D_{max}$ with a single loop covering all 200 sensor nodes and splits the loop accordingly. As a consequence, the coherence guarantee $C_g$ converges below the new value of $D_{max}$, which shows that SENSE correctly identified that it needs to adjust the sensing loop. At the same time, SENSE immediately reduces the coherence estimate $C_e$ as much as possible under the constraint $C_g \leq D_{max}$.

**Scenario B: Increasing $D_{max}$.** In Figure 3.19a at time Ⓑ, we change the system internal threshold $D_{max}$ back to its initial value, which enables SENSE to adapt by merging sensing loops. SENSE correctly detects that we can now fulfill the constraint $C_g \leq D_{max}$ with a single loop covering all 200 sensor nodes and merges the two sensing

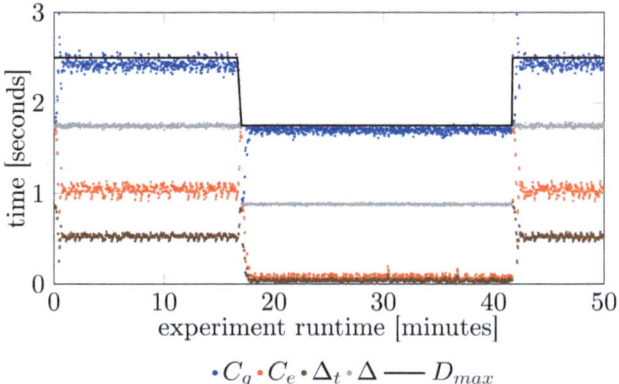

$$\cdot C_g \cdot C_e \cdot \Delta_t \cdot \Delta \ —— D_{max}$$

FIGURE 3.20: Evolution of coherence guarantees and estimates for changing incoherence limits ($D_{max}$). Results with periodic scheduling.

loops accordingly. As a consequence, the coherence guarantee $C_g$ converges below the new value of $D_{max}$.

**Impact of Read Scheduling.** We executed the experiment with two read scheduling techniques, *Schedule Next Read* and *Periodic Scheduling*. The resulting plots are identical, except that *Schedule Next Read* achieves smaller deviations from the desired read times ($\Delta_t$), because we can schedule sensor reads at optimal times with respect to future request times. For reference, we include the plot for periodic sampling in Figure 3.20. As we show in Figure 3.19b, *Schedule Next Read* reduces the number of required sensor reads by more than 99% compared to periodic scheduling because we can schedule exactly one sensor read per sensor and requested tuple.

**Discussion.** We observe that SENSE optimizes the coherence estimate of tuples while keeping the coherence guarantee within a user-defined upper limit. Thereby, SENSE adapts quickly to changes (i.e., network conditions and coherence requirements) and splits and merges sensing loops as required. Pre-scheduling sensor reads reduces the number of required reads drastically compared to reading values periodically.

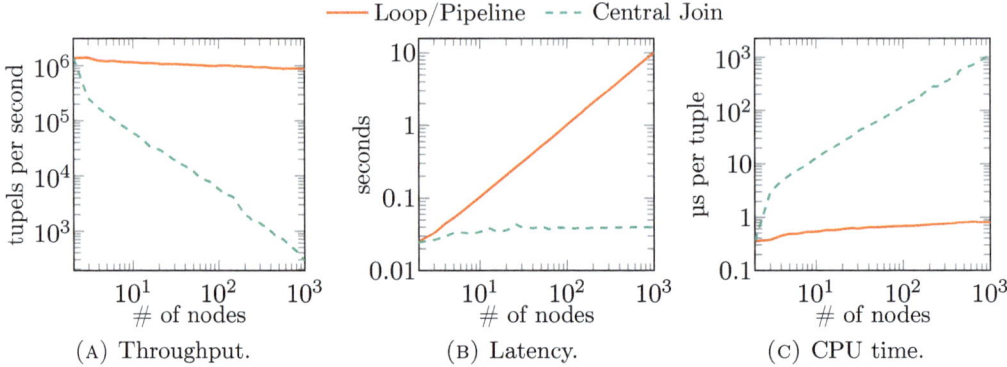

(A) Throughput.  (B) Latency.  (C) CPU time.

FIGURE 3.21: Performance Evaluation on the Loop Node.

### 3.9.3   Throughput, Latency, and CPU Load

In order to evaluate the performance of a sensing loop, we measure throughput, latency, and CPU utilization of loop nodes, which are the bottleneck for these measures. Individual sensor nodes in the same sensing loop always face the same load independent of the number of nodes in the loop. The latency includes the network latency for transmitting values from sensors to a central node (central join) and for transmitting values in a loop.

**Throughput.**   We observe in Figure 3.21a that a central join solution does not scale to thousands of sensors like we expect in upcoming IoT applications. The throughput decreases for larger numbers of sensors because matching values form many sensors to coherent tuples centrally requires many timestamp lookups and comparisons. Our pipeline-based solution overcomes this problem because it drastically reduces the number of inputs which need to be joined at a central node.

**Latency.**   Figure 3.21b shows the latency between the desired read time of a tuple and the time the systems returns the tuple to the user. The latency in sensing loops scales linearly with the number of sensor nodes (i.e. with the number of hops). A central join topology has a much smaller latency than a sensing loop because it requires only one hop from sensors to the central node. In general, transmission times dominate the latency of both approaches rather than computation times. Please note that our experiment shows the latency with sustained throughputs. Thus, central joins achieve smaller latencies with a much smaller throughput than sensing loops.

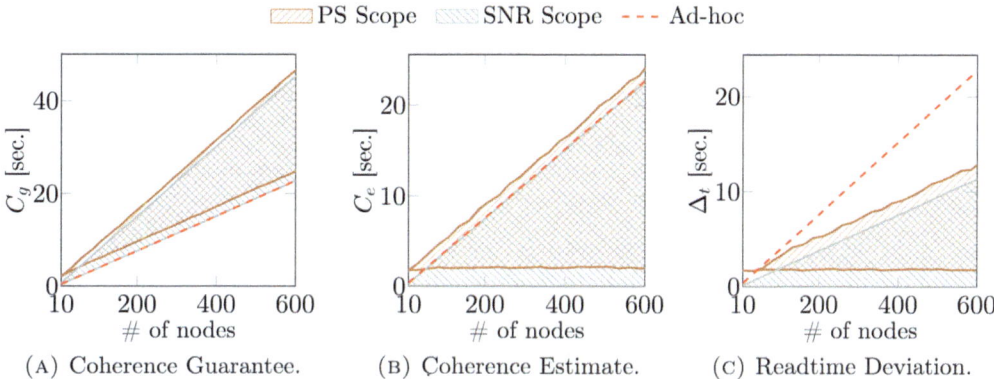

FIGURE 3.22: Evaluation of coherence measures.

**CPU Utilization.** Sensing loops reduce the CPU utilization at a central node significantly compared to central join topologies. Since the sensing loop provides a complete sensor data tuple, the remaining computation at the loop node is limited to calculating $C_e$, $C_g$, $\alpha$, and $\mu$ (remember Algorithm 5 from Page 77). In contrast, a central join of individual sensor values must match each incoming value with values of other sensors and check if it can output a complete tuple.

**Discussion.** Central join topologies are limited by their CPU performance which limits the sustained throughput. Sensing loops are limited by their latency which results from accumulated hop times between sensor nodes. The strength of our solution is the adaptive combination of both approaches: multiple sensing loops combined by a central join. We can see in Figure 3.21 that a sensing loop can acquire values from 100 sensors with less than two seconds latency. A central join can combine inputs from 100 sensing loops with a throughput of 5000 tuples per second. Hence, we can acquire values from 10000 sensors with a latency below 3 seconds and guaranteed time coherence below 2 seconds.

### 3.9.4 Coherences and Read Time Deviations

In this experiment, we analyze the impact of the number of nodes in one sensing loop on coherence guarantees, coherence estimates, read time deviations, and the related trade-offs. In Figure 3.22, we show the optimization scopes for coherence guarantees (Figure 3.22a), coherence estimates (Figure 3.22b), and read time deviations (Figure 3.22c).

We simulate average hop times of 38ms between sensors nodes and select the loop start time $l_s$ as request time $t$ for tuples. We show the optimization scopes for periodic scheduling (PS), schedule next read (SNR), and ad-hoc reading.

**Coherence Guarantee.** The smallest possible coherence guarantee is the roundtrip time $\Delta$ which increases linearly with the loop length. We achieve this optimum if all nodes provide a value with the same age $\alpha$. With SNR, we can achieve the optimal coherence guarantee because we can schedule sensor reads precisely with respect to following requests. Ad-hoc reading always results in $\alpha=0$ on all nodes which also leads to an optimal coherence guarantee. Periodic Scheduling (PS) leads to slightly worse guarantees, because it adds a deviation between the optimal read time and the read time which is available in the history buffer. The worst case coherence guarantee results from solely optimizing for coherence estimates, which means that we select values read exactly at the request time $t$ (according to sensor node clocks). In this case, the difference between $\alpha_{min}$ and $\alpha_{max}$ equals $\Delta$ and the coherence guarantee increases to $2\Delta$ accordingly.

**Coherence Estimate.** The optimal coherence estimate results from selecting values which were read exactly at the request time $t$ as described above. We can achieve this optimum with SNR because we can schedule sensor reads precisely at future request times. Periodic reading adds a deviation between the optimal read time and the read time available in the sensor node buffer which explains the slight shift of the optimization scope. The largest coherence estimate results from optimizing solely for the coherence guarantee. In this case, $\alpha_{min}=\alpha_{max}$ and $C_e \approx \Delta$ assuming correctly synchronized sensor node clocks. Ad-hoc reading results in the worst-case coherence estimate because it reads when it receives tuples without considering the request time.

**Read Time Deviation.** The read time deviation $\Delta_t$ is the maximum difference between the request time $t$ and any read time of a value contained in the result tuple. We regularly tune the parameter $\alpha$ to minimize $\Delta_t$ (remember Figure 3.13 from Page 74). Figure 3.22c shows the impact of this optimization. Both, periodic scheduling and schedule next read, achieve $\Delta_t \approx C_e/2$, which is the optimum. In contrast, reading ad-hoc doubles $\Delta_t$ because of the missing $\alpha$-optimization.

**Discussion.** Our experiment illustrates the best-cases and worst-cases for $C_e$, $C_g$, and $\Delta_t$ as well as the scope of the $C_e$-$C_g$-tradeoff. Schedule next read (SNR) achieved

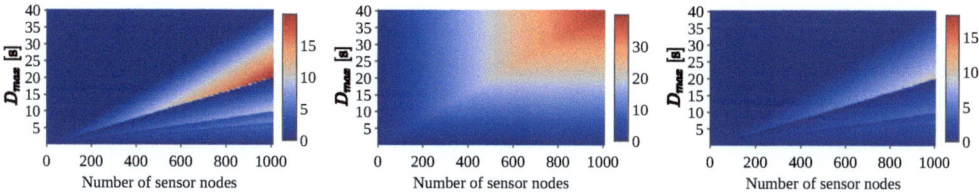

(A) Coherence Estimate ($C_e$)  (B) Coherence Guarantee ($C_g$)  (C) Read Time Deviation ($\Delta_t$)

FIGURE 3.23: Coherence measures depending on loop lengths and $D_{max}$.

slightly better results because of precise scheduling of sensor reads with respect to future requests. A naive solution which reads ad-hoc achieves an optimal $C_g$, at the cost of a worst-case $C_e$ and a doubled read time deviation. In contrast, our solution adapts the tradeoff between $C_e$ and $C_g$ flexibly with respect to user-defined coherence requirements.

### 3.9.5   Large Scale Parameter Exploration

In this experiment, we evaluate whether our results carry over to a large parameter space. We provide a quantitative analysis of the impact of the number of sensor nodes in a sensing loop and the coherence requirements ($D_{max}$) on the coherence measures ($C_g$, $C_e$, and $\Delta_t$). For each measure, we show a dedicated heatmap in Figure 3.23. Overall, the heatmaps show the results of 57600 experiments with a simulated duration of 66 minutes per experiment and a mean hop time of 20ms. We show $D_{max}$ on the y-axis, the amount of sensors on the x-axis, and coherence measures as heatmap colors.

**Coherence Estimate.**   In Figure 3.23a, we show the coherence estimates depending on $D_{max}$ and the number of sensors. We observe diagonal lines which correspond to loop splits. Above these lines, the system optimizes strongly for $C_g$ to keep $C_g \leq D_{max}$. In exchange, $C_e$ increases which explains the increasing values for $C_e$ when approaching the split. Directly below the lines which indicate loop splits, the system can optimize strongly for $C_e$ without violating $C_g \leq D_{max}$ which results in the best (i.e., smallest) values for $C_e$.

**Coherence Guarantee.**   In Figure 3.23b, we show the coherence guarantees for the same experiments. One can observe that pipeline splits are barely visible in this plot. This shows that our system always utilizes $D_{max}$ to relax $C_g$ and to optimize for $C_e$. At the same time, we observe that our system does not violate $D_{max}$. For smaller numbers of sensors, the system does not need to fully utilize $D_{max}$ for achieving an optimal $C_e$, which explains the blue area in the upper left corner of Figures 3.23a and 3.23b.

**Read Time Deviation.** Figure 3.23c shows the read time deviation $\Delta_t$ for our experiments. Similar to the results presented in the previous section, we achieve $\Delta_t \approx C_e/2$, which is the optimal result for $\Delta_t$. This proves that the loop node chooses the optimal value for $\alpha$.

**Discussion.** The presented heatmaps verify that SENSE achieves the desired results not only for selected combinations of parameters, but for a wide range of setups. Our solution optimizes $C_e$ without violating $C_g \leq D_{max}$. Pipeline splits take place as required to ensure this behavior (Figure 3.23a). The system utilizes the upper limit for coherence guarantees ($D_{max}$) to relax $C_g$ and to optimize $C_e$ as much as possible (Figure 3.23b). The read time deviation is about $C_e/2$, which proves an optimal selection of $\alpha$ (Figure 3.23c).

## 3.10   Related Work

Time coherence was studied in different contexts before. Srinivasan et al. discuss the *temporal coherence* of virtual data warehouses which work as cache for data sources [167]. Deolasee et al. propose an adaptive push-pull method to maintain the coherence of such cached data copies efficiently [51]. Agrawal et al. discuss techniques to smartly select up to date (temporal coherent) cached data copies for serving client requests [4]. All these works consider the coherence between data sources and several copies of these sources. In contrast, our work focuses on acquiring time coherent tuples which contain values from many distributed sensor nodes.

TiNA addresses temporal coherence-aware in-network aggregation [23, 154]. Sensors transmit new readings only if values changed more than a given tolerance. This allows for trading off energy consumption in sensor networks against the quality of data [155]. Similarly, adaptive sampling techniques [67, 59, 186] monitor the change of sensor values and transmit new measurements only if they are sufficiently different from previous ones. None of these techniques provides time coherence guarantees for result tuples which we introduce in this chapter. Instead, they focus on reducing the required update frequency of sensor values and aggregates.

The term coherence was also used in the context of fusing data from several sensors (i.e., sources) to one logically coherent data base [99, 117, 118]. This multi-sensor fusion is independent of time coherence and builds on the logical consistence of values from different sources instead.

Precise clock synchronization can be an alternative to our solutions if one controls a complete sensor network [6, 50, 105, 194]. However, we experienced in our Raspberry Pi testbed, that even if we control all sensor nodes, it is hard to always ensure precise synchronization among all nodes. For example, many public network providers block access to NTP servers to prevent DDOS attacs originating form their network [44]. With the large number of sensor nodes in the IoT, which are operated by diverse users and organizations, it is impossible to ensure complete synchronization among all clocks. Instead, sensor nodes connect to many different reference clocks and use diverse synchronization techniques with variable precision. The techniques presented in this chapter address these issues by detecting and quantifying clock offsets. We actively tune the coherence of sensor data tuples, isolate struggling nodes (e.g., nodes with large clock offset), and provide guaranteed time coherence for result tuples.

Diverse works propose clock synchronization techniques or synchronization optimizations [104, 106, 109, 128, 140, 163, 165]. In this chapter, we use synchronized clocks for coherence estimates wherever possible. However, in the IoT, we need to provide additional coherence guarantees which are independent of clock synchronization and address failure cases where one or many sensor node clocks are not perfectly synchronized.

Madden et al. introduce *acquisitional query processing* and show the benefits of interleaving data gathering operations with data manipulation operations in TinyDB [121]. They further extend TinyDB with efficient in-network aggregation [119]. Shrivastava et al. extend the scope of TinyDB with complex aggregations and range queries [160]. Our example pipeline in Figure 3.8, shows how our solution complements TinyDB and acquisitional query processing. We replace ad-hoc sensor reads with a sophisticated pipeline join which ensures time coherent result tuples. Riahi et al. consider the efficient data acquisition from many sensors and optimize data gathering based on application requests [149]. However, they do not discuss the time coherence of result tuples.

## 3.11 Conclusion

Upcoming IoT applications gather values from thousands of distributed sensors. Currently, these applications rely on clock synchronization among sensor nodes and clock offsets cause undetected result errors. We propose SENSE, the first system for sensor data acquisition that quantifies the time coherence of result tuples, provides synchronization independent coherence guarantees, and supports user-defined incoherence limits.

The core of SENSE are sensing loops, which gather sensor values sequentially from a set of sensors. To ensure scalability and to enforce incoherence limits, SENSE dynamically splits and merges sensing loops with respect to time coherence and latency requirements. Our results show that SENSE scales to thousands of sensor nodes and reliably optimizes the coherence estimate of tuples while keeping the coherence guarantee below a user-defined upper limit. Thereby, SENSE quickly adapts to changed network conditions and coherence requirements.

SENSE serves as sensor control layer of our end-to-end architecture and accesses sensor values through the read scheduler which we introduced in Chapter 2. Thereby, SENSE operates as intermediate layer between sensor nodes and stream analysis systems which prevents bottlenecks in stream analysis systems caused by central stream joins. Instead of individual time-value-pairs, SENSE outputs complete input tuples which represent coherent snapshots of sensor values. In the next chapter, we show how stream analysis systems aggregate sensor data tuples produced by SENSE.

# 4

# Efficient Window Aggregation with General Stream Slicing

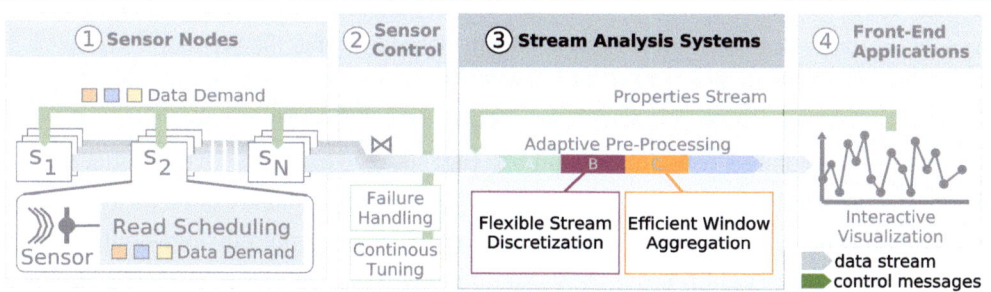

FIGURE 4.1: Scope of Chapter 4 - Flexible Stream Discretization and Efficient Window Aggregation in Stream Analysis Systems.

In this chapter, we optimize window aggregation, a common bottleneck in stream analysis systems. The rise of the IoT leads to an increasing number of applications that require aggregates over an increasing amount of data. To ensure scalability, it is crucial to share partial aggregates among all applications. To this end, we present the first general stream slicing technique for window aggregation. Our technique shares partial aggregates among all applications, prevents redundant computations, and automatically adapts to workload characteristics, to improve performance without sacrificing its general applicability. As a prerequisite, we identify workload characteristics that affect the performance and applicability of aggregation techniques. Our experiments show that general stream slicing outperforms alternative concepts by up to an order of magnitude.

## 4.1 Introduction

The need for real-time analysis shifts an increasing number of data analysis tasks from batch to stream processing. To be able to process queries over unbounded data streams, users typically formulate queries that compute aggregates over bounded subsets of a stream, called windows. Examples of such queries on windows are average vehicle speeds per minute, monthly revenue aggregations, or statistics of user behavior for online sessions. The transformation from streams to windows is called *stream discretization*.

Large computation overlaps caused by sliding windows and multiple concurrent queries lead to redundant computations and inefficiency. Consequently, there is an urgent need for *general* and *efficient* window aggregation in industry [199, 170, 29]. In this chapter, we contribute a general solution, which not only improves performance but also widens the applicability with respect to window types, time domains, aggregate functions, and out-of-order processing. Our solution is generally applicable to all data flow systems that adopt a tuple-at-a-time processing model (e.g., Apache Storm [177], Apache Flink [7, 35], and other Apache Beam-based systems [5, 11]).

To calculate aggregates of overlapping windows, the database community has been working on *aggregation techniques* such as B-Int [14], Pairs [102], Panes [111], RA [173] and Cutty [36]. These techniques compute partial aggregates for overlapping parts of windows and reuse these partial aggregates to compute final aggregates for overlapping windows. We believe that these techniques are not widely adopted in open-source streaming systems for two main reasons: first, the literature on streaming window aggregation is fragmented and, second, every technique has its own assumptions and limitations. As a consequence, it is not clear for researchers and practitioners under which conditions which streaming window aggregation techniques should be used.

General purpose streaming systems require a window operator that is applicable to many types of aggregation workloads. At the same time, the operator should be as efficient as specialized techniques, which support selected workloads only.

As our first contribution, we classify existing aggregation techniques with respect to their underlying concepts and their applicability (Section 4.3). We then identify and define the workload characteristics which may or may not be supported by existing specialized window aggregation techniques (Section 4.4). Those characteristics are: i) *window types* (e.g., sliding, session, tumbling), ii) *windowing measures* (e.g., time or tuple-count), iii) *aggregate functions* (e.g., associative, holistic), and iv) *stream order*.

We identify stream slicing as a concept on top of which window aggregation can be implemented efficiently. Consequently, our second main contribution is *a general stream slicing technique* (Section 4.5). Existing slicing-based techniques do not support complex window types such as session windows [102, 111], do not consider out-of-order processing [36], or limit the type of aggregation functions [36, 102, 111]. With general stream slicing, we provide a single, generally applicable, and highly efficient solution for streaming window aggregation. Our solution inherits the performance of specialized techniques, which use stream slicing, and generalizes stream slicing to support diverse workloads. Because we integrate all workloads into one general solution, we enable aggregate sharing among all queries with different window types (sliding, sessions, user-defined, etc.) and window measures (e.g., tuple-count or time). Our solution to general stream slicing is available as open source library[1].

General stream slicing breaks down slicing into three operations on slices, namely `merge`, `split`, and `update`. Specific workload characteristics influence the cost of each operation and how often operations are performed. By taking into account the workload characteristics, our slicing technique i) stores the tuples themselves only when it is required, which saves memory and ii) minimizes the number of slices that are created, stored, and recomputed. One can extend our techniques with additional aggregations and window types without changing the three core slicing operations. Thus, these core operations may be tuned by system experts while users can still implement custom windows and aggregations.

The contributions of this chapter are as follows:

1. We identify the workload characteristics which impact the applicability and performance limitations of existing aggregation techniques (Section 4.4).

2. We contribute *general stream slicing*, a generally applicable and highly efficient solution for streaming window aggregation in dataflow systems (Section 4.5).

3. We evaluate the performance implications of different use-case characteristics and show that general stream slicing is generally applicable while offering better performance than existing approaches (Section 4.7).

The remainder of this chapter is structured as follows: We first provide background information in Section 4.2 and present concepts of aggregation techniques in Section 4.3. We then present our contributions in Section 4.4, 4.5, and 4.7 and discuss related work in Section 4.8 before we conclude in Section 4.9.

---

[1]Open-Source-Repository: `https://github.com/TU-Berlin-DIMA/scotty-window-processor`

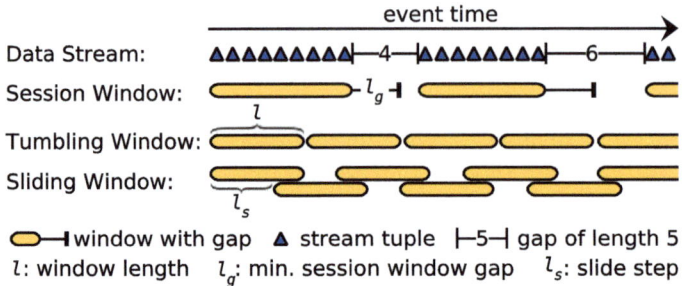

FIGURE 4.2: Common Window Types.

## 4.2 Preliminaries

Streaming window aggregation involves special terminology with respect to window types, timing, stream order, and data expiration. This section revisits terms and definitions, which are required for the remainder of this chapter.

**Window Types.** A window type refers to the logic based on which systems derive finite windows from a continuous stream (stream discretization). There exist diverse window types ranging from common sliding windows to more complex data-driven windows [75]. We address the diversity of window types with a classification in Section 4.4.4. For now, we limit the discussion to *tumbling* (or *fixed*), *sliding*, and *session* windows (Figure 4.2) which we use in subsequent examples. A *tumbling* window splits the time into segments of equal length $l$. The end of one window marks the beginning of the next window. *Sliding* windows, in addition to the length $l$, also define a slide step of length $l_s$. This length determines how often a new window starts. Consecutive windows overlap when $l_s < l$. In this case, tuples may belong to multiple windows. A *session* window typically covers a period of activity followed by a period of inactivity [5]. Thus, a session window times out (ends) if no tuple arrives for some time gap $l_g$. Typical examples of sessions are taxi trips, browser sessions, and ATM interactions.

**Notion of Time.** One can define windows on different measures such as times and tuple-counts. The *event-time* of a tuple is the time when an event was captured and the *processing-time* is the time when an operator processes a tuple [5, 35]. Technically, an event-time is a timestamp stored in the tuple and processing-time refers to a system clock. If not indicated otherwise, we refer to event-time windows in our examples because applications typically define windows on event-time.

**Stream Order.**   Input tuples of a stream are in-order if they arrive chronologically with respect to their event-times, otherwise, they are out-of-order [5, 114]. In practice, streams regularly contain out-of-order tuples because of transmission latencies, network failures, or temporary sensor outages. We differentiate in-order tuples from out-of-order tuples and in-order streams from out-of-order streams. Let a stream $S$ consist of tuples $s_1, s_2, s_3, ...$ where the subscripts denote the order in which an operator processes the tuples. Let the event-time of any tuple $s_x$ be $t_e(s_x)$.

- A tuple $s_x$ is *in-order* if $\nexists y : t_e(s_y) > t_e(s_x) \wedge y < x$.

- A stream is in-order iff all its tuples are in-order tuples.

**Punctuations, Watermarks, and Allowed Lateness.**   *Punctuations* are annotations embedded in a data stream [188]. Systems use punctuations for different purposes: *low-watermarks* (in short *watermarks*) indicate that no tuple will arrive with a timestamp smaller than the watermark's timestamp [5]. Many systems use watermarks to control how long they wait for out-of-order tuples before they output a window aggregate [11]. *Window punctuations* mark window starts and endings in the stream [68, 82]. The *allowed lateness*, specifies how long systems store window aggregates. If an out-of-order tuple arrives after the watermark, but in the allowed lateness, we output updated aggregates.

**Partial Aggregates and Aggregate Sharing.**   The key idea of partial aggregation is to compute aggregates for subsets of the stream as intermediate results. These intermediate results are *shared* among overlapping windows to prevent repeated computation [14, 102, 203]. In addition, one can compute partial aggregates incrementally when tuples arrive [173]. This reduces the memory footprint if a technique stores few partial aggregates instead of all stream tuples in the allowed lateness. It also reduces the latency because aggregates are pre-computed when windows end[2].

---

[2] We say that a window *ends* when the systems has to output the aggregate for a window. When processing in-order streams, a window *ends* as soon as the time progresses beyond the end-timestamp of the window. When processing out-of-order streams, a window *ends* as soon as the watermark progresses beyond the end-timestamp of the window.

## 4.3 Window Aggregation Concepts

In this section, we survey concepts for streaming window aggregation and give an intuition for each solution's memory usage, throughput, and latency. We provide a detailed comparison of all concepts in our experiments. Techniques which support out-of-order streams store values for an *allowed lateness* (see above). In the following discussion, we refer to allowed lateness only. Techniques which do not process out-of-order tuples, store values for the duration of the longest window.

Table 4.1 on Page 109 provides an overview of all techniques we discuss in the following subsections. We denote the number of values (i.e., tuples) as $|\blacktriangle|$, the number of slices as $|\text{\tiny\textbf{⬤}}|$, and the number of windows in the allowed lateness as $|\text{win}|$. We further denote the size of a tuple in bytes as $\text{size}(\blacktriangle)$, the size of a slice including an aggregate as $\text{size}(\text{\tiny\textbf{⬤}})$, the size of an aggregate as $\text{size}(\bullet)$, and the size of a bucket as $\text{size}(\text{⌐})$. The size of slices and buckets covers metadata such as their start and end timestamps and hashes. The metadata is of equal size for all buckets and slices.

### 4.3.1 Tuple Buffer

A tuple buffer (Table 4.1, Row 1) is a straightforward solution, which does not share partial aggregates.

The *throughput* of a tuple buffer is fair as long as there are few or no concurrent windows (i.e., no window overlaps), and there are few or no out-of-order tuples. Window overlaps decrease the throughput because of repeated aggregate computations. Out-of-order tuples decrease the throughput because of memory copy operations, which are required for inserting values in the middle of a sorted ring buffer.

The *latency* of a tuple buffer is high because aggregates are computed lazily. Thus, all aggregate computations contribute to the latency when the window ends.

A tuple buffer stores all tuples for the allowed lateness, which is $|\blacktriangle|\cdot\text{size}(\blacktriangle)$. Thus, the more tuples we process per time, the higher the memory consumption and the higher the memory copy overhead for out-of-order tuples.

### 4.3.2 Aggregate Trees

Aggregate trees such as FlatFAT [173] and B-INT [14] store partial aggregates in a tree structure and share them among overlapping windows (Table 4.1, Row 2).

| | Memory Usage | Example |
|---|---|---|
| 1.<br>Tuple<br>Buffer | $\lvert\blacktriangle\rvert\cdot\texttt{size}(\blacktriangle)$ | |
| 2.<br>Aggregate<br>Tree | $\lvert\blacktriangle\rvert\cdot\texttt{size}(\blacktriangle)$<br>$+(\lvert\blacktriangle\rvert-1)\cdot\texttt{size}(\bullet)$ | |
| 3.<br>Aggregate<br>Buckets | $\lvert\text{win}\rvert\cdot\texttt{size}(\bullet)$<br>$+\lvert\text{win}\rvert\cdot\texttt{size}(\textvisiblespace)$ | |
| 4.<br>Tuple<br>Buckets | $\lvert\text{win}\rvert\cdot[\texttt{avg}(\blacktriangle \text{ per win.})$<br>$\cdot\texttt{size}(\blacktriangle)+\texttt{size}(\textvisiblespace)]$ | |
| 5.<br>Lazy<br>Slicing | $\lvert\text{slice}\rvert\cdot\texttt{size}(\text{slice})$ | |
| 6.<br>Eager<br>Slicing | $\lvert\text{slice}\rvert\cdot\texttt{size}(\text{slice})$<br>$+(\lvert\text{slice}\rvert-1)\cdot\texttt{size}(\bullet)$ | |
| 7.<br>Lazy<br>Slicing<br>on tuples | $\lvert\blacktriangle\rvert\cdot\texttt{size}(\blacktriangle)$<br>$+\lvert\text{slice}\rvert\cdot\texttt{size}(\text{slice})$ | |
| 8.<br>Eager<br>Slicing<br>on tuples | $\lvert\blacktriangle\rvert\cdot\texttt{size}(\blacktriangle)$<br>$+\lvert\text{slice}\rvert\cdot\texttt{size}(\text{slice})$<br>$+(\lvert\text{slice}\rvert-1)\cdot\texttt{size}(\bullet)$ | |

Legend: ▲ Tuple   ● Aggregate   ⬭ Slice incl. Aggregate   ⏝ Bucket
An explanation of symbols and notations can be found on top of Page 108
and in the List of Notation starting on Page 162.

TABLE 4.1: Memory Usage and Visualization of Aggregation Techniques.

FlatFAT stores a binary tree of partial aggregates on top of stream tuples (leaves) which roughly doubles the memory consumption.

In-order tuples require $\log(|\blacktriangle|)$ updates of partial aggregates in the tree. Thus, the *throughput* is decreases logarithmically when the number of tuples in the allowed lateness increases. Out-of-order tuples decrease the throughput drastically: they require the same memory copy operation as in tuple buffers. In addition, they cause a rebalancing of the aggregate tree and the respective aggregate updates.

The *latency* of aggregate trees is much lower than for tuple buffers because they can compute final aggregates for windows from pre-computed partial aggregates. Thus, only a few final aggregation steps remain when windows end [158].

### 4.3.3 Buckets

Li et al. introduce *Window-ID* (WID) [112, 113, 114], a bucket-per-window approach which is adopted by many systems with support for out-of-order processing [5, 11, 35]. Each window is represented by an independent bucket. A system assigns tuples to buckets (i.e., windows) based on event-times, independently from the order in which tuples arrive [114]. Buckets do not utilize aggregate sharing. Instead, they compute aggregates for each bucket independently.

Systems can compute aggregates for buckets incrementally [173]. This leads to very low *latencies* because the final window aggregate is pre-computed when windows end.

We consider two versions of buckets. *Tuple buckets* keep individual tuples in buckets (Table 4.1, Row 4). This leads to data replication for overlapping buckets. *Aggregate buckets* store partial aggregates in buckets plus some overhead (e.g., start and end times), but no tuples (Table 4.1, Row 3). We prefer to store aggregates instead of individual tuples to reduce the memory footprint. However, some use-cases (e.g., holistic aggregates over count-based windows) require us to keep individual tuples in memory.

Buckets process in-order tuples as fast as out-of-order tuples for most use-cases: they assign the tuple to buckets and incrementally compute the aggregate of these buckets. The throughput bottleneck for buckets are overlapping windows. For example, one sliding window with $l = 20$s and $l_s = 2$s results in 10 overlapping windows (i.e., buckets) at any time. This causes 10 aggregation operations for each input tuple.

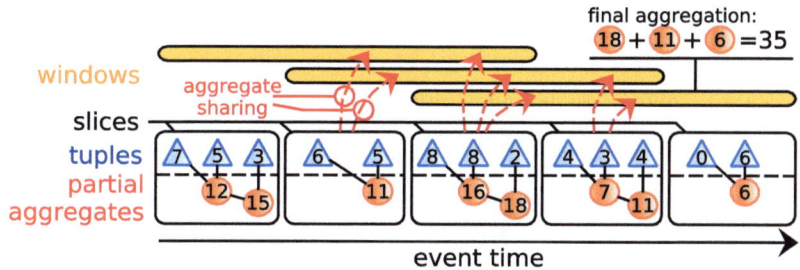

FIGURE 4.3: Example Aggregation with Stream Slicing.

## 4.3.4  Stream Slicing

Slicing techniques divide (i.e., *slice*) a data stream into non-overlapping chunks of data (i.e., *slices*) [102, 111]. The system computes a partial aggregate for each slice. When windows end, the system computes window aggregates from slices.

We show stream slicing with an example in Figure 4.3. Slicing techniques compute partial aggregates incrementally when tuples arrive (bottom of Figure 4.3). We show multiple intermediate aggregates per slice to illustrate the workflow.

Partial aggregates (i.e., slices) are shared among overlapping windows which avoids redundant computations. In Figure 4.3, dashed arrows mark multiple uses of slices. In contrast to aggregate trees and buckets, slicing techniques require just one aggregation operation per tuple because each tuple belongs to exactly one slice. This results in a high *throughput* for in-order as well as out-of-order tuples.

Similar to aggregate trees, the *latency* of stream slicing techniques is low because only a few final aggregation steps are required when a window ends. We consider a lazy and an eager version of stream slicing. The lazy version of stream slicing stores slices including partial aggregates (Table 4.1, Row 5). The eager version stores a tree of partial aggregates on top of slices to further reduce latencies (Table 4.1, Row 6). Both variants compute aggregates of slices incrementally when tuples arrive. The term *lazy* refers to the lazy computation of aggregates for combinations of slices.

There are usually many tuples per slice ($|\bullet| \ll |\blacktriangle|$) which leads to huge memory savings compared to aggregate trees and tuple buffers. Some use-cases such as holistic aggregates over count-based windows require us to keep individual tuples in addition to aggregates (Table 4.1, Row 7 and 8). In these cases, stream slicing requires more memory than tuple buffers, but saves memory compared to buckets and aggregate trees.

We focus on stream slicing because it offers a good combination of high throughputs, low latencies, and memory savings. Moreover, our experiments show that slicing techniques scale to many concurrent windows, high ingestion rates, and high fractions of out-of-order tuples. We create slices such that they can be shared among all queries.

## 4.4 Workload Characterization

In this section, we identify workload characteristics which either limit the applicability of aggregation techniques or impact their performance. These characteristics are the basis for subsequent sections in which we generalize stream slicing.

### 4.4.1 Characteristic 1: Stream Order

Out-of-order streams increase the complexity of window aggregation, because out-of-order tuples can require changes in the past. For example, tuple buffers and aggregate trees process in-order tuples efficiently using a ring buffer (FIFO principle) [173]. Out-of-order tuples break the FIFO principle and require memory copy operations in buffers.

We differentiate whether or not out-of-order processing is required for a use-case. For techniques which support out-of-order processing, we study how the fraction of out-of-order tuples and the delay of such tuples affect the performance.

### 4.4.2 Characteristic 2: Aggregation Function

We classify aggregation functions with respect to their algebraic properties. Our notation splits the aggregation in incremental steps and is consistent with related works [173, 36]. We write input values as lower case letters, the operation which adds a value to an aggregate as $\oplus$, and the operation which removes a value from an aggregate as $\ominus$. E.g., if we compute a sum, $\oplus$ corresponds to the arithmetic $+$ and $\ominus$ corresponds to the arithmetic $-$. We first adopt three algebraic properties used by Tangwongsan et al. [173]. These properties focus on the incremental computation of aggregates:

$$(1)\ \textit{Associativity:}\ (x \oplus y) \oplus z = x \oplus (y \oplus z)\ \ \forall\, x, y, z$$

$$(2)\ \textit{Invertibility:}\ (x \oplus y) \ominus y = x\ \ \forall\, x, y$$

$$(3)\ \textit{Commutativity:}\ x \oplus y = y \oplus x\ \ \forall\, x, y$$

Stream slicing requires *associative* aggregate functions because it computes partial aggregates per slice which are shared among windows. This requirement is inherent for all techniques which share partial aggregates [14, 36, 102, 111, 173]. Our general slicing approach does not require invertibility or commutativity, but exploits these properties if possible to increase performance.

We further adopt the classification of aggregations in *distributive*, *algebraic*, and *holistic* [74]. Aggregations such as sum, min, and max are *distributive*. Their partial aggregates equal the final aggregates of partials and have a constant size. An aggregation is *algebraic* if its partial aggregates can be summarized in an intermediate result of fixed size. The final aggregate is computed from this intermediate result. The remainder of aggregations, which have an unbounded size of partial aggregates, is *holistic*.

### 4.4.3   Characteristic 3: Windowing Measure

Windows can be specified using different measures (also called *time domains* [30] or WATTR [112]). For example, a tumbling window can have a length of 5 minutes (time-measure), or a length of 10 tuples (count-measure). To simplify the presentation, we refer to *timestamps* in the rest of this chapter. However, bear in mind that a timestamp can actually be a time, a tuple count, or any other monotonically increasing measure [36]:

- **Time-Based Measures:** Common time-based measures are *event-time* and *processing-time* as introduced in Section 4.2.

- **Arbitrary Advancing Measures** are a generalization of event-times. Typically, it is irrelevant for a stream processor if *"timestamps"* actually represent a time or another advancing measure. Examples of other advancing measures are transaction counters in a database, kilometers driven by a car, and invoice numbers.

- **Count-Based Measures** (also called *tuple-based* [112] or *tuple-driven* [30]) refer to a tuple counter. For example, a window can start at the 100th and end at the 200th tuple of a stream. Count-based measures cause challenges when combined with out-of-order processing: If tuples are ordered with respect to their event-times and a tuple arrives out-of-order, it changes the count of all other tuples which have a greater event-time. This changes the aggregates of all count-based windows which start or end after the out-of-order tuple.

If we process multiple queries which use different window-measures, timestamps are represented as vectors which contain multiple measures as dimensions. This representations allows for slicing the stream with respect to multiple dimensions (i.e., measures) while slices are still shared among all queries [33, 36].

### 4.4.4 Characteristic 4: Window Type

We classify window types with respect to the *context* (or *state*) which is required to know where windows start and end. We adopt the classification in context free (CF), forward-context aware (FCA), and forward-context free (FCF) introduced by Li et al. [112]. Here we present those classes along with the most common window types belonging to them.

- **Context Free (CF).** A window type is context free if one can tell all start and end timestamps of windows without processing any tuples. Common *sliding* and *tumbling* windows are context free because we can compute all start and end timestamps a priori based on the parameters $l$ and $l_s$.

- **Forward Context Free (FCF).** Windows are forward context free, if one can tell all start and end timestamps of windows up to any timestamp $t$, once all tuples up to this timestamp $t$ have been processed. An example are *punctuation-based* windows where punctuations mark start and end timestamps [68]. Once we processed all tuples up to $t$ (including out-of-order tuples), we also processed all punctuations before $t$ and, thus, we know all start and end positions up to $t$.

- **Forward Context Aware (FCA).** The remaining window types are forward context aware. Such window types require us to process tuples after a timestamp $t$ in order to know all window start and end timestamps before $t$. An example of such windows are *Multi-Measure Windows* which define their start and end timestamps on different measures. For example, *output the last 10 tuples (count-measure) every 5 seconds (time-measure)* is forward context aware: we need to process tuples up to a window end in order to compute the window begin.

## 4.5 General Stream Slicing

We now present our general stream slicing technique which supports high-performance aggregation for multiple queries with diverse workload characteristics. General stream

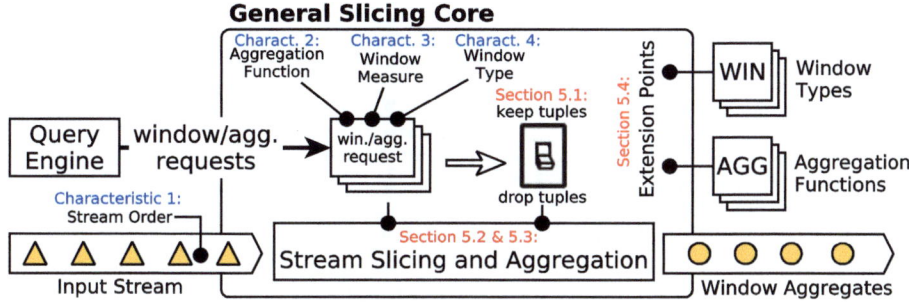

FIGURE 4.4: Architecture of General Stream Slicing.

slicing replaces alternative operators for window aggregation without changing their input or output semantics. Our technique minimizes the number of partial aggregates (saving memory), reduces the final aggregation steps when windows end (reducing latency), and avoids redundant computation for overlapping windows (increasing throughput). The main idea behind our technique is to exploit workload characteristics (Section 4.4) and to automatically adapt aggregation strategies. Such adaptivity is a highly desired feature of an aggregation framework: current non-adaptive techniques fail to support multiple window types, process in-order streams only, cannot share aggregates among windows defined on different measures, lack support for holistic aggregations, or incur dramatically reduced performance in exchange for being generally applicable.

**Approach Overview.** Figure 4.4 depicts an overview of our general slicing and aggregation technique. Users specify their queries in a high-level language, such as a flavor of stream SQL or a functional API. The query translator observes the characteristics of a query (i.e., window type, aggregate function, and window measure) as well as the characteristics of input streams (in-order vs. out-of-order streams) and forwards them to our aggregator. Once those characteristics are given to our aggregator, our general slicing technique adapts automatically to the given workload characteristics.

More specifically, general slicing detects if individual tuples need to be kept in memory (to ensure generality) or if they can be dropped after computing partial aggregates (to improve performance). We further discuss this in Section 4.5.1. Moreover, the stream slicing component automatically decides when it needs to apply our three fundamental slicing operations: merge, split, and update (discussed in Section 4.5.2). Queries can be added or removed from the aggregator and due to that, the workload characteristics

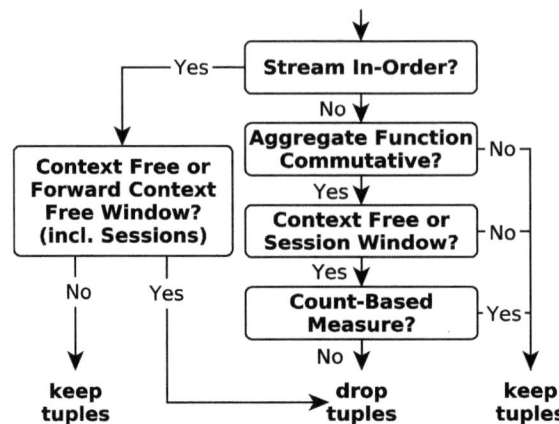

FIGURE 4.5: Decision Tree - Which workload characteristics require storing individual tuples in memory?

can change. To this end, our aggregator adapts on the fly. General slicing has extension points that can be used to implement user-defined window types and aggregations (discussed in Section 4.5.4).

### 4.5.1 Storing Tuples vs. Partial Aggregates

Existing aggregation techniques achieve generality by storing all input tuples and by computing high-level partial aggregates [14, 173]. Specialized techniques, on the other hand, only store (partial) aggregates. A general slicing technique needs to decide when to store what, according to workload characteristics of each of the queries that it serves. In this section, we discuss how we match the performance of specialized techniques, by choosing on-the-fly whether to keep tuples or to store partial aggregates only.

For example, consider an aggregation function which is non-commutative ($\exists x, y : x \oplus y \neq y \oplus x$) defined over an unordered stream. When an out-of-order tuple arrives, we need to recompute aggregates from the source tuples, in order to retain the correct order of the aggregation. Thus, one would have to store the actual tuples for possible later use. Storing all tuples for the whole duration of the allowed lateness requires more memory, but allows for computing arbitrary windows from stored tuples. The decision tree in Figure 4.5 summarizes when storing source tuples is required depending on different workload characteristics.

**In-order Streams.** For in-order streams, we drop tuples for all context free (CF) and forward context free (FCF) windows but must keep tuples if we process forward context aware (FCA) windows. For such windows, forward context leads to additional window start or end timestamps. Thus, we must be able to compute partial aggregates for arbitrary timestamp ranges from the originally stored tuples.

**Out-of-order Streams.** For out-of-order streams, we need to keep tuples if at least one of the following conditions is true:

1. **The aggregation function is non-commutative.**

   An out-of-order tuple changes the order of the incremental aggregation, which forces us to recompute the aggregate using source tuples. For in-order processing, the commutativity of aggregation functions is irrelevant, because tuples are always aggregated in-order. Thus, there is no need to store source tuples in addition to partial aggregates.

2. **The window is neither context free nor a session window.**

   In combination with out-of-order tuples, all context aware windows require tuples to be stored. This is because out-of-order tuples change backward context, which can lead to additional window start or end timestamps. Such additional start and end timestamps require to split slices and to recompute the respective partial aggregates from the original tuples. Session windows are an exception, because they are context aware, but never require recomputing aggregates, as we will show in Section 4.6.

3. **The query uses a count-based window measure.**

   An out-of-order tuple (see definition in Section 4.2) changes the count of all succeeding tuples. Thus, the last tuple of each window shifts to its succeeding window.

### 4.5.2 Slice Management

Stream slicing is the fundamental concept that allows us to build partial aggregates and share them among concurrently running queries and overlapping windows. In this section, we introduce three fundamental operations which we can perform on slices.

**Slice Metadata.** A slice stores its start timestamp ($t_{\texttt{start}}$), its end timestamp ($t_{\texttt{end}}$), and the timestamp of the first ($t_{\texttt{first}}$) and last tuple it contains ($t_{\texttt{last}}$). Note that the timestamps of the first and last tuples do not need to conincide with the start and end timestamps of a slice. For instance, consider a slice $A$ that starts at $t_{\mathtt{start}}(A) = 1$ and ends at $t_{\mathtt{end}}(A) = 10$, but the first (earliest) tuple contained is timestamped as $t_{\mathtt{first}}(A) = 2$ and its last/latest one as $t_{\mathtt{last}}(A) = 9$. Note that the *timestamp* can refer not only to actual time, but to any measure presented in Section 4.4.3.

We identify three fundamental operations which we perform on stream slices. These operations are *i*) *merging* of two slices into one, *ii*) *splitting* one slice into two, and *iii*) *updating* the state of a slice (i.e., aggregate and metadata updates). In the following paragraphs, we discuss `merge`, `split`, and `update` as well as the impact of our workload characteristics on each operation. We use upper case letters to name slices and corresponding lower case letters for slice aggregates.

**Merge.** Merging two slices $A$ and $B$ happens in three steps:

1. Update the end of $A$ such that $t_{\mathtt{end}}(A) \leftarrow t_{\mathtt{end}}(B)$.

2. Update the aggregate of $A$ such that $a \leftarrow a \oplus b$.

3. Delete slice $B$, which is now merged into $A$.

Steps one and three have a constant computational cost. The complexity of the second step ($a \leftarrow a \oplus b$) depends on the type of aggregate function. For instance, the cost is constant for algebraic and distributive functions such as `sum`, `min`, and `avg` because they require just a few basic arithmetic operations. Holistic functions such as quantiles can be more complex to compute. Except from the type of aggregation function, no other workload characteristics impact the complexity of the merge operation. However, stream order and window types influence when and *how often* we merge slices. We discuss this influence in Section 4.5.3.

**Split.** Splitting a slice $A$ at timestamp $t$ requires three steps:

1. Add slice $B$: $t_{\mathtt{start}}(B) \leftarrow t + 1$ and $t_{\mathtt{end}}(B) \leftarrow t_{\mathtt{end}}(A)$.

2. Update the end of $A$ such that $t_{\mathtt{end}}(A) \leftarrow t$.

3. Recompute the aggregates of $A$ and $B$.

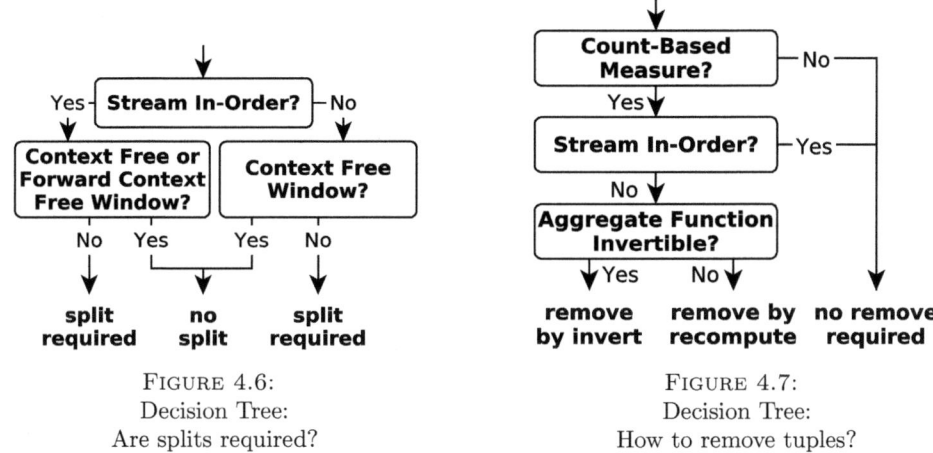

FIGURE 4.6:
Decision Tree:
Are splits required?

FIGURE 4.7:
Decision Tree:
How to remove tuples?

Note that splitting slices is an expensive operation because it requires recomputing slice aggregates from scratch. Moreover, if splitting is required, we need to keep individual tuples in memory to enable the recomputation.

We show in Figure 4.6 when split operations are required. For in-order streams, only forward context aware (FCA) windows require split operations. For such windows, we split slices according to a window's start and end timestamp as soon as we process the required forward context. In out-of-order data streams, all context aware windows can require split operations because out-of-order tuples contain backward context. We never split slices for context free windows such as tumbling and sliding ones.

**Update.** Updating a slice can involve adding in-order tuples, adding out-of-order tuples, removing tuples, or changing metadata ($t_{\mathsf{start}}$, $t_{\mathsf{end}}$, $t_{\mathsf{first}}$, and $t_{\mathsf{last}}$).

Metadata changes are simple assignments of new values to the existing variables. Adding a tuple to a slice requires one incremental aggregation step ($\oplus$), with the exception of processing out-of-order tuples with a non-commutative aggregation function. For this, we recompute the aggregate of the slice from scratch to retain the order of aggregation steps.

For some workloads we need to remove tuples from slices. We show in Figure 4.7 when and how we remove tuples from slices. Generally, a remove operation is required only if a window is defined on a count-based measure and if we process out-of-order tuples. An out-of-order tuple changes the count of all succeeding tuples. This requires

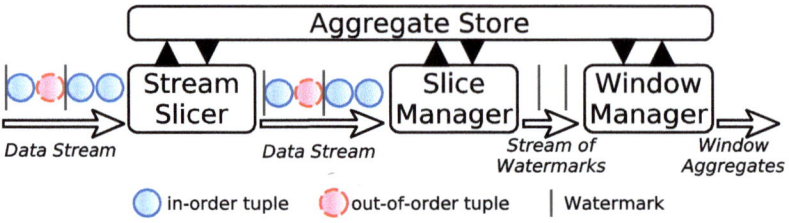

FIGURE 4.8: The Stream Slicing and Aggregation Process.

us to shift the last tuple of each slice one slice further, starting at the slice of the out-of-order tuple. If the aggregation function is invertible, we exploit this property by performing an incremental update. Otherwise, we have to recompute the slice aggregate from scratch. If the out-of-order tuple has a small delay, such that it still belongs to the latest slice, we can simply add the tuple without performing a remove operation.

### 4.5.3   Processing Input Tuples

The stream slicing and aggregation logic (bottom of Figure 4.4) consists of four components, which we show in Figure 4.8. The Aggregate Store is our shared data structure, which is accessed by the Stream Slicer to create new slices, by the Slice Manager to update slices, and by the Window Manager to compute window aggregates.

The input stream can contain in-order tuples, out-of-order tuples, and watermarks. Note that in-order tuples can either arrive from an in-order stream (i.e., one that is guaranteed to never contain an out-of-order tuple) or from an out-of-order stream (i.e., one that does not guarantee in-order arrival). If the the stream is in-order (i.e., all tuples are in-order tuples), there is no need to ingest watermarks. Instead, we output windows directly, since there is no need to wait for potentially delayed tuples.

**Step 1 - The Stream Slicer.**   The Stream Slicer initializes new slices on-the-fly when in-order tuples arrive [102]. In an in-order stream, it is sufficient to start slices when windows start [36]. In an out-of-order stream, we also need to start slices when windows end, to allow for updating the last slice of windows later on with out-of-order tuples. We always cache the timestamp of the next upcoming window edge and compare in-order tuples with this timestamp. As soon as the timestamp of a tuple exceeds the cached timestamp, we start a new slice and cache the timestamp of the next edge. This is highly efficient because the majority of tuples do not end a slice and require just one comparison of timestamps.

The Stream Slicer does not process out-of-order tuples and watermarks but forwards them directly to the Slice Manager. This is possible because the slices for out-of-order tuples have already been initialized by previous in-order tuples.

**Step 2 - The Slice Manager.** The Slice Manager is responsible for triggering all `split`, `merge`, and `update` operations on slices.

First, the Slice Manager checks whether a `merge` or `split` operation is required. We always merge and split slices such that all slice edges match window edges and vice versa. This guarantees that we maintain the minimum possible number of slices [33, 36, 180].

In an out-of-order stream, context aware windows can cause `merge`s or `split`s. In an in-order stream, only forward context aware windows can cause these operations. Context free windows never require `merge` or `split` operations, as the window edges are known in advance and slices never need to change.

In-order tuples can be part of the forward context which indicates window start or end timestamps earlier in the stream. When processing forward context aware windows, we check if the new tuple changes the context such that it introduces or removes window start or end timestamps. In such case, we perform the required `merge` and `split` operation to match the new slice and window edges. Out-of-order tuples can change forward and backward context, such that a `merge` operation or `split` operation are required.

If the new context causes new window edges and, thus, `merge` or `split` operations, we notify the Window Manager, which outputs window aggregates up to the current watermark.

Finally, the Slice Manager adds the new tuple to its slice and updates the slice aggregate accordingly. In-order tuples always belong to the current slice and are added with an incremental aggregate update [173]. For out-of-order tuples, we look up the slice which covers the timestamp of the out-of-order tuple and add the tuple to this slice. For commutative aggregation functions, we add the new tuple with an incremental aggregate update. For non-commutative aggregation functions, we need to recompute the aggregate from individual tuples to retain the correct order.

**Step 3 - The Window Manager.** The Window Manager computes the final aggregates for windows from slice aggregates.

When processing an in-order stream, the Window Manager checks if the tuple it processes is the last tuple of a window. Therefore, each tuple can be seen as a watermark which has the timestamp of the tuple. If a window ended, the window manager computes and outputs the window aggregate (final aggregation step).

For out-of-order streams, we wait for the watermark (see Section 4.2) before we output results of windows which ended before a watermark.

The Slice Manager notifies the Windows Manager when it performs `split`, `merge`, or `update` operation on slices. Upon such notification, the Window Manager performs two operations:

1. If an out-of-order tuple arrives within the allowed lateness but after the watermark, the tuple possibly changes aggregates of windows which were output before. Thus, the Window Manager outputs updates for these window aggregates.

2. If a tuple changes the context of context aware windows such that new windows end before the current watermark, the window manager computes and outputs the respective aggregates.

**Parallelization.** We parallelize stream processing with key partitioning, which is the common approach used in stream processing systems [84] such as Flink [35], Spark [16], and Storm [177]. Key partitioning enables intra-node as well as inter-node parallelism and, thus, results in good scalability. Since our generic window aggregation is a drop in replacement for the window aggregation operator, the input and output semantics of the operator remains unchanged. Thus, neither the query interface nor optimizations unrelated to window aggregations are affected.

### 4.5.4 User-Defined Windows and Aggregations

Our architecture decouples the general logic of stream slicing from the concrete implementation of window types and aggregation functions. This makes it easy to add window types and aggregation functions, as no changes are required in the slicing logic. In this section, we describe how we implement aggregation functions and window types.

#### 4.5.4.1 Implementing Aggregation Functions

We adopt the same approach of incremental aggregation introduced by Tangwongsan et al. [173]. Each aggregation type consists of three functions: *lift*, *combine*, and *lower*. In addition, aggregations may implement an *invert* function. We now discuss the concept behind these functions, and refer the reader to the original paper for an overview of different aggregations and their implementation.

**Lift.** The *lift* function transforms a tuple to a partial aggregate. For example, consider an average computation. If a tuple $\langle t, v \rangle$ contains its timestamp $t$ and a value $v$, the *lift* function will transform it to $\langle \mathtt{sum} \leftarrow v, \mathtt{count} \leftarrow 1 \rangle$, which is the partial aggregate of that one tuple.

**Combine.** The *combine* function ($\oplus$) computes the combined aggregate from partial aggregates. Each incremental aggregation step results in one call of the *combine* function.

**Lower.** The *lower* function transforms a partial aggregate to a final aggregate. In our example, the lower function computes the average from sum and count:

$$\langle \mathtt{sum}, \mathtt{count} \rangle \mapsto \mathtt{sum}/\mathtt{count}$$

**Invert.** The optional *invert* function removes one partial aggregate from another with an incremental operation.

In this work, we consider holistic aggregation functions which have an unbounded size of partial aggregates. A widely used holistic function is the computation of quantiles. For instance, windowed quantiles are the basis for billing models of content delivery networks and transit-ISPs [53, 85]. For quantile computations, we sort tuples in slices to speed up succeeding merge operations and apply run length encoding to save memory [152].

### 4.5.4.2 Implementing Different Window Types

We use a common interface for the in-order slicing logic of all windows. We extend this interface with additional methods for context-aware windows. One can add additional window types by implementing the respective interface.

**Context Free Windows.** The slicing logic for context free windows depends on in-order tuples only. When a tuple is processed, the slicing core initializes all slices up to the timestamp of that tuple. Our interface for context free windows has two methods: The first method has the following signature:

```
long getNextEdge(long timestamp)
```

123

The method receives a timestamp as parameter and returns the next window edge (begin or end timestamp) after this timestamp. We use this method to retrieve the next window edge for on-the-fly stream slicing (Step 1 in subsection 4.5.3). For example, a tumbling window with length $l$ would return $timestamp + l - (timestamp \bmod l)$.

The second method triggers the final window aggregation according to a watermark and has the following signature:

```
void triggerWin(Callback c, long prevWM, long currWM)
```

The Window Manager calls this method when it processes a watermark. `c` is a callback object, `prevWM` is the timestamp of the previous watermark and `currWM` is the timestamp of the current watermark. The method reports all windows which ended between `prevWM` and `currWM` by calling

```
c.triggerWin(longstartTime, long endTime).
```

This callback to the Window Manager triggers the computation and output of the final window aggregate.

**Context Aware Windows.**   Context aware windows use the same interface as context free windows to trigger the initialization of slices when processing in-order tuples. In addition, context aware windows require to keep a state (i.e., context) in order to derive window start and end timestamps when processing out-of-order tuples. We initialize context aware windows with a pointer to the Aggregate Store. This prevents redundancies among the state of the shared aggregator and the window state. When the Slice Manager processes a tuple, it notifies context aware windows by calling

```
window.notifyContext(callbackObj, tuple).
```

This method can then add and remove window start and end timestamps through the callback object and the Slice Manager splits and merges slices as required to match window start and end timestamps. We detect whether or not a window is context aware based on the interface which is implemented by the window specification. We provide examples for different context free and context aware window implementations in our open source repository[3].

---

[3]Open-Source-Repository: `https://github.com/TU-Berlin-DIMA/scotty-window-processor`

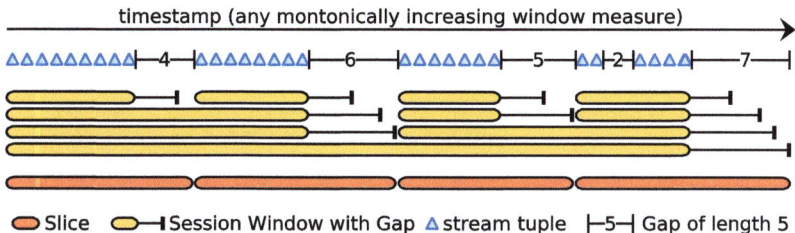

FIGURE 4.9: Session Window Aggregate Sharing.

# 4.6 Stream Slicing for Session Windows

Recently, session windows evolved to a common window type supported by programming models such as Apache Beam [11] and the Dataflow Model [5]. Many systems implement these models and process session windows in addition to sliding and tumbling windows [10, 36, 205]. In this section, we take a close look on session windows and show that session window aggregation benefits from stream slicing.

## 4.6.1 Aggregate Sharing for Session Windows

We show an example for session window stream slicing in Figure 4.9. The example has four session windows with the minimum gaps $l_g = 3$, 5, 6, and 7. We make five observations based on our example:

1. Multiple session window queries with different gaps can share slices and, thus, partial aggregates.

2. Session windows would also share slices with other types of windows.

3. Sessions of a single query have no overlap. Thus, a single session window query cannot benefit from aggregate sharing.

4. Slices can cover the gaps between sessions because gaps do not cover any tuples by definition. Respectively, a partial aggregate which covers a session and a gap is equal to an aggregate which covers the session only.

5. The slicing logic solely depends on one session window - the one with the smallest gap. All session windows with larger gaps are compositions of the slices made for the session window with the smallest minimum gap. In our example $\mathtt{min}(l_g) = 3$.

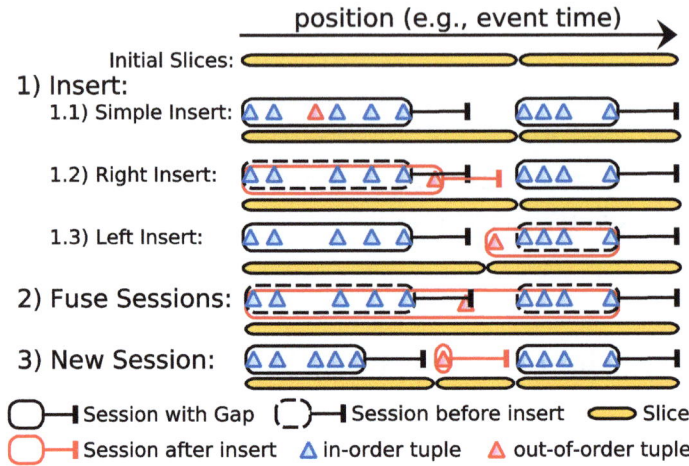

FIGURE 4.10: Out-of-order Processing with Session Windows.

We utilize the observations above and create slices with respect to the session window with the smallest gap only. This allows for creating stream slices with a constant workload, which is independent from the number concurrent sessions.

### 4.6.2 Session Windows on Out-Of-Order Streams

Stream slicing for session windows is more complex than for sliding or tumbling windows, because session windows are context aware. Thus, we do not know start and end positions of sessions up front. Instead, start and end positions of sessions depend on the gaps between the tuples we process.

Out-of-order tuples either belong to an existing session (update), fuse sessions (merge), or form new sessions (split). We show all cases in Figure 4.10. Interestingly, we can rewrite all required split operations to update operations. Thus, we completely prevent expensive slice splits and do not need to store tuples in additions to aggregates when processing session windows. If an out-of-order tuple belongs to an existing session (Case 1.1) or extends a session at the session end (Case 1.2), we insert the tuple into the respective slice (one update). Thereby, the start and end times of slices remain unchanged. If an out-of-order tuple extends a session at the session start (Case 1.3), we change session edges respectively and add the tuple (two updates). An out-of-order tuple can also fuse two sessions. This is the case whenever the gap between sessions shrinks below the minimum session gap (Case 2). Fusing sessions also combines the slices of the sessions (one merge). Finally, an out-of-order tuple can form a new session on its own if its gap on both sides is larger than the minimum session gap (Case 3). In this case, we split a slice between sessions (i.e., within the gap). Because gaps contain no data by definition, we can create a new slice which contains the out-of-order tuple and and update the end of the existing slice without changing its aggregate (one update).

## 4.7 Evaluation

In this section, we evaluate the performance of general stream slicing and compare stream slicing with alternative techniques introduced in Section 4.3.

### 4.7.1 Experimental Setup

**Setup.** We implement all techniques on Apache Flink v1.3. We run our experiments on a VM with 6 GB main memory and 8 processing cores with 2.6 GHz.

**Metrics.** In our experiments, we report throughput, latency, and memory consumption. We measure throughput as in the Yahoo Streaming Benchmark implementation for Apache Flink [41, 191]. We determine latencies with the JMH benchmarking suite [137]. JMH provides precise latency measurements on JVM-based systems. We use the *ObjectSizeCalculator* of Nashorn to determine memory footprints [138].

**Baselines.** We compare an eager and a lazy version of general stream slicing with non-slicing techniques from Section 4.3: As representative for aggregate trees, we implement FlatFAT [173]. For the buckets technique, we use the implementation of Apache Flink [35]. For tuple buffers, we use an implementation based on a ring buffer array. We also include Pairs [102] and Cutty [36] as specialized slicing techniques where possible.

**Data.** We replay real-world sensor data from a football match [133] and from manufacturing machines [90]. The original data sets track the position of the football with 2000 and the machine states with 100 updates per second. We generate additional tuples based on the original data to simulate higher ingestion rates [77]. We add 5 gaps per minute to separate sessions. This is representative for the ball possession moving from one player to another[4]. If not indicated differently, we show results for the football data. The results for other data sets are almost identical because the performance depends on workload characteristics rather than data characteristics.

**Queries.** We base our queries (i.e., window length, slide steps, etc.) on the workload of a live-visualization dashboard which is built for the football data we use [183]. If not indicated differently, we use the `sum` aggregation in Sections 4.7.2 and Section 4.7.3. In Section 4.7.4, we use the M4 aggregation technique [93] to compress the data stream for visualization. M4 computes four algebraic aggregates per window (i.e., minimum, maximum, first and last value of each window). We show in Section 4.7.3.2 how the performance differs among diverse aggregation functions. Because we do not change the input and output semantics of the window and aggregation operation, there is no impact on upstream or downstream operations. We ensure that windowing and aggregation are the bottleneck and, thus, we measure the performance of aggregation techniques.

We do not alternate between tumbling and sliding windows because they lead to identical performance: For example, 20 concurrent tumbling window queries cause 20 concurrent windows (1 window for each query at any time). This is equivalent to a single sliding window with a window length of 20 seconds and and a slide step of one second (again 20 concurrent windows). In the following, we refer to *concurrent windows* instead of *concurrent tumbling window queries*. *Sliding window queries* yield identical results if they imply the same number of *concurrent windows*.

**Structure.** We split our evaluation in three parts. First, we compare stream slicing and alternative approaches with respect to their throughput, latency, and memory footprint (Section 4.7.2). Second, we study the impact of each workload characteristic introduced in Section 4.4 (Section 4.7.3). Third, we integrate general slicing in Apache Flink and show the performance gain for a concrete application (Section 4.7.4). Sections 4.7.2 and 4.7.3 focus on the performance per operator instance. Section 4.7.4 studies the parallelization.

---

[4]The DEBS 2013 Grand Challenge defines *ball possession* as follows: *"A player (and thereby his respective team) can obtain the ball whenever the ball is in his proximity and he hits it. A ball is in proximity of the player when it is less than one meter away from him. The distance of one meter applies to the distance between the sensor within the ball and any of the two sensors in the player's shin guards. A ball is hit whenever its acceleration or velocity peaks. A ball will stay in the possession of a given player until another player hits it, the ball leaves the field, or the game is stopped. Specifically, a ball may leave the player's proximity and will still remain in his possession."* [133]

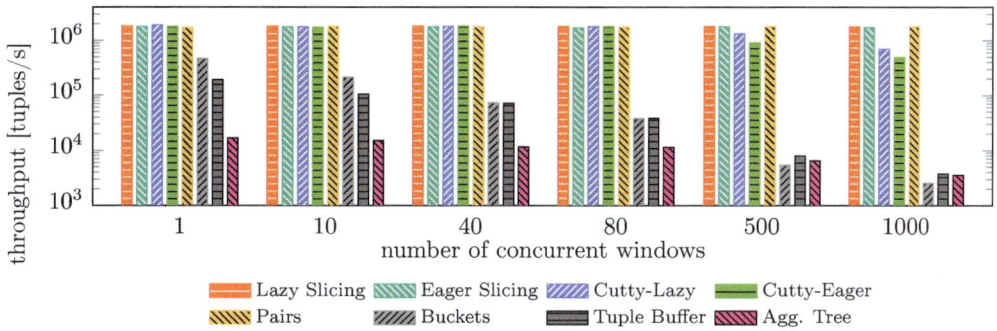

FIGURE 4.11: In-order Processing with Context Free Windows.

## 4.7.2 Stream Slicing Compared to Alternatives

We now compare stream slicing with alternative techniques discussed in Section 4.3. We first study the throughput for in-order processing on context-free windows in Section 4.7.2.1. Our goal is to understand the performance of stream slicing compared to alternative techniques, including specialized slicing techniques. In Section 4.7.2.2, we evaluate how the throughput changes in the presence of out-of-order tuples and context-aware windows. In Section 4.7.2.3, we evaluate the memory footprint and in Section 4.7.2.4 the latency of different techniques.

### 4.7.2.1 Throughput

**Workload.** We execute multiple concurrent tumbling window queries with equally distributed lengths from 1 to 20 seconds. These window lengths are representative of window aggregations which facilitate plotting line charts at different zoom levels (Application of Section 4.7.3). We chose Pairs [102] and Cutty [36] as example slicing techniques because Pairs is one of the first and most cited techniques and Cutty offers a high generality with respect to window types.

**Results.** We show our results in Figure 4.11. All three slicing techniques process millions of tuples per second and scale to large numbers of concurrent windows.

Buckets achieves orders of magnitude less throughput than Slicing techniques and does not scale to large numbers of concurrent windows. The reason is that we must assign each tuple to all concurrent buckets (i.e., windows). Thus, tuples belong to

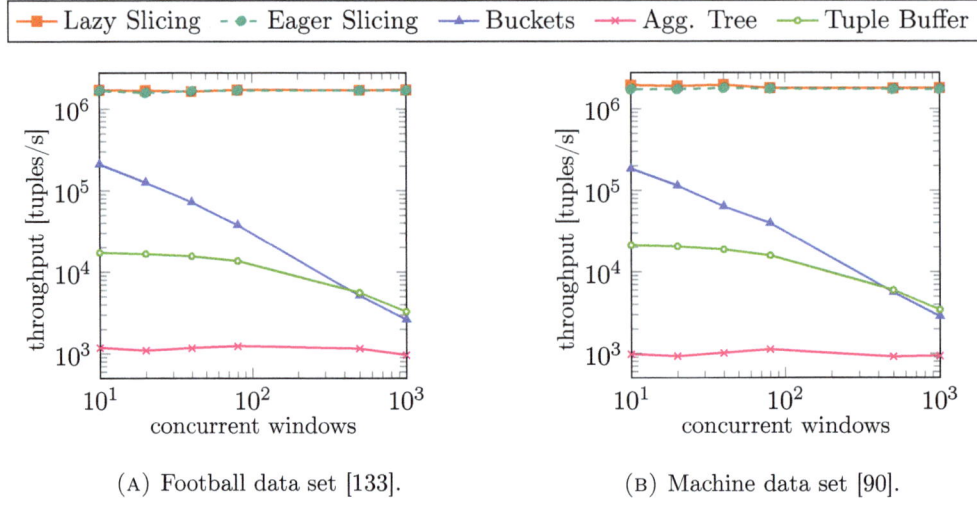

(A) Football data set [133].　　　　(B) Machine data set [90].

FIGURE 4.12: Increasing the number of concurrent windows including 20% out-of-order tuples and session windows.

up to 1000 buckets causing 1000 redundant aggregation steps per tuple. In contrast, slicing techniques always assign tuples to exactly one slice. Similar to buckets, the tuple buffer causes redundant aggregation steps for each window as we compute each window independently. Aggregate Trees show a throughput which is orders of magnitude smaller than the one of slicing techniques. This is because each tuple requires several updates in the tree.

**Summary.** We observe that slicing techniques outperform alternative concepts with respect to throughput and scale to large numbers of concurrent windows.

### 4.7.2.2 Throughput under Constraints

We now analyze the throughput under constraints, i.e., including out-of-order tuples and context-aware windows.

**Workload.** The workload remains the same as before but we add a time-based session window ($l_g = \mathtt{1sec.}$) as representative for a context-aware window. We add 20% out-of-order tuples with random delays between 0 and 2 seconds.

**Results.** We show the results in Figure 4.12 on Page 130. Slicing techniques achieve an order of magnitude higher throughput than alternative techniques, which do not use stream slicing. Moreover, slicing scales to large numbers of concurrent windows with almost constant throughput. This is because the per-tuple complexity remains constant: we assign each tuple to exactly one slice. Lazy Slicing has the highest throughput (1.7 Million tuples/s) because it uses stream slicing and does not compute an aggregate tree. Eager Slicing achieves slightly lower throughput than Lazy Slicing. This is due to out-of-order tuples which cause updates in the aggregate tree. Buckets show the same performance decrease as in the previous experiment. The performance decrease for the Tuple Buffer is intensified due to out-of-order inserts in the ring buffer array. Aggregate Trees process less than 1500 tuples/s with 20% out-of-order tuples. This is because out-of-order tuples require expensive leaf inserts in the aggregate tree (rebalance and update of inner nodes). Eager slicing seldom faces this issue because it stores slices instead of tuples in the aggregate tree. The majority of out-of-order tuples falls in an existing slice, which prevents rebalancing. We exemplary show our results on two different datasets for this experiment. Because the performance depends on workload characteristics rather than data characteristics, the results are almost identical. We omit similar results for different data sets in the following experiments and focus on the impact of workload characteristics.

**Summary.** For workloads including out-of-order tuples and context-aware windows, we observe that general stream slicing outperforms alternative concepts with respect to throughput and scales to large numbers of concurrent windows.

### 4.7.2.3 Memory Consumption

We now study the memory consumption of different techniques with four plots: In Figures 4.13a and 4.13c on Page 132, we vary the number of slices in the allowed lateness and fix the number of tuples in the allowed lateness to 50 thousand. In Figures 4.13b and 4.13d on Page 132, we vary the number of tuples and fix the number of slices to 500. We experimentally compare time-based and count-based windows. Our measurements include all memory required for storing partial aggregates and metadata, such as the start and end times of slices.

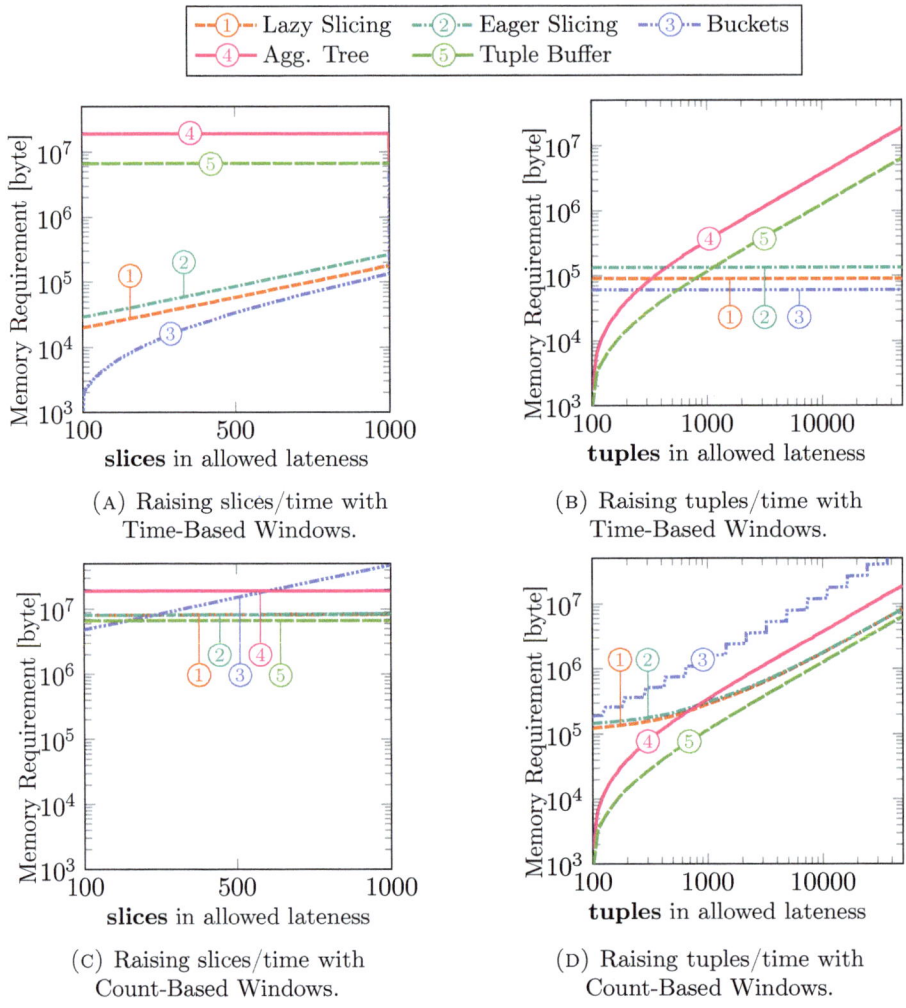

(A) Raising slices/time with
Time-Based Windows.

(B) Raising tuples/time with
Time-Based Windows.

(C) Raising slices/time with
Count-Based Windows.

(D) Raising tuples/time with
Count-Based Windows.

FIGURE 4.13: Memory Experiments with Out-of-order Streams.

**Results for Time-Based Windows.** Figures 4.13a and 4.13b show the memory consumption for time-based windows, which do not require us to store individual tuples. For Stream Slicing and Buckets, the memory footprint increases linearly with the number of slices in the allowed lateness. The memory footprint is independent from the number of tuples. The opposite holds for Tuple Buffers and Aggregate Trees. Slicing techniques store just one partial aggregate per slice, while buckets store one partial aggregate per window. Tuple Buffers and Aggregate Trees store each tuple individually.

**Results for Count-Based Windows.** Figures 4.13c and 4.13d show the memory consumption for count-based windows, which require individual tuples to be stored. The experiment setup is the same as in Figures 4.13a and 4.13b.

The memory consumption of all techniques increases with the number of tuples in the allowed lateness, because we need to store all tuples for processing count-based windows on out-of-order streams (Figure 4.13d). Starting from 1000 tuples in the allowed lateness, the memory consumed by tuples dominates the overall memory requirement. Accordingly, all curves become linear and parallel. Buckets show a stair shape because of the underlying hash map implementation [195]. Slicing techniques start at roughly $10^5$ byte which is the space required to store 500 slices. The memory footprint of buckets also increases with the number of slices because more slices correspond to more window buckets (Figure 4.13c). Each bucket stores all tuples it contains which leads to duplicated tuples for overlapping buckets.

**Summary.** When we can drop individual tuples and store partial aggregates only (Figure 4.13a and 4.13b), the memory consumptions of slicing and buckets depends only on the number of slices in the allowed lateness. In this case, stream slicing and buckets scale to high ingestion rates with almost constant memory utilization. If we need to keep individual tuples (Figure 4.13c and 4.13d), storing tuples dominates the memory consumption.

#### 4.7.2.4 Latency

The output latency for window aggregates depends on the aggregation technique, the number of entries (tuples or slices) which are stored, and the aggregation function. In Figure 4.14 on Page 134, we show the latency for different situations.

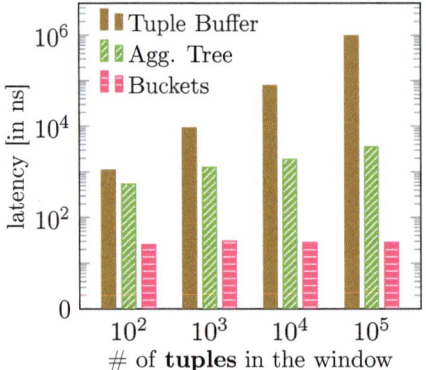

(A) Latency for **sum** with **tuple-dependent** techniques.

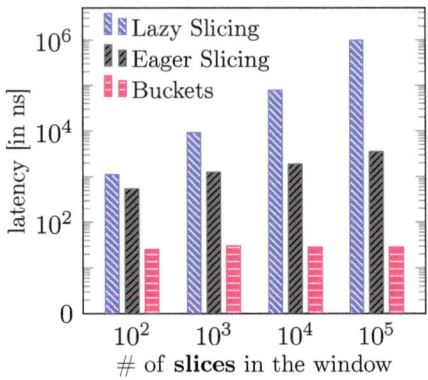

(B) Latency for **sum** with **slice-dependent** techniques.

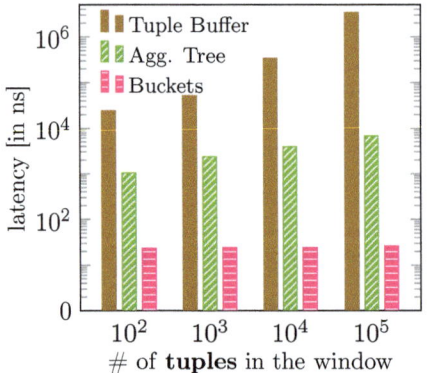

(C) Latency for **median** with **tuple-dependent** techniques.

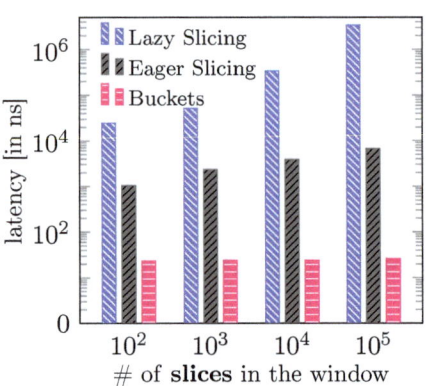

(D) Latency for **median** with **slice-dependent** techniques.

FIGURE 4.14: Output Latency of Aggregate Stores.

**Distributive and Algebraic Aggregation.**   For the sum aggregation (Figure 4.14a), Lazy Slicing and Tuple Buffer exhibit up to 1ms latency for $10^5$ entries (no matter if $10^5$ tuples or $10^5$ slices). Eager Slicing and Aggregate Trees show latencies below $5\mu s$. Buckets achieve latencies below 30ns. Lazy aggregation has higher latencies because it computes final aggregates upon request. Eager Aggregation uses precomputed partial aggregates from an aggregate tree which reduces the latency. Buckets pre-compute the final aggregate of each window and store aggregates in a hash map which leads to the lowest latency.

**Holistic Aggregation.**   The latencies for the holistic median aggregation (Figure 4.14c) are in the same order of magnitude and follow the same trends. Buckets exhibit the same latencies as before because they precompute the aggregate for each bucket. Thus, a more complex holistic aggregation decreases the throughput but does not increase the latency. The latency of slicing techniques increases for the median aggregation, because we combine partial aggregates to final aggregates when windows end. This combine step is more expensive for holistic aggregates than for algebraic ones.

**Summary.**   We observe a trade-off between throughput and latency. Lazy aggregation has the highest throughput and the highest latency. Eager aggregation has a lower throughput but achieves microsecond latencies. Buckets provide latencies in the order of nanoseconds but have an order of magnitude less throughput.

## 4.7.3   Studying Workload Characteristics

We measure the impact of the workload characteristics from Section 4.4 on the performance of general slicing. For comparison, we also show the best alternative techniques.

### 4.7.3.1   Impact of Stream Order

In this experiment, we investigate the impact of the amount of out-of-order tuples and the impact of the delay of out-of-order tuples on throughput (Figure 4.15 on Page 136). We use the same setup as for the throughput experiments in Section 4.7.2.2 with 20 concurrent windows.

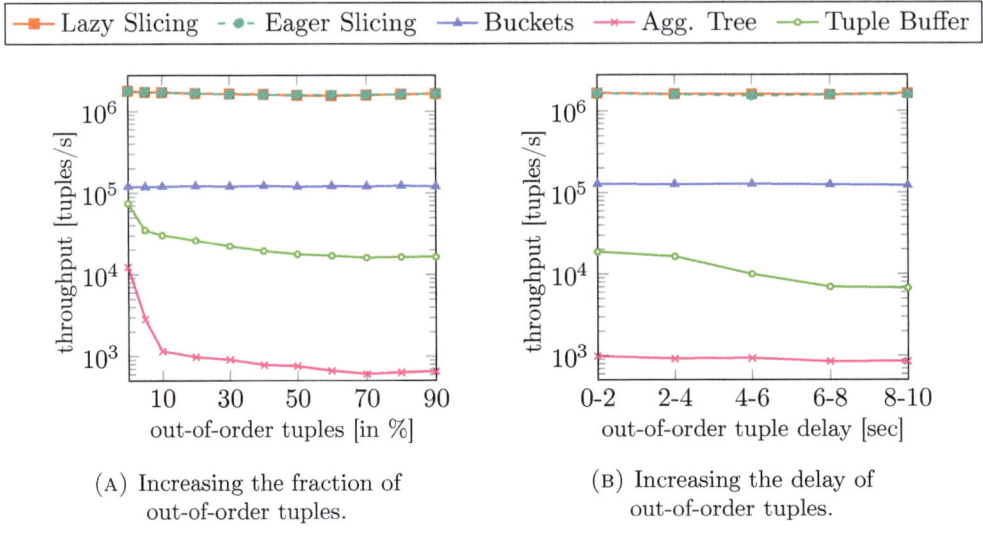

FIGURE 4.15: Impact of Stream Order on the Throughput.

**Out-of-order Performance.** In Figure 4.15a, we increase the fraction of out-of-order tuples. Slicing and Buckets process out-of-order tuples as fast as in-order tuples. The throughput of the other techniques decreases when processing more out-of-order tuples.

Slicing techniques process out-of-order tuples efficiently because they perform only one slice update per out-of-order tuple. Eager slicing also updates its aggregate tree. This update has a low overhead because there are just a few hundred slices in the allowed lateness and, accordingly, there are just a few tree levels which require updates. Aggregate Trees on tuples have a much larger number of tree levels because they store tuples instead of slices as leaf nodes.

Buckets have a constant throughput as in the previous experiments. Tuple Buffers and Aggregate Trees exhibit a throughput decay when processing out-of-order tuples. Tuple Buffers require expensive out-of-order inserts in the sorted buffer array. Aggregate Trees require inserting past leaf nodes in the aggregate tree. This causes a rebalancing of the tree and the respective re-computation of aggregates. Eager Slicing seldom faces this issue (see Section 4.7.2.2).

**Delay Robustness.** In Figure 4.15b, we increase the delay of out-of-order tuples. We use equally distributed random delays within the ranges specified on the horizontal axis.

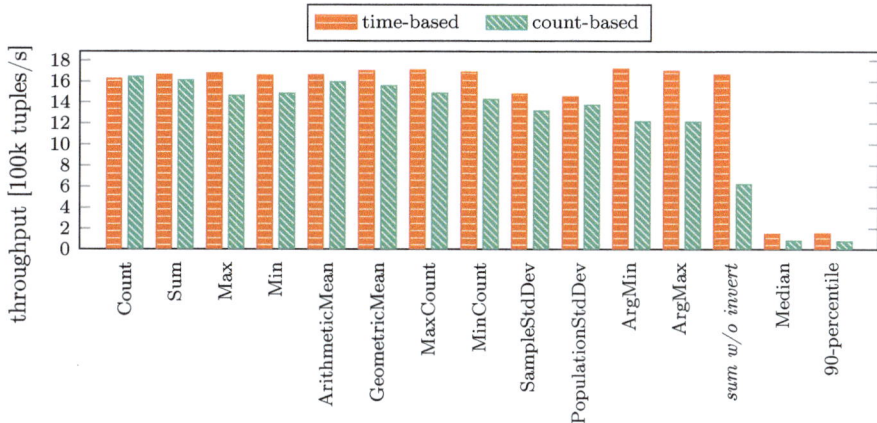

FIGURE 4.16: Impact of Aggregation Types on Throughput.

All techniques except Tuple Buffers are robust against increasing delays. Slicing techniques always update one slice when they process a tuple. Small delays can sightly increase the throughput compared to longer delays if out-of-order tuples still belong to the most recent slice. In this case, we require no lookup operations to find the correct slice. The throughput of Buckets is independent of the delay because Flink stores buckets in a hashmap. The throughput of the tuple buffer decreases with increasing delay of out-or-order tuples, because the lookup and update costs in the sorted buffer array increase.

**Summary.** Stream slicing and Buckets scale with constant throughput to large fractions of out-of-order tuples and are robust against high delays of these tuples.

### 4.7.3.2 Impact of Aggregation Functions

We now study the throughput of different aggregation functions using the same setup as before (20 concurrent windows, 20% out-of-order tuples, delays between 0 and 2 seconds) in Figure 4.16. We differentiate time-based and count-based windows to show the impact of invertibility. We implement the same aggregation functions as Tangwongsang et al. [173]. The original publication provides a discussion of these functions and an overview of their algebraic properties. We additionally study the median and the 90-percentile as examples for holistic aggregation. Moreover, we study a naive version of the sum aggregation which does not use the invertibility property. This allows for making a deduction with respect to not invertible aggregations in general.

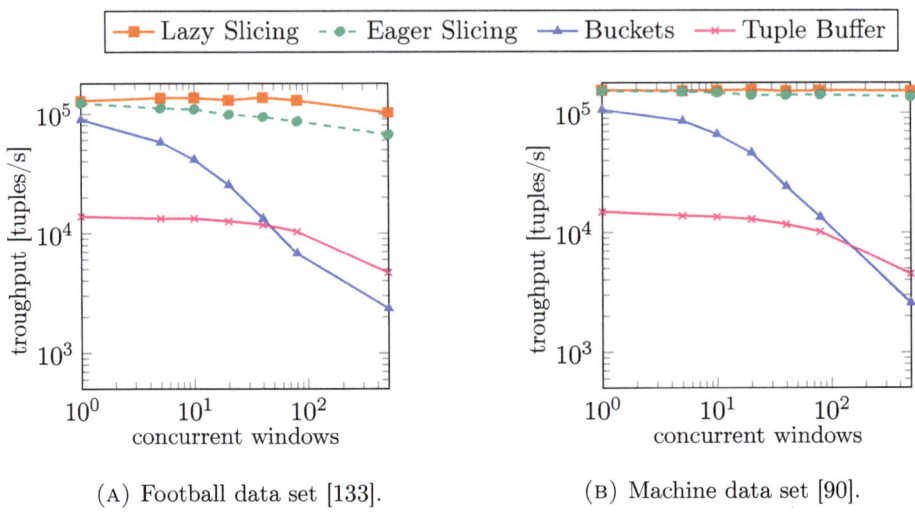

(A) Football data set [133].          (B) Machine data set [90].

FIGURE 4.17: Throughput for Median Aggregation.

**Time-Based Windows.** For time-based windows, the throughput is similar for all algebraic and distributive aggregations with small differences due to different computational complexities of the aggregations. Holistic aggregations (median and 90-percentile) show a much lower throughput because they require to keep all tuples in memory and have a higher complexity.

**Count-Based Windows.** We observe lower throughputs than for time-based windows, which is because of out-of-order tuples. For count-based windows, an out-of-order tuple changes the sequence id (count) of all later tuples. Thus, we need to shift the last tuple of each slice to the next slice. This operation has low overhead for invertible aggregations because we can subtract and add tuples from aggregates. The operation is costly for not invertible aggregations because it requires the recomputation of the slice aggregate. Time-based windows do not require an invert operation because out-of-order tuples only change the sequence id (count) of later tuples but not the timestamps.

**Impact of invertibility.** There is a big difference between the performance for different not invertible aggregations on count-based windows. Although Min, Max, MinCount, MaxCount, ArgMin, and ArgMax are not invertible, they have a small throughput decay compared to time-based windows (Figure 4.16). This is because most invert operations

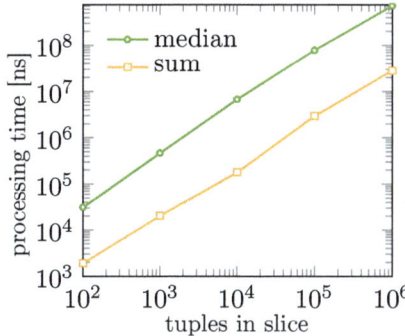

FIGURE 4.18: Processing Time for Recomputing Aggregates.

do not affect the aggregate and, thus, do not require a recomputation. For example, it is unlikely that the tuple we shift to the next slice is the maximum of the slice. If the maximum remains unchanged, max, MaxCount, and ArgMax do not require a recomputation. In contrast, the sum w/o invert function shows the performance decay for a not invertible function which always requires a recomputation when removing tuples.

**Impact of Holistic Aggregations.** In Figure 4.16, we observe that holistic aggregations have a much lower throughput than algebraic and distributive aggregations. In Figure 4.17 on Page 138, we show that stream slicing still outperforms alternative approaches for these aggregations. The reason is that stream slicing prevents redundant computations for overlapping windows by sorting values within slices and by applying run length encoding. In contrast, Buckets and Tuple Buffer compute each window independently. The machine data set shows slightly higher throughputs because the aggregated column has only 37 distinct values compared to 84232 distinct values in the football dataset. Fewer distinct values increase the savings achieved by run length encoding. Aggregate trees (not shown) can hardly compute holistic aggregates. They maintain partial aggregates for all inner nodes of a large tree which is extremely expensive for holistic aggregations.

**Summary.** On time-based windows, stream slicing performs diverse distributive and algebraic aggregations with similarly high throughputs. Considering count-based windows and out-of-order tuples, invertible aggregations lead to higher throughputs than not invertible ones.

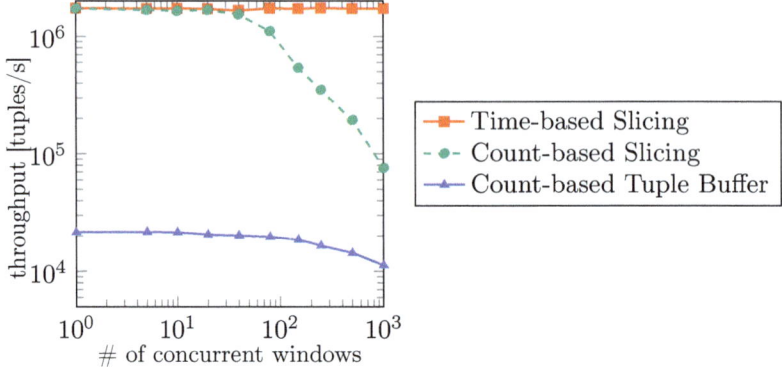

FIGURE 4.19: The Impact of Different Window Measures.

### 4.7.3.3   Impact of Window Types

The window type impacts the throughput if we process context-aware windows because these windows potentially require split operations. Note that context aware windows cover arbitrary user-defined windows which makes it impossible to provide a general statement on the throughput for all these windows. Thus, we evaluate the time required to recompute aggregates for slices of different sizes when a split operation is performed (Figure 4.18 on Page 139). Given a context aware window, one can estimate the throughput decay based on the number of split operations required and the time required for recomputing aggregates after splits. We show the sum aggregation as representative for an algebraic function and the median as example for a holistic function.

The processing time for the recomputation of an aggregate increases linearly with the number of tuples contained in the aggregate. If split operations are required to process a context aware window, a system should monitor the overhead caused by split operations and adjust the maximum size of slices accordingly. Smaller slices require more memory and cause repeated aggregate computation when calculating final aggregates for windows. In exchange, the aggregates of smaller slices are cheaper to recompute when we split slices.

### 4.7.3.4   Impact of Window Measures

We compare different window measures in Figure 4.19. We use the same setup as before (20% out-of-order tuples with delays between 0 and 2 seconds).

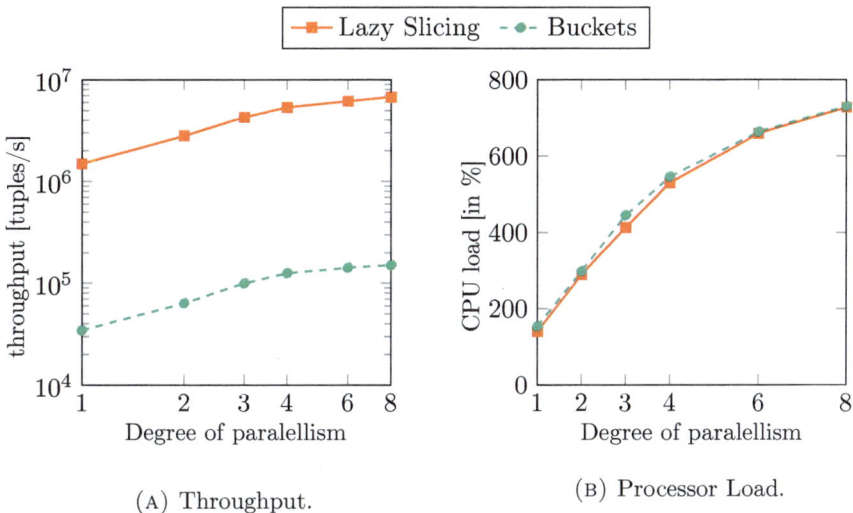

(A) Throughput.

(B) Processor Load.

FIGURE 4.20: Parallelizing the workload of a live-visualization dashboard (80 concurrent windows per operator instance).

**Time-Based Windows.** For time-based windows, the throughput is independent from the number of concurrent windows as discussed in our throughput analysis in Section 4.7.2.2. The throughput for arbitrary advancing measures is the same as for time-based measures because they are processed identically [36].

**Count-Based Windows.** The throughput for count-based windows is almost constant for up to 40 concurrent windows and decays linearly for larger numbers. For up to 40 concurrent windows, most slices are larger than the delay of tuples. Thus, out-of-order tuples still belong to the current slice and require no slice updates. The more windows we add, the smaller our slices become. Thus, out-of-order tuples require an increasing number of updates for shifting tuples between slices which reduces the throughput. Tuple buffers are the fastest alternative to Slicing in our experiment. For 1000 concurrent windows, slicing is still an order of magnitude faster than tuple buffers.

**Summary.** The throughput of time-based windows stays constant whereas the throughput of count-based windows decreases with a growing number of concurrent windows.

### 4.7.4 Parallel Stream Slicing

In this experiment, we study stream slicing on the example of our dashboard application [183] which uses the M4 aggregation [93]. We vary the degree of parallelism to show the scalability with respect to the number of cores. We compare Lazy Slicing with Buckets which are used in Flink.

**Results.** In Figure 4.20 on Page 141, we increase the number of parallel operator instances of the windowing operation (degree of parallelism). The throughput scales linearly up to a degree of parallelism of four (Figure 4.20a). Up to this degree, each parallel operator instance runs on a dedicated core with other tasks (data source operator, writing outputs, operating system overhead, etc.) running on the remaining four cores. For higher degrees of parallelism the throughput and the CPU load increase logarithmically, approaching the full 800% CPU utilization (Figure 4.20b). Slicing achieves an order of magnitude higher throughput than buckets, because it prevents assigning tuples to multiple buckets (cf. Section 4.7.2.1). The memory consumption scaled linearly with the degree of parallelism for both techniques.

**Summary.** We conclude that stream slicing and buckets scale linearly with the number of cores for our application.

## 4.8 Related Work

**Optimizing Window Aggregations.** Our general slicing techniques utilizes features of existing techniques such as on-the-fly slicing [102], incremental aggregation [173], window grouping [78, 79], and user-defined windows [36]. However, general stream slicing offers a unique combination of generality and performance. One can extend other slicing techniques based on this chapter to reach similar generality and performance. Existing slicing techniques such as Pairs [102] and Panes [111] are limited to tumbling and sliding windows. Cutty can process user-defined window types, but does not support out-of-order processing [36]. Several publications optimize sliding window aggregations focusing on different aspects such as incremental aggregation [27, 70, 173] or worst-case constant time aggregation [172]. Hirzel et al. conclude that one needs to decide on a concrete algorithm based on the aggregation, window type, latency requirements, stream order, and sharing requirements because each specialized algorithm addresses a different set of requirements [83]. Instead of alternating between different algorithms, we provide a single solution which is generally applicable and allows for adding aggregation functions and window types without changing the core of our technique. Our solutions can be integrated in open source streaming systems such as Apache Flink [35], Spark [205], and Storm [177].

**Stream Processing in Batches.** In contrast to our techniques, which adopts a tuple-at-a-time processing approach, several works split streams in batches of data which they process in parallel [21, 100, 204]. For example, D-Streams [204] processes mini-batches of data, which are combined to windows. This requires the *slide step* and *range* of sliding windows to be multiples of the batch size. SABER introduces *window fragments* to decouple *slide* and *range* of sliding windows from the batch size [100]. However, in contrast to our work, SABER does not consider aggregate sharing among queries. Balkesen et al. use panes to share aggregates among overlapping windows [21]. None of these works addresses the general applicability with respect to workload characteristics.

**Complementary Techniques.** Weaving optimizes execution plans to reduce the overall computation costs for concurrent window aggregate queries [78, 79, 157]. We use a similar approach to fuse window aggregation queries when window edges match. This optimization is orthogonal to the generalization of slicing which is the focus of this chapter. Huebsch et al. study multiple query optimization when aggregating several data streams which arrive at different nodes [86]. General stream slicing complements this work with an increased per-node performance. Truviso proposes an alternative technique based on independent stream partitions to correct outputs when tuples arrive after the watermark [101]. While our work focuses on slicing streams and computing partial aggregations for slices, recent publications of Shein et al. further accelerate the final aggregation step which is required when windows end [158, 159]. Trill [39] is an analytics system that supports streaming, historical, and exploratory queries in the same system. Trill supports incremental aggregation and performs aggregations on snapshots, the state of the window at a certain point in time.

## 4.9 Conclusion

Stream slicing is a technique for streaming window aggregation which provides high throughputs and low latencies with a small memory footprint. We contribute a generalization of stream slicing with respect to four key workload characteristics: Stream (dis)order, aggregation types, window types, and window measures. Our general slicing technique dynamically adapts to these characteristics, for example, by exploiting the invertibility of an aggregation or the absence of out-of-order tuples.

Our experimental evaluation reveals that general slicing is highly efficient without limiting generality. It scales to a large number of concurrent windows and consistently outperforms state-of-the-art techniques in terms of throughput. Furthermore, it efficiently supports application scenarios with large fractions of out-of-order tuples, tuples with high delays, time-based and count-based window measures, context-aware windowing, and holistic aggregation functions. Finally, we observed that the throughput of general slicing scales linearly with the number of processing cores.

In the next chapter, we integrate our flexible stream discretization and window aggregation technique into an adaptive pre-processing pipeline for front-end applications.

# 5

# Interactive Real-Time Visualization for Streaming Data

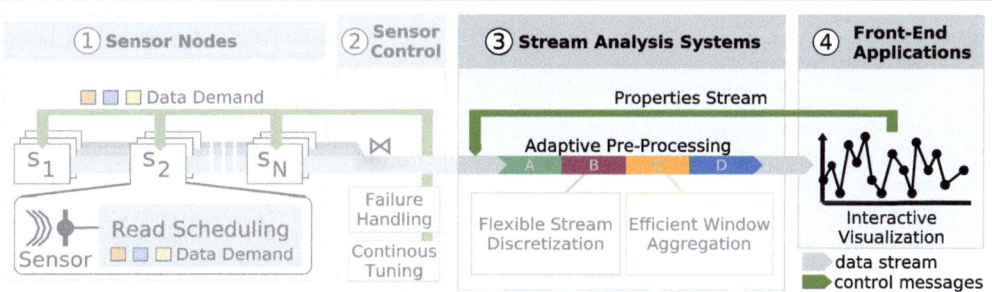

FIGURE 5.1: Scope of Chapter 5 - Connecting Stream Analysis Systems and Front-End Applications.

In this chapter, we connect stream analysis systems with front-end applications (Figure 5.1). We visualize the football data, which we also used in the preceding chapters. Window discretization and aggregation (Chapter 4) are core steps of an adaptive pre-processing pipeline in our example application. We present $I^2$, an interactive development environment that coordinates running cluster applications and corresponding visualizations such that only the currently depicted data points are processed and transferred. To this end, we present an algorithm for the real-time visualization of time series, which is proven to be correct and minimal in terms of transferred data. Moreover, we show how cluster programs can adapt to changing visualization properties at runtime to allow for interactive data exploration on data streams.

## 5.1  Introduction

The amount of available real-time data increases rapidly with the growth of the IoT. Such data is provided in the form of continuous data streams and includes various kinds of information including stock prices, Twitter messages, Wikipedia edits, weather data, and GPS positions. Systems such as Apache Flink, Apache Spark and Apache Storm can process huge amounts of data with low latencies in a cluster to provide real-time analysis. Nevertheless, the development of analysis programs for these platforms remains a complex task, which requires iterative refinements and adaptations to address changing user request and to allow for discovering the input data.

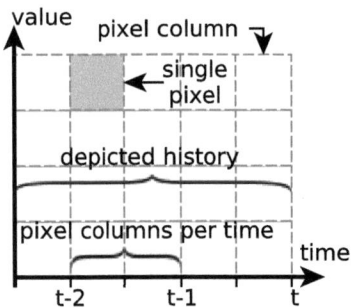

FIGURE 5.2: The tradeoff between depicted history and plot precision.

A visualization of the incoming datastream can provide insights to support refinements and adaptations, but visualizing big data in real-time is a challenge itself. Since display capabilities are limited to a certain plot resolution (height and width of the screen) and local processing capabilities (e.g., a browser), it is usually impossible or unnecessary to show all individual data points from a high bandwidth data stream. For example, even though a time series may consist of 2000 measurements per second, the visualization of a second in a line chart is limited to a certain amount of pixel columns. Thus, a user has to trade off between the length of the displayed history (time span covered on the time axis) and the resolution of the provided plot (pixel columns per time) as shown in Figure 5.2.

Interestingly, it is proven that the amount of data which is required to plot a correct line chart depends only on the number of pixel columns and not on the data. Jugel et al. [93] derive standard SQL queries from a given plot resolution and provide a loss-free plot from only four values per pixel column which reduces the computational load of the system. We show how the same values can be computed in a parallel dataflow program to allow for the live visualization of incoming streaming data. Additionally, we handle differences between event time and processing time, as well as tuples arriving out-of-order, which makes processing streaming data a more complex task.

We integrate the efficient live visualization of time series as line chart together with other types of visualizations in $I^2$, our interactive development environment, which connects distributed data analysis programs with the visualization of the results. The name $I^2$ emphasizes two types of interactivity: *(i)* through code changes and *(ii)* through an interactive visualization GUI. With $I^2$, developers can change and deploy the code of analysis pipelines and corresponding result visualizations in a one-click fashion. Moreover, running applications adapt to changes in the visualization, e.g., if the user zooms into a map, and ensure that only the data points which are depicted in the current visualization are processed and transferred towards the front end. As a result, $I^2$ decreases the workload in the cluster backend as well as the visualization front end. $I^2$ is available online as open source project[1].

Summarizing, the contributions of this chapter are:

1. We present an interactive environment for visualization supported development of streaming cluster applications.

2. We show that our solution significantly reduces the amount of processed and transferred data, while still providing loss-free visualizations.

3. We provide an algorithm for the live visualization of time series in line charts, which is proven to be correct and minimal in terms transferred data.

We demonstrate $I^2$ with a front-end application for real-time sport analytics. Therefore, we explore the data set from the DEBS 2013 Grand Challenge [133] which we also used in the previous chapters of the thesis. This data set consists of more than 2.6 GB sensor data recorded at a football match with up to 2000Hz sampling rates. The data provides detailed real-time information about all players as well as the ball.

In the remainder of this chapter, we first present our solution for the visualization of time-series in line charts in Section 5.2. We then present the over-all architecture of $I^2$ in Section 5.3 and our example application in Section 5.4. We present related work in Section 5.6 and conclude in Section 5.7

---

[1]Open Source Repository: `https://github.com/TU-Berlin-DIMA/i2`

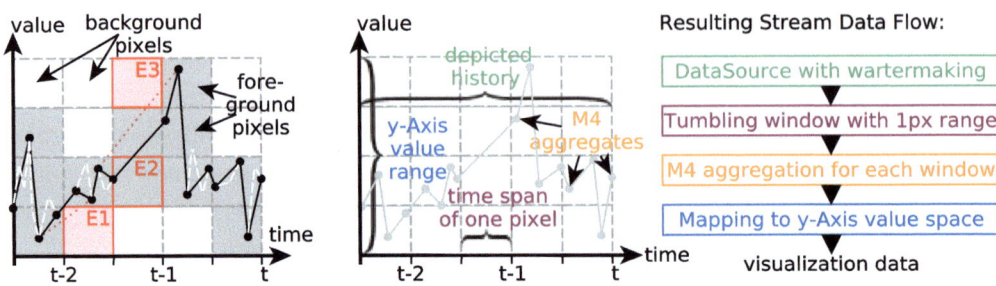

FIGURE 5.3:
The M4 aggregation technique
for time-series data.

FIGURE 5.4:
Deriving a stream data flow program for the real-time
visualization of time-series data with M4.

## 5.2 Visualization of Time Series

High volume time series data is omnipresent in many domains such as banking, weather data, facility monitoring, or, as in our example, sport analytics. A naive approach for the visualization of time series would send all available data points towards the front-end, which causes the visualization to crash, in case the amount of input data increases as we will show in Section 5.4. The M4 aggregation technique [93] overcomes this limitation and constantly transfers just four values per pixel column. Furthermore, M4 is proven to provide loss-free plots compared to plots of the original data.

Figure 5.3 illustrates the key concepts of the M4 aggregation. For each pixel column, M4 finds the minimum and maximum value as well as the first and the last value (minimum and maximum timestamp). All pixels which are crossed by the line connecting the extracted data points are colored and, thus, become foreground pixels. The intuitive approach to take only the minimum and maximum values into consideration would be insufficient. This would result in the red dotted line in Figure 5.3 and cause the pixel errors E1, E3 (wrongly colored) as well as E2 (not colored).

In $I^2$, we want to visualize streaming data in real-time. While M4 only considers finite data stored in a relational database, the real-time requirement adds several new challenges: instead of standard SQL queries, we now need *parallelizable processing pipelines*. Due to network delays and failures, there might be a gap between event time (the point in time a measure is taken) and processing time (the point in time the data is processed). Since data points may arrive out-of-order, we can never guarantee that the data for a pixel column is complete and possibly need to update past pixel columns in

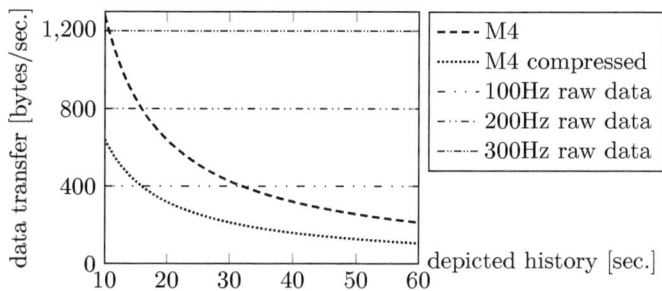

FIGURE 5.5: The required bandwidth for an 800x600px plot.

case of delayed input data. We address these challenges, as we derive a complete stream processing pipeline from a given plot resolution and the length of the depicted history, as shown in Figure 5.4 on Page 148. The pipeline mainly consists of four steps, each of which can be executed as an operator with possibly multiple parallel instances. These four steps form the adaptive pre-processing pipeline which we also show in our overall architecture (Figure 5.1 on Page 145).

**Watermarks.** Watermarks flow through the pipeline alongside the regular data and propagate the progress of event time. A watermark of time $t_w$ means that no later processed event will have a timestamp $t_e < t_w$. We input watermarks at the data source of our pipeline to mark the smallest timestamp which is still covered by the live plot. Hence, we update pixel columns in case data arrives out-of-order. However, we avoid the unnecessary processing of out-of-order data that arrives so late that the corresponding pixel column of the live chart is no longer displayed.

**Windowing.** We apply a time window function, which splits the stream into finite data chunks spanning the time of one pixel column. We then compute the M4 aggregates over these windows, and respectively for each pixel column.

**Value compression.** Finally, we map the results of the aggregation to the value space of the y-axis, which allows us to represent each value with less bytes. Figure 5.5 shows the savings in the input bandwidth of the visualization assuming an 800x600px plot, showing 4 byte integer values. Note that the bandwidth required by M4 is independent from the frequency of the underlying raw data and solely depends on the length of the depicted history. The longer the depicted history, the more data is aggregated into one pixel column, which causes the required bandwidth to decrease. In the next section, we show how our streaming ready M4 aggregation pipeline is integrated into the overall architecture of the I$^2$ development environment.

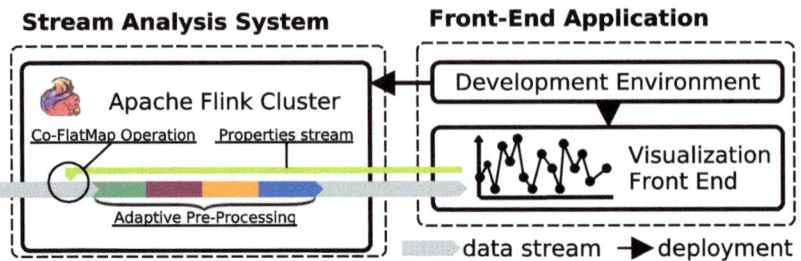

FIGURE 5.6: $I^2$ architecture overview.

## 5.3 $I^2$ Development Environment

The $I^2$ development environment aims to seamlessly connect live data visualization with the development of streaming data analysis pipelines. Therefore, we directly link a development environment and result visualizations within a single front-end (Figure 5.6). Developers can deploy data analysis pipelines as well as visualizations in a one-click fashion. While the visualization is provided within the same GUI as the code editor, the analytics pipeline is deployed on an Apache Flink cluster to be capable of processing high bandwidth streams in parallel.

**Apache Flink** [7, 35] is an open source platform for big data batch and stream processing. The basis of Flink is a fault tolerant execution engine. Programs are represented as operator graphs and the full processing pipeline is executed concurrently. Thus, the output tuples of an operator can be processed immediately by succeeding operators. Flink allows operators to have state. An asynchronous snapshot algorithm [34] ensures exactly once processing guarantees even in case of failures. Flink fits perfectly to $I^2$ since we need stateful operators to store current visualization parameters, and low latency processing to quickly adapt running jobs to changes.

**Apache Zeppelin.** The $I^2$ front-end is based on Apache Zeppelin [12], which we extended to support automatic data reduction depending on current visualization parameters. In general, Zeppelin aims to support quick development by enabling interactive analytics in web based notebooks. It is similar to IPython [139], but focuses on big data and distributed computing. Zeppelin notebooks are data driven, interactive, and can be edited collaboratively by multiple users. Moreover, Zeppelin supports a variety of

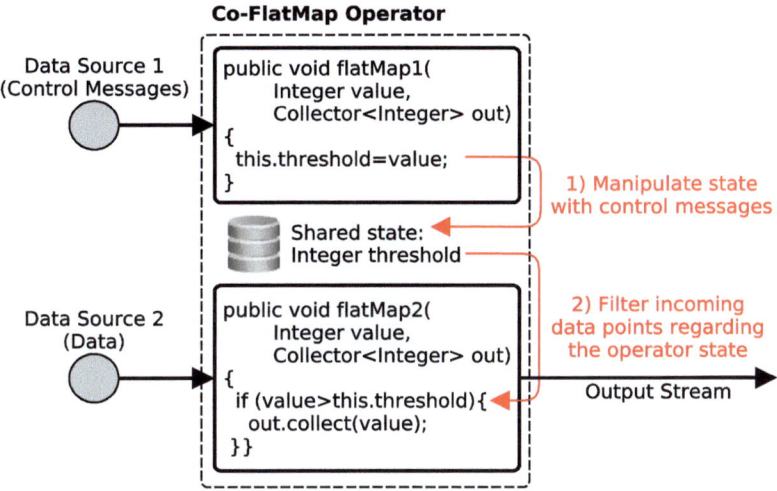

FIGURE 5.7: A runtime adaptive filter operator
for variable thresholds in Apache Flink.

execution back ends. In addition to classical dashboards, Zeppelin allows for developing
source code, submitting jobs directly to the cluster, and retrieving results immediately.

**Runtime Adaptive Operators.** $I^2$ informs running Flink jobs about changes of the
visualization parameters. For example, if the user zooms into a map or changes the
length of the depicted history of a time series plot. The running cluster program has
to adapt to such changes with low latency in order to immediately provide the required
data for the visualization. Since a redeployment of a job in the cluster can take more
than a minute, we need to adapt jobs at runtime.

We push changes of the visualization parameters as control messages in a separate
stream to the running Flink job. Only the type of an operator (e.g., filter or aggregation)
is defined a priori, while we allow to adjust the parameters of the operator (e.g., filter
predicate or aggregate function) on the fly at runtime. We use Flink's CoMap operators
merge control messages and the actual data points in a runtime-adaptive operator.

Flink's CoMap operators consume two input streams while input items from each
stream are processed by separate *user defined functions* (UDFs). Nevertheless, both
UDFs can access a shared operator state which is used to communicate between them.

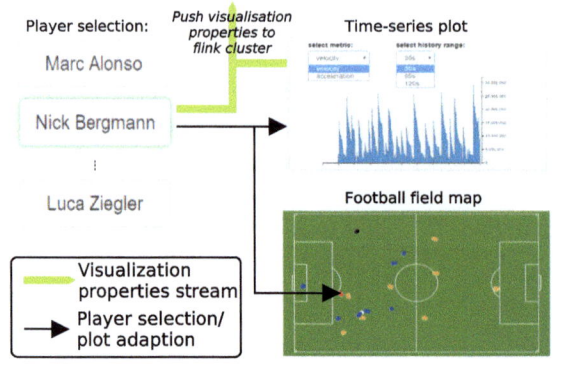

(A) Interactive Dashboard          (B) Development Environment

FIGURE 5.8: Selected screenshots from the $I^2$ demonstration.

Figure 5.7 shows how we can utilize a CoFlatMap operator to adapt to changed properties: in this example, one input stream consists of control messages containing changes to the threshold of a filter operation. The responsible UDF saves the current threshold as operator state (Figure 5.7, Step 1). Each value from the actual data stream is compared to the currently stored threshold and all smaller values are filtered out (Figure 5.7, Step 2). In general, arbitrary changes to a selection criteria, aggregation function, windowing semantics, and other operations are possible using this architecture.

## 5.4 Example Application

We provide an example application to allow for experiencing the fast visualization supported development with $I^2$. This covers the development of the Flink job running in the cluster as well as changing the visualizations, which are part of the front-end application. Our example application continuously shows the savings in terms of the transferred data volume, which are achieved by $I^2$. When we increase the data rates of the input streams, $I^2$ will hide that workload from the visualization front-end. Without using $I^2$ the front end would first become unresponsive and finally crash due to an overload.

**Data.** We replay the data set which was provided with the DEBS Grand Challenge 2013 [133]. This data set consists of sensor data, which was recorded at a football match. The speed, acceleration, and position of the ball are tracked with a frequency of 2000Hz. In addition, each player has two sensors close to his shoes which are tracked with a 200Hz frequency. In total, roughly 15.000 data points are provided per second.

**Use Case.** We show an interactive dashboard to analyze the performance of individual players in detail. Users can either select a player manually or automatically follow the ball possession, which involves detecting peaks in the measures of the ball sensor as well as correlating these peaks with the data from the player sensors. Our dashboard shows different metrics (e.g, acceleration and speed) for the selected player as well as the player's current position on the football field (Figure 5.8a on Page 152).

**Interactivity.** Our application demonstrates the two types of interactivity in $I^2$:

1. Visualization properties can be changed easily in the dashboard and the running Flink job adapts with low latency to, e.g., changes in the player selection or the length of the depicted history of line charts.

2. Interactive code changes allow an even more flexible data exploration and the rapid development of cluster applications. The code for the visualizations can be adapted and directly deployed without a need to restart the running Flink job. One can also adapt the running Flink job. For example, one can connect an additional data source, e.g., for twitter messages, and these messages can be correlated with the data we used before. The extended Flink job is directly deployed to the cluster with just one click.

$I^2$ and our example application are available online as open source project[2] and as ready-to-run docker container[3].

## 5.5 Evaluation

We first try to run the dashboard of our example applications without using $I^2$, meaning that no data reduction is applied and all data - roughly 15.000 tuples/sec. - are transferred towards the front-end. As shown in Figure 5.9 (left) on Page 154, the UI works only for a short moment before it becomes unresponsive due to a CPU overload.

---

[2]Project Website: `https://tu-berlin-dima.github.io/i2/`
[3]Docker Hub Link: `https://hub.docker.com/r/tuberlindima/i2/`

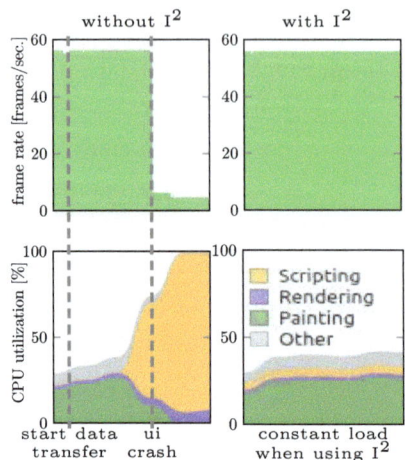

FIGURE 5.9: I² Performance Monitoring.

We now run the same dashboard with I², pushing the current visualization properties to the running Flink job, as described in Section 5.3. This information is then used by Flink to apply different data reduction techniques: knowing the currently selected player enables adaptive filtering as shown in Figure 5.7, and knowing the plot resolution of line charts allows to apply the M4 aggregation technique we presented in Section 5.2. The soccer field map combines different data reduction techniques. We reduce the precision of the position reports based on the plot resolution, and at the same time apply load shedding [174] to reduce the data rate to the current frame rate of the visualization. As shown on Figure 5.9 (right), the presented dashboard runs fluently when using I² with close to 60 frames per second and a CPU utilization below 50%.

We exemplarily compare the performance of I² for the dashboard described above (Figure 5.9). Our experiment shows that the data traffic, the memory utilization, the CPU load, and the frame rate remain constant throughout the game when I² is active. Switching off I² causes the visualization to become unresponsive immediately due to the massive amount of arriving data. With I² activated, the bottleneck is no longer the visualization, but the throughput (i.e., input bandwidth) of the used Flink cluster.

## 5.6  Related Work

In contrast to existing data exploration techniques [88], $I^2$ combines three functionalities within a single environment:

1. Rapid development and deployment of cluster applications with streaming data.

2. Automatic adaptation of running cluster jobs to changed visualization properties.

3. Efficient reduction of data to prevent overload of the visualization front-end.

While other solution require an additional intermediate layer between database and visualization [22], $I^2$ directly integrates into data analysis applications.

Many other approaches use sampling strategies for data reduction to enable fast visualizations of huge amounts of data [2, 3, 98, 164]. In contrast to $I^2$, these techniques disregard physical display properties and do not cover live plots of streaming data. Moreover, sampling-based visualizations are usually lossy compared to plots of the original data, while the M4-based visualization of $I^2$ is proven to be loss-free [93].

Wu et al. [198] take into account visualization properties and automatically derive SQL-queries, but use a domain specific query language. In contrast, $I^2$ works with any query language integrated in Apache Zeppelin.

## 5.7  Conclusion

We connect stream analysis systems and front-end applications through the $I^2$ development environment. $I^2$ enables two types of interactivity: first, the user can specify real-time analysis programs and change them on-the-fly. Second, the interactive visualization of the results adapts currently running cluster applications without a need to restart. Using $I^2$, the amount of data points to be processed and transferred to the front end can be reduced significantly without quality loss, enabling the live visualization of high bandwidth data streams. The capabilities of $I^2$ have been shown in an interactive example application using real-world sensor data which was recorded at a football match. The front-end application presented in this section completes our end-to-end processing pipeline for IoT sensor data. In the remaining chapters, we present additional contributions in Chapter 6 and conclude the thesis in Chapter 7.

# 6

# Additional Contributions

This chapter summarizes additional research contributions which have been made by the author while working on this thesis. These additional contributions are not part of the thesis contents, but closely related to the thesis topic or the systems used in this thesis.

**Stream Processing Techniques.** We presented additional techniques for efficient data stream processing in the following four publications:

1. Paris Carbone, **Jonas Traub**, Asterios Katsifodimos, Seif Haridi, Volker Markl: *Cutty: Aggregate Sharing for User-Defined Windows.* ACM International on Conference on Information and Knowledge Management (CIKM), 2016.

2. Philipp Marian Grulich, René Saitenmacher, **Jonas Traub**, Sebastian Breß, Tilmann Rabl, Volker Markl: *Scalable Detection of Concept Drifts on Data Streams with Parallel Adaptive Windowing.* International Conference on Extending Database Technology (EDBT), 2018.

3. Ahmed Awad, **Jonas Traub**, Sherif Sakr: *Adaptive Watermarks: A Concept Drift-based Approach for Predicting Event-Time Progress in Data Streams.* International Conference on Extending Database Technology (EDBT), 2019.

4. Philipp Marian Grulich, **Jonas Traub**, Sebastian Breß, Asterios Katsifodimos, Tilmann Rabl, and Volker Markl: *Generating Reproducible Out-of-Order Data Streams.* ACM International Conference on Distributed and Event-based Systems (DEBS), 2019.

The paper *Cutty: Aggregate Sharing for User-Defined Windows* [36], introduces the concept of *user-defined windows (UDWs)*, a programming model that allows for defining custom stream discretization, i.e., custom window types. Cutty uses stream slicing to combine stream discretization with window aggregation and to share partial aggregates among concurrent queries. Our general stream slicing technique presented in Chapter 4 supports user-defined windows and adds support for out-of-order processing, additional aggregation types, and forward context aware windows.

In the paper *Scalable Detection of Concept Drifts on Data Streams with Parallel Adaptive Windowing* [76], we address the problem of efficient concept drifts detection on high-velocity data streams. Concept drift detection methods such as adaptive windowing (ADWIN) [28] allow for detecting concept drifts on the fly in order to prevent wrong results. We examine ADWIN in detail and point out its throughput bottlenecks. We then introduce several parallelization alternatives to address these bottlenecks. Our optimizations lead to a speedup of two orders of magnitude.

The paper *Adaptive Watermarks: A Concept Drift-based Approach for Predicting Event-Time Progress in Data Streams* [19] applies the ADWIN algorithm to decide when to generate watermarks which indicate the progress of event time in a streaming systems. We use ADWIN to detect changes in the data arrival frequency and changes in delays of out-of-order tuples. Compared to common periodic watermark generation, our adaptive watermarks achieve a lower average latency, by triggering windows earlier, and a lower rate of dropped elements, by delaying watermarks when expecting out-of-order data.

The publication *Generating Reproducible Out-of-Order Data Streams* [77] focuses on evaluating modern stream processing systems in a reproducible manner. We present an open source stream generator which generates reproducible and deterministic out-of-order streams based on real data files, simulating arbitrary fractions of out-of-order tuples and their respective delays.

**Apache Flink.** The Apache Flink stream analysis system was used in Chapters 4 and 5 of this thesis. We presented Apache Flink in two publications:

1. Tilmann Rabl, **Jonas Traub**, Asterios Katsifodimos, and Volker Markl:
   *Apache Flink in current research.*
   it-Information Technology, 58(4):157-165, De Gruyter Oldenbourg, 2016.

2. **Jonas Traub**, Tilmann Rabl, Fabian Hueske, Till Rohrmann, Volker Markl:
   *Die Apache Flink Plattform zur parallelen Analyse von Datenströmen und
   Stapeldaten.*
   Proceedings of the LWA Workshops: KDML, FGWM, IR, and FGDB, 2015.

The paper *Apache Flink in current research* [145] provides an overview of the Apache
Flink system and presents how Flink is used in current research projects. The German
paper *Die Apache Flink Plattform zur parallelen Analyse von Datenströmen und Stapel-
daten* [182] presents Flink to the German database community. The author of this thesis
also presented the research related to Apache Flink at the BOSS Workshop at the 42th
International Conference on Very Large Data Bases (VLDB) 2016 in New Delhi, at the
DB2 User Group Meeting 2015 at the IBM Böblingen Research Lab, at the 2nd BMBF
Big Data All Hands Meeting (BDAHM) and the 2nd Smart Data Innovation Conference
(SDIC) 2017 at KIT Karlsruhe (joint conferences), and as panelist at the BIRTE Work-
shop at the 44th International Conference on Very Large Data Bases (VLDB) 2018 in
Rio de Janeiro.

**Modern Hardware.** The following two publications focus on emerging modern hardware and their application in the context of databases and stream processing:

1. Steffen Zeuch, Bonaventura Del Monte, Jeyhun Karimov, Clemens Lutz, Manuel
   Renz, **Jonas Traub**, Sebastian Breß, Tilmann Rabl, Volker Markl: *Analyzing
   Efficient Stream Processing on Modern Hardware.* Proceedings of the International
   Conference on Very Large Data Bases (PVLDB), 2019.

2. Tobias Behrens, Viktor Rosenfeld, **Jonas Traub**, Sebastian Breß, Volker Markl:
   *Efficient SIMD Vectorization for Hashing in OpenCL.*
   International Conference on Extending Database Technology (EDBT), 2018.

In the paper *Analyzing Efficient Stream Processing on Modern Hardware* [207], we conduct an extensive experimental analysis of current SPEs and SPE design alternatives
optimized for modern hardware. Based on our analysis, we describe a set of design
changes to the common architecture of SPEs to scale-up on modern hardware. We show
that the single-node throughput can be increased by up to two orders of magnitude compared to state-of-the-art SPEs by applying specialized code generation, fusing operators,
batch-style parallelization, and optimized windowing.

In the paper *Efficient SIMD Vectorization for Hashing in OpenCL* [24], we add vectorized hashing primitives to OpenCL and show that these primitives are competitive to low-level APIs on CPUs and Xeon Phis. Hashing is at the core of many database operators. Vectorization uses *Single Instruction Multiple Data* (SIMD) instructions to process multiple data elements at once. Applying vectorization to hash tables results in promising speedups, but requires processor dependent low-level APIs. OpenCL provides a higher abstraction and avoids processor dependencies.

**Sensor Simulation.** Realistically emulating IoT infrastructure involving a large number of heterogeneous sensors is important to enable IoT related research. We address this issue in one publication which presents the Resense framework:

1. Dimitrios Giouroukis, Julius Hülsmann, Janis von Bleichert, Morgan Geldenhuys, Tim Stullich, Felipe Gutierrez, **Jonas Traub**, Kaustubh Beedkar and Volker Markl:
   *Resense: Transparent Record and Replay of Sensor Data in the Internet of Things.*
   International Conference on Extending Database Technology (EDBT), 2019.

Existing research on emulating sensors is often tailored to specific hardware and/or software, which makes it difficult to reproduce and extend. In contrast, Resense [72] emulates senors on the operating system level, and allows for managing experiments on sensor node testbeds independent of the hardware and/or software under test.

# 7

# Conclusion

The architecture presented in this thesis combines stream processing infrastructure with extensions needed in the IoT era. Thereby, the thesis addresses major challenges that arise from a growing number of sensors and sensor nodes, as well as a growing amount of sensor data. We analyze all layers of the infrastructure stack and identify missing control interfaces between these layers. By establishing these control interfaces, we solve scalability issues and significantly improve efficiency. This lays the foundation for shared data infrastructures in the IoT era. Our end-to-end architecture contributes to systems that serve as public or private IoT clouds, covering the full processing pipeline from sensors to front-end applications.

Our research unites aspects of network management and distributed processing from a data management perspective. We connect stream analysis systems with sensor nodes and introduce all required means to produce data streams based on the data demands of applications. We further connect front-end applications and stream analysis jobs, such that stream processing jobs running on streaming clusters can adapt at runtime to application needs. The demand-driven acquisition of streaming data is fundamentally different from existing approaches, which acquire as much data as possible without considering data demands. We found that demand-based data acquisition not only prevents costly system scale-out and data transfer charges, but also reduces latencies by reducing the amount of data that streaming systems have to process for detecting events of interest. We believe that the connection of networking, distributed processing, and data management issues in the context of the IoT opens a new field of research with great potential for novel features and performance optimizations.

# Future Research

This thesis lays the foundation for future research in several directions. In Chapter 2, we introduced user-defined sampling functions (UDSFs). These functions allow for defining data demands of applications flexibly. We have shown that UDSFs can express diverse sampling techniques such as adaptive sampling, periodic sampling, and model-based sampling [87]. A future research goal is to automate the selection of optimal read time tolerances and penalty functions for read requests posted by UDSFs. This goes beyond existing adaptive sampling techniques, which adapt when and how often they read from a sensor, but do not optimize how much read time deviation they allow and how they penalize these read time deviations. We investigated the *automatic tuning of read-time tolerances for on-demand data streaming* in a master's thesis [110]. Initial experiments with three different data sets show promising savings in sensor reads using an automatic selection of read time tolerances. We plan to extend this work to ease the decision for appropriate read time tolerances for users of our read scheduler.

While working on this thesis, we observed that there is no common benchmark that evaluates the efficiency of data gathering and transmission systems in the IoT. Existing IoT benchmarks focus on the performance of stream analysis systems with respect to typical IoT applications, but disregard the efficiency of the preceding data acquisition [15, 161, 162]. We investigated the idea to provide *a benchmark for adaptive data collection in the IoT* in a master's thesis [47]. We design a benchmark based on the New York taxi dataset [134] which evaluates the efficiency of the data acquisition for different scenarios. An extended version of our benchmark, in combination with the Resense framework for managing sensor node testbeds [72], would be highly valuable for comparing data gathering and transmission approaches in the IoT.

This thesis makes the case for demand-based data stream gathering, processing, and transmission. Therefore, we move away from monolithic architectures and connect all layers of the infrastructure stack. This connection enables an end-to-end optimization of processing pipelines starting at sensors and reaching to front-end applications. Novel IoT database systems can incorporate data gathering, data transmission, and central stream analysis and, thereby, gain diverse new opportunities for novel query optimization techniques. The architecture presented in this thesis is a first step towards an end-to-end database system for the IoT era and will become a part of the NebulaStream platform for application and data management in the IoT [206].

# List of Notations

## CHAPTER 4

## CHAPTER 5

# List of Figures

# List of Tables

# Bibliography

[1] Karl Aberer, Manfred Hauswirth, and Ali Salehi. Infrastructure for data processing in large-scale interconnected sensor networks. In *IEEE International Conference on Mobile Data Management*, pages 198–205, 2007.

[2] Sameer Agarwal, Henry Milner, Ariel Kleiner, Ameet Talwalkar, Michael Jordan, Samuel R Madden, Barzan Mozafari, and Ion Stoica. Knowing when you're wrong: building fast and reliable approximate query processing systems. In *Proceedings of the ACM SIGMOD International Conference on Management of Data*, pages 481–492, 2014.

[3] Sameer Agarwal, Barzan Mozafari, Aurojit Panda, Henry Milner, Samuel R Madden, and Ion Stoica. BlinkDB: queries with bounded errors and bounded response times on very large data. In *Proceedings of the ACM European Conference on Computer Systems*, pages 29–42. ACM, 2013.

[4] Shweta Agrawal, Krithi Ramamritham, and Shetal Shah. Construction of a temporal coherency preserving dynamic data dissemination network. In *IEEE Real-Time Systems Symposium (RTSS)*, 2004.

[5] Tyler Akidau, Robert Bradshaw, Craig Chambers, Slava Chernyak, Rafael J Fernández-Moctezuma, Reuven Lax, Sam McVeety, Daniel Mills, Frances Perry, Eric Schmidt, et al. The dataflow model: A practical approach to balancing correctness, latency, and cost in massive-scale, unbounded, out-of-order data processing. *Proceedings of the International Conference on Very Large Data Bases (PVLDB)*, 8(12):1792–1803, 2015.

[6] Ian F Akyildiz, Weilian Su, Yogesh Sankarasubramaniam, and Erdal Cayirci. A survey on sensor networks. *IEEE Communications Magazine*, 40(8):102–114, 2002.

[7] Alexander Alexandrov, Rico Bergmann, Stephan Ewen, Johann-Christoph Freytag, Fabian Hueske, Arvid Heise, Odej Kao, Marcus Leich, Ulf Leser, Volker Markl,

Felix Naumann, Mathias Peters, Astrid Rheinländer, Matthias J. Sax, Sebastian Schelter, Mareike Höger, Kostas Tzoumas, and Daniel Warneke. The Stratosphere platform for big data analytics. *VLDB Journal*, 23(6):939–964, 2014.

[8] Rajagopal Ananthanarayanan, Venkatesh Basker, Sumit Das, Ashish Gupta, Haifeng Jiang, Tianhao Qiu, Alexey Reznichenko, Deomid Ryabkov, Manpreet Singh, and Shivakumar Venkataraman. Photon: Fault-tolerant and scalable joining of continuous data streams. In *Proceedings of the ACM SIGMOD International Conference on Management of Data*, pages 577–588, 2013.

[9] Kiam Heong Ang, Gregory Chong, and Yun Li. PID control system analysis, design, and technology. *IEEE Transactions on Control Systems Technology*, 13(4):559–576, 2005.

[10] Apache Apex. Enterprise-grade unified stream and batch processing engine. 2018. Accessed Dec. 2018, https://apex.apache.org/ (project website).

[11] Apache Beam. An advanced unified programming model. 2018. Accessed Dec. 2018, https://beam.apache.org/ (project website).

[12] Apache Zeppelin. Web-based notebook that enables data-driven, interactive data analytics and collaborative documents with sql, scala and more. 2018. Accessed Dec. 2018, http://zeppelin.apache.org/ (project website).

[13] Arvind Arasu, Shivnath Babu, and Jennifer Widom. The CQL continuous query language: semantic foundations and query execution. *VLDB Journal*, 15(2):121–142, 2006.

[14] Arvind Arasu and Jennifer Widom. Resource sharing in continuous sliding-window aggregates. *Proceedings of the International Conference on Very Large Data Bases (PVLDB)*, pages 336–347, 2004.

[15] Martin Arlitt, Manish Marwah, Gowtham Bellala, Amip Shah, Jeff Healey, and Ben Vandiver. IoTAbench: an internet of things analytics benchmark. In *Proceedings of the ACM/SPEC International Conference on Performance Engineering*, pages 133–144, 2015.

[16] Michael Armbrust, Tathagata Das, Joseph Torres, Burak Yavuz, Shixiong Zhu, Reynold Xin, Ali Ghodsi, Ion Stoica, and Matei Zaharia. Structured streaming: A

declarative API for real-time applications in Apache Spark. In *Proceedings of the ACM SIGMOD International Conference on Management of Data*, pages 601–613, 2018.

[17] Karl Johan Åström and Tore Hägglund. *PID controllers: theory, design, and tuning*, volume 2. Instrument Society of America, 1995.

[18] Karl Johan Åström and Richard M Murray. *Feedback systems: an introduction for scientists and engineers*. Princeton university press, 2010.

[19] Ahmed Awad, Jonas Traub, and Sherif Sakr. Adaptive watermarks: A concept drift-based approach for predicting event-time progress in data streams. In *Proceedings of the International Conference on Extending Database Technology (EDBT)*, 2019.

[20] Andreas Bader, Oliver Kopp, and Michael Falkenthal. Survey and comparison of open source time series databases. *Datenbanksysteme für Business, Technologie und Web (BTW)*, 2017.

[21] Cagri Balkesen and Nesime Tatbul. Scalable data partitioning techniques for parallel sliding window processing over data streams. In *International Workshop on Data Management for Sensor Networks (DMSN)*, 2011.

[22] Leilani Battle, Michael Stonebraker, and Remco Chang. Dynamic reduction of query result sets for interactive visualizaton. In *IEEE International Conference on Big Data*, pages 1–8, 2013.

[23] Jonathan Beaver, Mohamed A Sharaf, Alexandros Labrinidis, and Panos K Chrysanthis. Power-aware in-network query processing for sensor data. In *Proceedings of the Hellenic Data Management Symposium (HDMS)*, 2003.

[24] Tobias Behrens, Viktor Rosenfeld, Jonas Traub, Sebastian Breß, and Volker Markl. Efficient SIMD vectorization for hashing in OpenCL. In *Proceedings of the International Conference on Extending Database Technology (EDBT)*, pages 489–492, 2018.

[25] Andreea Berfield and Daniel Mossé. Efficient scheduling for sensor networks. In *IEEE International Conference on Mobile and Ubiquitous Systems*, pages 1–8, 2006.

[26] Remi Bergsma. How accurately can the Raspberry Pi keep time? In *Remi Bergsma's blog*, 2013. Accessed Dec. 2018, https://blog.remibergsma.com/2013/05/12/how-accurately-can-the-raspberry-pi-keep-time/.

[27] Pramod Bhatotia, Umut A Acar, Flavio P Junqueira, and Rodrigo Rodrigues. Slider: Incremental sliding window analytics. In *Proceedings of the International Middleware Conference*, pages 61–72. ACM, 2014.

[28] Albert Bifet and Ricard Gavalda. Learning from time-changing data with adaptive windowing. In *Proceedings of the SIAM international conference on data mining*, pages 443–448, 2007.

[29] Brice Bingman. Poor performance with sliding time windows. In *Flink Jira Issues (Accessed Dec. 2018, issues.apache.org/jira/browse/FLINK-6990)*, 2018.

[30] Irina Botan, Roozbeh Derakhshan, Nihal Dindar, Laura Haas, Renée J. Miller, and Nesime Tatbul. Secret: A model for analysis of the execution semantics of stream processing systems. *Proceedings of the International Conference on Very Large Data Bases (PVLDB)*, 3(1-2):232–243, 2010.

[31] E Brockmeyer, HL Halstrøm, Arne Jensen, and Agner Krarup Erlang. The life and works of A. K. Erlang. 1948.

[32] Fatos Bytyci and Maja Zuvela. Serbia, Kosovo power grid row delays european clocks. *Reuters*, 2018. Accessed Dec. 2018, https://www.reuters.com/article/serbia-kosovo-energy/serbia-kosovo-power-grid-row-delays-european-clocks-idUSL5N1QP2FF.

[33] Paris Carbone. *Scalable and Reliable Data Stream Processing*. PhD thesis, KTH Royal Institute of Technology, 2018.

[34] Paris Carbone, Gyula Fóra, Stephan Ewen, Seif Haridi, and Kostas Tzoumas. Lightweight asynchronous snapshots for distributed dataflows. *arXiv*, 2015.

[35] Paris Carbone, Asterios Katsifodimos, Stephan Ewen, Volker Markl, Seif Haridi, and Kostas Tzoumas. Apache Flink: Stream and batch processing in a single engine. *Bulletin of the IEEE Computer Society Technical Committee on Data Engineering*, 38(4):28–38, 2015.

[36] Paris Carbone, Jonas Traub, Asterios Katsifodimos, Seif Haridi, and Volker Markl. Cutty: Aggregate sharing for user-defined windows. In *Proceedings of the ACM International on Conference on Information and Knowledge Management*, pages 1201–1210, 2016.

[37] Kevin Carter and William Streilein. Probabilistic reasoning for streaming anomaly detection. In *IEEE Statistical Signal Processing Workshop*, pages 377–380, 2012.

[38] Ufuk Celebi. How Apache Flink handles backpressure. *Data Artisans Blog*, 2015. Accessed Feb. 2019, https://www.da-platform.com/blog/how-flink-handles-backpressure.

[39] Badrish Chandramouli, Jonathan Goldstein, Mike Barnett, Robert DeLine, Danyel Fisher, John C Platt, James F Terwilliger, and John Wernsing. Trill: A high-performance incremental query processor for diverse analytics. *Proceedings of the International Conference on Very Large Data Bases (PVLDB)*, 8(4):401–412, 2014.

[40] Yen-Kuang Chen. Challenges and opportunities of Internet of Things. In *Asia and South Pacific Design Automation Conference (ASP-DAC)*, pages 383–388, 2012.

[41] Sanket Chintapalli, Derek Dagit, Bobby Evans, Reza Farivar, Thomas Graves, Mark Holderbaugh, Zhuo Liu, Kyle Nusbaum, Kishorkumar Patil, Boyang Jerry Peng, and Paul Poulosky. Benchmarking streaming computation engines: Storm, Flink and Spark streaming. In *IEEE International Parallel and Distributed Processing Symposium Workshops (IPDPSW)*, pages 1789–1792, 2016.

[42] David Chu, Amol Deshpande, Joseph M Hellerstein, and Wei Hong. Approximate data collection in sensor networks using probabilistic models. In *IEEE International Conference on Data Engineering (ICDE)*, pages 48–48, 2006.

[43] Razvan Cristescu, Baltasar Beferull-Lozano, Martin Vetterli, and Roger Wattenhofer. Network correlated data gathering with explicit communication: NP-completeness and algorithms. *IEEE Transactions on Networking (ToN)*, 14(1):41–54, 2006.

[44] Jakub Czyz, Michael Kallitsis, Manaf Gharaibeh, Christos Papadopoulos, Michael Bailey, and Manish Karir. Taming the 800 pound gorilla: The rise and decline of NTP DDoS attacks. In *Proceedings of the Conference on Internet Measurement*, pages 435–448. ACM, 2014.

[45] Abhinandan Das, Johannes Gehrke, and Mirek Riedewald. Approximate join processing over data streams. In *Proceedings of the ACM SIGMOD International Conference on Management of Data*, pages 40–51, 2003.

[46] Anirban DasGupta. Poisson processes and applications. In *Probability for Statistics and Machine Learning: Fundamentals and Advanced Topics*, pages 437–462. Springer New York, 2011.

[47] Vianney de Cibeins. A benchmark for adaptive data collection in the Internet of Things. Master's thesis, Technische Universität Berlin, 2017.

[48] Corrado De Fabritiis, Roberto Ragona, and Gaetano Valenti. Traffic estimation and prediction based on real time floating car data. In *IEEE Intelligent Transportation Systems Conference (ITSC)*, pages 197–203, 2008.

[49] Jeffrey Dean and Sanjay Ghemawat. MapReduce: simplified data processing on large clusters. *Communications of the ACM*, 51(1):107–113, 2008.

[50] Alan Demers, Johannes Gehrke, Rajmohan Rajaraman, Niki Trigoni, and Yong Yao. The Cougar project: a work-in-progress report. *ACM Sigmod Record*, 32(4):53–59, 2003.

[51] Pavan Deolasee, Amol Katkar, Ankur Panchbudhe, Krithi Ramamritham, and Prashant Shenoy. Adaptive push-pull: disseminating dynamic web data. In *Proceedings of the ACM International Conference on World Wide Web*, pages 265–274, 2001.

[52] Amol Deshpande, Carlos Guestrin, Samuel R Madden, Joseph M Hellerstein, and Wei Hong. Model-driven data acquisition in sensor networks. *Proceedings of the International Conference on Very Large Data Bases (PVLDB)*, pages 588–599, 2004.

[53] Xenofontas Dimitropoulos, Paul Hurley, Andreas Kind, and Marc Ph Stoecklin. On the 95-percentile billing method. In *Passive and Active Network Measurement (PAM)*, pages 207–216. Springer, 2009.

[54] Leandro D'Orazio, Filippo Visintainer, and Marco Darin. Sensor networks on the car: State of the art and future challenges. In *IEEE Design, Automation & Test in Europe Conference & Exhibition (DATE)*, pages 1–6, 2011.

[55] Benjamin Dowling, Douglas Stebila, and Greg Zaverucha. Authenticated network time synchronization. In *USENIX Security Symposium*, pages 823–840, 2016.

[56] Partha Dutta, Vivek Mhatre, Debmalya Panigrahi, and Rajeev Rastogi. Joint routing and scheduling in multi-hop wireless networks with directional antennas. In *IEEE International Conference on Computer Communications*, pages 1–5, 2010.

[57] Lasse Eriksson and Heikki N Koivo. Tuning of discrete-time PID controllers in sensor network based control systems. In *IEEE International Symposium on Computational Intelligence in Robotics and Automation (CIRA)*, pages 359–364, 2005.

[58] Liyue Fan and Li Xiong. Adaptively sharing time-series with differential privacy. *arXiv*, 2012.

[59] Liyue Fan and Li Xiong. Real-time aggregate monitoring with differential privacy. In *Proceedings of the ACM International Conference on Information and Knowledge Management*, pages 2169–2173. ACM, 2012.

[60] Liyue Fan and Li Xiong. An adaptive approach to real-time aggregate monitoring with differential privacy. *IEEE Transactions on Knowledge and Data Engineering*, 26(9):2094–2106, 2014.

[61] Liyue Fan, Li Xiong, and Vaidy Sunderam. FAST: differentially private real-time aggregate monitor with filtering and adaptive sampling. In *Proceedings of the ACM SIGMOD International Conference on Management of Data*, pages 1065–1068, 2013.

[62] Xiaolin Fang, Hong Gao, Jianzhong Li, and Yingshu Li. Application-aware data collection in wireless sensor networks. In *IEEE International Conference on Computer Communications*, pages 1645–1653, 2013.

[63] Elena Fasolo, Michele Rossi, Jorg Widmer, and Michele Zorzi. In-network aggregation techniques for wireless sensor networks: A survey. *IEEE Wireless Communications*, 14(2):70–87, 2007.

[64] National Institue for Standards and Technology. NIST Authenticated NTP Service. Created 2010, Updated 2017. Accessed Feb. 2019, https://www.nist.gov/pml/time-and-frequency-division/time-services/nist-authenticated-ntp-service.

[65] Behrouz A Forouzan and Sophia Chung Fegan. *TCP/IP protocol suite*. McGraw-Hill Higher Education, 2002.

[66] Paul Fremantle. A reference architecture for the Internet of Things. *WSO2 White paper*, 2014.

[67] Elena I Gaura, James Brusey, Michael Allen, Ross Wilkins, Dan Goldsmith, and Ramona Rednic. Edge mining the Internet of Things. *IEEE Sensors Journal*, 13(10):3816–3825, 2013.

[68] Buğra Gedik. Generic windowing support for extensible stream processing systems. *Software: Practice and Experience (SPE)*, 44(9):1105–1128, 2014.

[69] Megan Geuss. European grid dispute resolved, lost 6 minutes returned to oven clocks. *ars Technica*, 2018. Accessed Dec. 2018, https://arstechnica.com/tech-policy/2018/04/european-grid-dispute-resolved-lost-6-minutes-returned-to-oven-clocks/.

[70] Thanaa M Ghanem, Moustafa A Hammad, Mohamed F Mokbel, Walid G Aref, and Ahmed K Elmagarmid. Incremental evaluation of sliding-window queries over data streams. *IEEE Transactions on Knowledge and Data Engineering (TKDE)*, 19(1):57–72, 2007.

[71] Dimitrios Giouroukis, Alexander Dadiani, Jonas Traub, Steffen Zeuch, and Volker Markl. A survey of adaptive sampling and filtering algorithms for the internet of things. In *Proceedings of the 14th ACM International Conference on Distributed and Event-based Systems*, pages 27–38, 2020.

[72] Dimitrios Giouroukis, Julius Hülsmann, Janis von Bleichert, Morgan Geldenhuys, Tim Stullich, Felipe Gutierrez, Jonas Traub, Kaustubh Beedkar, and Volker Markl. Resense: Transparent record and replay of sensor data in the Internet of Things. In *Proceedings of the International Conference on Extending Database Technology (EDBT)*, 2019.

[73] Google. Cloud prediction API - pricing and terms of service, accessed 05.05.17. prices: $0.50/1,000 predictions beyond the initial 10,000. 2017. https://cloud.google.com/prediction/pricing.

[74] Jim Gray, Surajit Chaudhuri, Adam Bosworth, Andrew Layman, Don Reichart, Murali Venkatrao, Frank Pellow, and Hamid Pirahesh. Data cube: A relational aggregation operator generalizing group-by, cross-tab, and sub-totals. *Data Mining and Knowledge Discovery (DMKDFD)*, 1(1):29–53, 1997.

[75] Michael Grossniklaus, David Maier, James Miller, Sharmadha Moorthy, and Kristin Tufte. Frames: data-driven windows. In *Proceedings of the ACM International Conference on Distributed and Event-based Systems (DEBS)*, 2016.

[76] Philipp Grulich, René Saitenmacher, Jonas Traub, Sebastian Breß, Tilmann Rabl, and Volker Markl. Scalable detection of concept drifts on data streams with parallel adaptive windowing. In *Proceedings of the International Conference on Extending Database Technology (EDBT)*, 2018.

[77] Philipp Grulich, Jonas Traub, Sebastian Breß, Asterios Katsifodimos, Tilmann Rabl, and Volker Markl. Generating reproducible out-of-order data streams. In *ACM International Conference on Distributed and Event-based Systems (DEBS)*, pages 256–257, 2019.

[78] Shenoda Guirguis, Mohamed A Sharaf, Panos K Chrysanthis, and Alexandros Labrinidis. Optimized processing of multiple aggregate continuous queries. In *Proceedings of the International Conference on Information and Knowledge Management*, pages 1515–1524. ACM, 2011.

[79] Shenoda Guirguis, Mohamed A Sharaf, Panos K Chrysanthis, and Alexandros Labrinidis. Three-level processing of multiple aggregate continuous queries. In *IEEE International Conference on Data Engineering (ICDE)*, pages 929–940, 2012.

[80] Pieter Hintjens. *ZeroMQ: messaging for many applications*. O'Reilly Media, Inc., 2013.

[81] Martin Hirzel, Henrique Andrade, Buğra Gedik, Gabriela Jacques-Silva, Rohit Khandekar, Vibhore Kumar, Mark Mendell, Howard Nasgaard, Scott Schneider, Robert Soulé, et al. IBM streams processing language: Analyzing big data in motion. *IBM Journal*, 57(3/4):7.1–7.11, 2013.

[82] Martin Hirzel, Henrique Andrade, Buğra Gedik, Vibhore Kumar, Giuliano Losa, Howard Nasgaard, Robert Soulé, and Kun-Lung Wu. SPL stream processing language specification. *IBM Research Report*, 2009.

[83] Martin Hirzel, Scott Schneider, and Kanat Tangwongsan. Sliding-window aggregation algorithms: Tutorial. In *Proceedings of the ACM International Conference on Distributed and Event-based Systems (DEBS)*, pages 11–14, 2017.

[84] Martin Hirzel, Robert Soulé, Scott Schneider, Buğra Gedik, and Robert Grimm. A Catalog of Stream Processing Optimizations. *ACM Computing Surveys*, 46(4):46, 2014.

[85] Kartik Hosanagar, John Chuang, Ramayya Krishnan, and Michael D Smith. Service adoption and pricing of content delivery network (CDN) services. *Management Science*, 54(9):1579–1593, 2008.

[86] Ryan Huebsch, Minos Garofalakis, Joseph M Hellerstein, and Ion Stoica. Sharing aggregate computation for distributed queries. In *Proceedings of the ACM SIGMOD International Conference on Management of Data*, pages 485–496, 2007.

[87] Julius Hülsmann, Jonas Traub, and Volker Markl. Demand-based sensor data gathering with multi-query optimization. *Proceedings of the VLDB Endowment*, 13(12):2801–2804, 2020.

[88] Stratos Idreos, Olga Papaemmanouil, and Surajit Chaudhuri. Overview of data exploration techniques. In *Proceedings of the ACM SIGMOD International Conference on Management of Data*, pages 277–281, 2015.

[89] Ankur Jain, Edward Y Chang, and Yuan-Fang Wang. Adaptive stream resource management using kalman filters. In *Proceedings of the ACM SIGMOD International Conference on Management of Data*, pages 11–22, 2004.

[90] Zbigniew Jerzak, Thomas Heinze, Matthias Fehr, Daniel Gröber, Raik Hartung, and Nenad Stojanovic. The DEBS 2012 grand challenge. In *Proceedings of the ACM International Conference on Distributed and Event-based Systems (DEBS)*, pages 393–398, 2012.

[91] Barbara Jorgensen. Electronic component shortages will worsen through Q4. *EPS News for Electronics Purchasing and the Supply Chain*, 2018. Accessed Dec. 2018, https://epsnews.com/2018/08/30/component-shortages-worsen/.

[92] Barbara Jorgensen. Electronic Component shortages: 'no end in sight'. *EPS News for Electronics Purchasing and the Supply Chain*, 2018. Accessed Dec. 2018, https://epsnews.com/2018/05/23/electronic-component-shortages/.

[93] Uwe Jugel, Zbigniew Jerzak, Gregor Hackenbroich, and Volker Markl. M4: a visualization-oriented time series data aggregation. *Proceedings of the International Conference on Very Large Data Bases (PVLDB)*, 7(10):797–808, 2014.

[94] Rudolph Emil Kalman. A new approach to linear filtering and prediction problems. volume 82, pages 35–45. American Society of Mechanical Engineers, 1960.

[95] Jeyhun Karimov, Tilmann Rabl, Asterios Katsifodimos, Roman Samarev, Henri Heiskanen, and Volker Markl. Benchmarking distributed stream processing engines. In *IEEE International Conference on Data Engineering (ICDE)*, 2018.

[96] Paul Keeler. Notes on the Poisson point process. *Tech. Report*, 2016.

[97] David G Kendall. *On the generalized "birth-and-death" process*, volume 19. Institute of Mathematical Statistics, 1948.

[98] Albert Kim, Eric Blais, Aditya Parameswaran, Piotr Indyk, Samuel R Madden, and Ronitt Rubinfeld. Rapid sampling for visualizations with ordering guarantees. *Proceedings of the International Conference on Very Large Data Bases (PVLDB)*, 8(5):521–532, 2015.

[99] Mieczyslaw M. Kokar and KH Kim. Review of multisensor data fusion architectures and techniques. In *Proceedings of the IEEE International Symposium on Intelligent Control (ISIC)*, pages 261–266, 1993.

[100] Alexandros Koliousis, Matthias Weidlich, Raul Castro Fernandez, Alexander L Wolf, Paolo Costa, and Peter Pietzuch. SABER: Window-based hybrid stream processing for heterogeneous architectures. In *Proceedings of the ACM SIGMOD International Conference on Management of Data*, pages 555–569, 2016.

[101] Sailesh Krishnamurthy, Michael J Franklin, Jeffrey Davis, Daniel Farina, Pasha Golovko, Alan Li, and Neil Thombre. Continuous analytics over discontinuous streams. In *Proceedings of the ACM SIGMOD International Conference on Management of Data*, pages 1081–1092, 2010.

[102] Sailesh Krishnamurthy, Chung Wu, and Michael Franklin. On-the-fly sharing for streamed aggregation. In *Proceedings of the ACM SIGMOD International Conference on Management of Data*, pages 623–634, 2006.

[103] Srdjan Krčo, Boris Pokrić, and Francois Carrez. Designing IoT architecture(s): A european perspective. In *IEEE World Forum on Internet of Things (WF-IoT)*, pages 79–84, 2014.

[104] Sandeep S Kulkarni, Murat Demirbas, Deepak Madappa, Bharadwaj Avva, and Marcelo Leone. Logical physical clocks. In *Proceedings of the International Conference on Principles of Distributed Systems (OPODIS)*, pages 17–32. Springer, 2014.

[105] V. S. Anil Kumar, Madhav V. Marathe, Srinivasan Parthasarathy, and Aravind Srinivasan. Algorithmic aspects of capacity in wireless networks. *ACM SIGMETRICS Performance Evaluation Review*, 33(1):133–144, 2005.

[106] Sami M Lasassmeh and James M Conrad. Time synchronization in wireless sensor networks: A survey. In *Proceedings of the IEEE SoutheastCon*, pages 242–245, 2010.

[107] Trong Nhan Le, Olivier Sentieys, Olivier Berder, Alain Pegatoquet, and Cecile Belleudy. Power manager with PID controller in energy harvesting wireless sensor networks. In *IEEE International Conference on Green Computing and Communications (GreenCom)*, pages 668–670, 2012.

[108] In Lee and Kyoochun Lee. The Internet of Things (IoT): Applications, investments, and challenges for enterprises. 58(4):431–440, 2015.

[109] Mei Leng and Yik-Chung Wu. On clock synchronization algorithms for wireless sensor networks under unknown delay. *IEEE Transactions on Vehicular Technology (TVT)*, 59(1):182–190, 2010.

[110] Chiao-Yun Li. Automatic tuning of read-time tolerances for on-demand data streaming. Master's thesis, Technische Universität Berlin, 2017.

[111] Jin Li, David Maier, Kristin Tufte, Vassilis Papadimos, and Peter A Tucker. No pane, no gain: efficient evaluation of sliding-window aggregates over data streams. *SIGMOD Record*, 34(1):39–44, 2005.

[112] Jin Li, David Maier, Kristin Tufte, Vassilis Papadimos, and Peter A Tucker. Semantics and evaluation techniques for window aggregates in data streams. In

*Proceedings of the ACM SIGMOD International Conference on Management of Data*, pages 311–322, 2005.

[113] Jin Li, Kristin Tufte, David Maier, and Vassilis Papadimos. AdaptWID: An adaptive, memory-efficient window aggregation implementation. *IEEE Internet Computing*, 12(6):22–29, 2008.

[114] Jin Li, Kristin Tufte, Vladislav Shkapenyuk, Vassilis Papadimos, Theodore Johnson, and David Maier. Out-of-order processing: A new architecture for high-performance stream systems. *Proceedings of the International Conference on Very Large Data Bases (PVLDB)*, 1(1):274–288, 2008.

[115] Ming Li, Tingxin Yan, Deepak Ganesan, Eric Lyons, Prashant Shenoy, Arun Venkataramani, and Michael Zink. Multi-user data sharing in radar sensor networks. In *ACM Conference on Embedded Networked Sensor Systems*, pages 247–260, 2007.

[116] Ning Lu, Nan Cheng, Ning Zhang, Xuemin Shen, and Jon W Mark. Connected vehicles: Solutions and challenges. *IEEE Internet of Things Journal*, 1(4):289–299, 2014.

[117] Ren C Luo and Michael G Kay. Multisensor integration and fusion in intelligent systems. *IEEE Transactions on Systems, Man, and Cybernetics*, 19(5):901–931, 1989.

[118] Ren C Luo, Chih-Chen Yih, and Kuo Lan Su. Multisensor fusion and integration: approaches, applications, and future research directions. *IEEE Sensors Journal*, 2(2):107–119, 2002.

[119] Samuel R Madden, Michael J Franklin, Joseph M Hellerstein, and Wei Hong. TAG: A tiny aggregation service for ad-hoc sensor networks. *ACM SIGOPS Operating Systems Review*, 36(SI):131–146, 2002.

[120] Samuel R Madden, Michael J Franklin, Joseph M Hellerstein, and Wei Hong. The design of an acquisitional query processor for sensor networks. In *Proceedings of the ACM SIGMOD International Conference on Management of Data*, pages 491–502, 2003.

[121] Samuel R. Madden, Michael J. Franklin, Joseph M. Hellerstein, and Wei Hong. TinyDB: an acquisitional query processing system for sensor networks. *ACM Transactions on Database Systems*, 30(1):122–173, 2005.

[122] Linux Programmer's Manual. *getrusage*. Accessed May 2018. http://man7.org/linux/man-pages/man2/getrusage.2.html.

[123] David Meyer. How a mysterious case of 'missing energy' caused europe's clocks to run 6 minutes slow. *Fortune*, 2018.

[124] David Mills. Network time protocol (version 2) specification and implementation. Network Working Group, University of Delaware, 1989.

[125] David Mills. Network time protocol (version 3) specification, implementation and analysis. Network Working Group, University of Delaware, 1992.

[126] David Mills, Jim Martin, Jack Burbank, and William Kasch. Network time protocol version 4: Protocol and algorithms specification. Internet Engineering Task Force (IETF), 2010.

[127] Daniele Miorandi, Sabrina Sicari, Francesco De Pellegrini, and Imrich Chlamtac. Internet of Things: vision, applications and research challenges. *Ad hoc networks*, 10(7):1497–1516, 2012.

[128] Pulkit A Misra, Jeffrey S Chase, Johannes Gehrke, and Alvin R Lebeck. Enabling lightweight transactions with precision time. *ACM SIGARCH Computer Architecture News*, 45(1):779–794, 2017.

[129] Gianmarco De Francisci Morales and Aristides Gionis. Streaming similarity self-join. *Proceedings of the International Conference on Very Large Data Bases (PVLDB)*, 9(10):792–803, 2016.

[130] Kannan M Moudgalya. Proportional, integral, derivative controllers. *Digital Control*, pages 301–325, 2007.

[131] Conor Muldoon, Niki Trigoni, and Greg MP O'Hare. Combining sensor selection with routing and scheduling in wireless sensor networks. International Workshop on Data Management for Sensor Networks, 2011.

[132] Rene Muller and Gustavo Alonso. Efficient sharing of sensor networks. In *IEEE International Conference on Mobile Adhoc and Sensor Systems*, pages 109–118, 2006.

[133] Christopher Mutschler, Holger Ziekow, and Zbigniew Jerzak. The DEBS 2013 grand challenge. In *Proceedings of the ACM International Conference on Distributed and Event-based Systems (DEBS)*, pages 289–294, 2013.

[134] New York City Taxi and Limousine Commission. Taxicab passenger enhancements project (TPEP). 2018. Accessed Dec. 2018, http://www.nyc.gov/html/tlc/html/industry/taxicab_serv_enh.shtml (project website).

[135] Ninja (Username). Time and timezone issues on Pi. In *Raspberry Pi on Stack-Exchange*, 2017. Accessed Dec. 2018, https://raspberrypi.stackexchange.com/questions/59860/time-and-timezone-issues-on-pi.

[136] NXP Semiconductors N.V. Pcf2127 accurate RTC with integrated quartz crystal for industrial applications. product data sheet. 2014.

[137] OpenJDK. JMH benchmarking suite project website. 2018. Accessed Dec. 2018, http://openjdk.java.net/projects/code-tools/jmh/.

[138] OpenJDK. Nashorn project, objectsizecalculator. 2018. Accessed Dec. 2018, http://openjdk.java.net/projects/nashorn/.

[139] Fernando Pérez and Brian E Granger. IPython: A system for interactive scientific computing. *Computing in Science & Engineering (CISE)*, 2007.

[140] Su Ping. Delay measurement time synchronization for wireless sensor networks. *Intel Research Berkeley Lab*, 6:1–12, 2003.

[141] Giuseppe Piro, Nicola Baldo, and Marco Miozzo. An LTE module for the ns-3 network simulator. In *Proceedings of the International Conference on Simulation Tools and Techniques (ICST)*, pages 415–422, 2011.

[142] IQD Frequency Products. TCVCXO specification; part no. + packaging: LFTVXO076344Reel/LFTVXO076344CUTT. product data sheet. 2017. Accessed Dec. 2018, https://eu.mouser.com/datasheet/2/741/LFTVXO076344Reel-1148063.pdf.

[143] Valentin Protschky, Christian Ruhhammer, and Stefan Feit. Learning traffic light parameters with floating car data. In *IEEE Intelligent Transportation Systems Conference*, pages 2438–2443, 2015.

[144] Friedrich Pukelsheim. The three sigma rule. *The American Statistician*, 48(2):88–91, 1994.

[145] Tilmann Rabl, Jonas Traub, Asterios Katsifodimos, and Volker Markl. Apache Flink in current research. *it-Information Technology*, 58(4):157–165, 2016.

[146] Abdullah Raouf. Minimize frequency drift in crystals. *ElectronicDesign*, 2013. Accessed Feb. 2109, https://www.electronicdesign.com/analog/minimize-frequency-drift-crystals.

[147] Usman Raza, Alessandro Camerra, Amy L Murphy, Themis Palpanas, and Gian Pietro Picco. What does model-driven data acquisition really achieve in wireless sensor networks? In *IEEE International Conference on Pervasive Computing and Communications*, pages 85–94, 2012.

[148] Felix Rempe, Philipp Franeck, Ulrich Fastenrath, and Klaus Bogenberger. Online freeway traffic estimation with real floating car data. In *IEEE Intelligent Transportation Systems Conference*, pages 1838–1843, 2016.

[149] Mehdi Riahi, Thanasis G. Papaioannou, Immanuel Trummer, and Karl Aberer. Utility-driven data acquisition in participatory sensing. In *Proceedings of the International Conference on Extending Database Technology (EDBT)*, pages 251–262. ACM, 2013.

[150] George F Riley and Thomas R Henderson. The ns-3 network simulator. In *Modeling and tools for network simulation*, pages 15–34. Springer, 2010.

[151] A Wayne Roberts and Dale E Varberg. *Convex functions*, volume 57. Academic Press, 1973.

[152] David Salomon. *Variable-length Codes for Data Compression*. Springer, 2007.

[153] Theodoor Scholte, Davide Balzarotti, and Engin Kirda. Have things changed now? An empirical study on input validation vulnerabilities in web applications. *Computers & Security*, 31(3):344–356, 2012.

[154] Mohamed A Sharaf, Jonathan Beaver, Alexandros Labrinidis, and Panos K Chrysanthis. TiNA: A scheme for temporal coherency-aware in-network aggregation. In *Proceedings of the ACM International Workshop on Data Engineering for Wireless and Mobile Access*, pages 69–76, 2003.

[155] Mohamed A Sharaf, Jonathan Beaver, Alexandros Labrinidis, and Panos K Chrysanthis. Balancing energy efficiency and quality of aggregate data in sensor networks. *VLDB journal*, 13(4):384–403, 2004.

[156] Mehdi Sharifzadeh and Cyrus Shahabi. Supporting spatial aggregation in sensor network databases. In *Proceedings of the ACM International Workshop on Geographic Information Systems*, pages 166–175, 2004.

[157] Anatoli U Shein, Panos K Chrysanthis, and Alexandros Labrinidis. F1: Accelerating the optimization of aggregate continuous queries. In *Proceedings of the ACM International on Conference on Information and Knowledge Management (CIKM)*, pages 1151–1160, 2015.

[158] Anatoli U Shein, Panos K Chrysanthis, and Alexandros Labrinidis. Flatfit: Accelerated incremental sliding-window aggregation for real-time analytics. In *Proceedings of the International Conference on Scientific and Statistical Database Management (SSDBM)*, 2017.

[159] Anatoli U Shein, Panos K Chrysanthis, and Alexandros Labrinidis. Slickdeque: High throughput and low latency incremental sliding-window aggregation. In *Proceedings of the International Conference on Extending Database Technology (EDBT)*, 2018.

[160] Nisheeth Shrivastava, Chiranjeeb Buragohain, Divyakant Agrawal, and Subhash Suri. Medians and beyond: new aggregation techniques for sensor networks. In *Proceedings of the International Conference on Embedded Networked Sensor Systems (Sensys)*, pages 239–249. ACM, 2004.

[161] Anshu Shukla, Shilpa Chaturvedi, and Yogesh Simmhan. RIoTBench: An IoT benchmark for distributed stream processing systems. *Concurrency and Computation: Practice and Experience*, 29(21):e4257, 2017.

[162] Anshu Shukla and Yogesh Simmhan. Benchmarking distributed stream processing platforms for IoT applications. In *Technology Conference on Performance Evaluation and Benchmarking*, pages 90–106. Springer, 2016.

[163] Mihail L Sichitiu and Chanchai Veerarittiphan. Simple, accurate time synchronization for wireless sensor networks. In *IEEE Wireless Communications and Networking Conference (WCNC)*, volume 2, pages 1266–1273, 2003.

[164] Lefteris Sidirourgos, Martin Kersten, and Peter Boncz. Scientific discovery through weighted sampling. In *IEEE International Conference on Big Data*, pages 300–306, 2013.

[165] Fikret Sivrikaya and Bülent Yener. Time synchronization in sensor networks: A survey. *IEEE network*, 18(4):45–50, 2004.

[166] Antonios Skordylis and Niki Trigoni. Jointly optimizing data acquisition and delivery in traffic monitoring VANETs. In *Proceedings of the ACM symposium on Applied Computing (SIGAPP)*, pages 2186–2190, 2009.

[167] R. Srinivasan, Chao Liang, and K. Ramamritham. Maintaining temporal coherency of virtual data warehouses. In *Proceedings of the IEEE Real-Time Systems Symposium (RTSS)*, pages 60–70, 1998.

[168] Andy Stanford-Clark and Hong Linh Truong. MQTT for sensor networks (MQTT-SN) protocol specification. *IBM Corporation*, 2013.

[169] Michael Stonebraker, Uğur Çetintemel, and Stan Zdonik. The 8 requirements of real-time stream processing. *ACM Sigmod Record*, 34(4):42–47, 2005.

[170] Leo Syinchwun. Lightweight event time window. In *Flink Jira Issues (Accessed Dec. 2018, issues.apache.org/jira/browse/FLINK-5387)*, 2016.

[171] Hideaki Takagi and Bernhard H. Walke. Derivation of formulas by queueing theory. In *Spectrum Requirement Planning in Wireless Communications: Model and Methodology for IMT-Advanced*, pages 201–217. Wiley, 2008.

[172] Kanat Tangwongsan, Martin Hirzel, and Scott Schneider. Low-latency sliding-window aggregation in worst-case constant time. In *Proceedings of the ACM International Conference on Distributed and Event-based Systems (DEBS)*, pages 66–77, 2017.

[173] Kanat Tangwongsan, Martin Hirzel, Scott Schneider, and Kun-Lung Wu. General incremental sliding-window aggregation. *Proceedings of the International Conference on Very Large Data Bases (PVLDB)*, 8(7):702–713, 2015.

[174] Nesime Tatbul, Uğur Çetintemel, Stan Zdonik, Mitch Cherniack, and Michael Stonebraker. Load shedding in a data stream manager. In *Proceedings of the International Conference on Very Large Data Bases (PVLDB)*, volume 29, pages 309–320, 2003.

[175] Alejandro Tauber. Electric clocks in europe have been running slow for over a month. *tnw*, 2018. Accessed Dec. 2018, https://thenextweb.com/eu/2018/03/06/electric-clocks-europe-running-slow-month/.

[176] Arsalan Tavakoli, Aman Kansal, and Suman Nath. On-line sensing task optimization for shared sensors. In *Proceedings of the ACM/IEEE International Conference on Information Processing in Sensor Networks*, pages 47–57, 2010.

[177] Ankit Toshniwal, Siddarth Taneja, Amit Shukla, Karthik Ramasamy, Jignesh M Patel, Sanjeev Kulkarni, Jason Jackson, Krishna Gade, Maosong Fu, Jake Donham, et al. Storm@twitter. In *Proceedings of the ACM SIGMOD International Conference on Management of Data*, pages 147–156, 2014.

[178] Jonas Traub, Sebastian Breß, Tilmann Rabl, Asterios Katsifodimos, and Volker Markl. Optimized on-demand data streaming from sensor nodes. In *Proceedings of the Symposium on Cloud Computing (SoCC)*, pages 586–597. ACM, 2017.

[179] Jonas Traub, Philipp Grulich, Alejandro Rodriguez Cuellar, Sebastian Breß, Asterios Katsifodimos, Tilmann Rabl, and Volker Markl. Efficient window aggregation with general stream slicing. In *Proceedings of the International Conference on Extending Database Technology (EDBT)*, 2019.

[180] Jonas Traub, Philipp Marian Grulich, Alejandro Rodriguez Cuellar, Sebastian Breß, Asterios Katsifodimos, Tilmann Rabl, and Volker Markl. Scotty: Efficient window aggregation for out-of-order stream processing. In *IEEE International Conference on Data Engineering (ICDE)*, pages 1300–1303, 2018.

[181] Jonas Traub, Julius Hülsmann, Sebastian Breß, Tilmann Rabl, and Volker Markl. SENSE: Scalable data acquisition from distributed sensors with guaranteed time coherence. 2019. arXiv 1912.04648; https://arxiv.org/abs/1912.04648.

[182] Jonas Traub, Tilmann Rabl, Fabian Hueske, Till Rohrmann, and Volker Markl. Die Apache Flink Plattform zur parallelen Analyse von Datenströmen und Stapeldaten. In *Proceedings of the LWA Workshops: KDML, FGWM, IR, and FGDB*, pages 403–408, 2015.

[183] Jonas Traub, Nikolaas Steenbergen, Philipp Grulich, Tilmann Rabl, and Volker Markl. I2: Interactive real-time visualization for streaming data. In *Proceedings of the International Conference on Extending Database Technology (EDBT)*, pages 526–529, 2017.

[184] Martin Treiber and Arne Kesting. *Trajectory and Floating-Car Data*. Springer, 2013.

[185] Niki Trigoni, Yong Yao, Alan Demers, Johannes Gehrke, and Rajmohan Rajaraman. Wave scheduling and routing in sensor networks. *ACM Transactions on Sensor Networks (TOSN)*, 3(1):2, 2007.

[186] Demetris Trihinas, George Pallis, and Marios D Dikaiakos. AdaM: An adaptive monitoring framework for sampling and filtering on IoT devices. In *IEEE International Conference on Big Data*, pages 717–726, 2015.

[187] Demetris Trihinas, George Pallis, and Marios D Dikaiakos. ADMin: Adaptive monitoring dissemination for the internet of things. In *IEEE Conference on Computer Communications (INFOCOM)*, pages 1–9, 2017.

[188] Peter A. Tucker, David Maier, Tim Sheard, and Leonidas Fegaras. Exploiting punctuation semantics in continuous data streams. *IEEE Transactions on Knowledge and Data Engineering (TKDE)*, 15(3):555–568, 2003.

[189] Daniela Tulone and Samuel R Madden. PAQ: Time series forecasting for approximate query answering in sensor networks. In *European Workshop on Wireless Sensor Networks*, pages 21–37. Springer, 2006.

[190] James Turnbull. *Monitoring with Prometheus*. Turnbull Press, 2018.

[191] Kostas Tzoumas, Stephan Ewen, and Robert Metzger. High-throughput, low-latency, and exactly-once stream processing with Apache Flink. 2015. Accessed Dec. 2018, https://data-artisans.com/blog/high-throughput-low-latency-and-exactly-once-stream-processing-with-apache-flink.

[192] LiveOverflow (user name). Don't trust time. *Security Flag GmbH on Youtube*, 2017. Accessed Feb. 2019, https://www.youtube.com/watch?v=ylfyezRhA5s.

[193] Rob van der Meulen. Gartner says 6.4 billion connected "things" will be in use in 2016, up 30 percent from 2015. *Gartner Newsroom Press Release*, 2015.

[194] Potdar Vidyasagar, Sharif Atif, and Chang Elizabeth. Wireless sensor networks: a survey. In *AINA Workshops*, volume 641, 2009.

[195] Mikhail Vorontsov. Memory consumption of popular Java data types - part 2. *Java Performance Tuning Guide*, 2013. Accessed Dec. 2018, http://java-performance.info/memory-consumption-of-java-data-types-2/.

[196] Kang Wang, Shuhua Chen, and Aimin Pan. Time and position spoofing with open source projects. *Black Hat Europe*, 2015.

[197] Liuping Wang, TJD Barnes, and William R Cluett. New frequency-domain design method for PID controllers. *IEE Proceedings-Control Theory and Applications*, 142(4):265–271, 1995.

[198] Eugene Wu, Leilani Battle, and Samuel R Madden. The case for data visualization management systems: Vision paper. *Proceedings of the VLDB Endowment*, 7(10):903–906, 2014.

[199] Jark Wu. Improve performance of sliding time window with pane optimization. In *Flink Jira Issues (Accessed Dec. 2018, issues.apache.org/jira/browse/FLINK-7001)*, 2017.

[200] Shili Xiang, Hock Beng Lim, and Kian-Lee Tan. Impact of multi-query optimization in sensor networks. In *Proceedings of the International Workshop on Data Management for Sensor Networks*, pages 7–12. ACM, 2006.

[201] Shili Xiang, Hock Beng Lim, Kian-Lee Tan, and Yongluan Zhou. Two-tier multiple query optimization for sensor networks. In *IEEE International Conference on Distributed Computing Systems*, pages 39–39, 2007.

[202] Shili Xiang, Wei Wu, and Kian-Lee Tan. Optimizing multiple data acquisition queries in sparse mobile sensor networks. In *IEEE International Conference on Mobile Data Management*, pages 137–146, 2012.

[203] Yuan Yu, Pradeep Kumar Gunda, and Michael Isard. Distributed aggregation for data-parallel computing: interfaces and implementations. In *Proceedings of the ACM SIGOPS Symposium on Operating Systems Principles*, pages 247–260, 2009.

[204] Matei Zaharia, Tathagata Das, Haoyuan Li, Scott Shenker, and Ion Stoica. Discretized streams: An efficient and fault-tolerant model for stream processing on large clusters. *Proceedings of the USENIX conference on Hot Topics in Cloud Ccomputing*, 12:10–10, 2012.

[205] Matei Zaharia, Reynold S Xin, Patrick Wendell, Tathagata Das, Michael Armbrust, Ankur Dave, Xiangrui Meng, Josh Rosen, Shivaram Venkataraman, Michael J Franklin, et al. Apache Spark: A unified engine for big data processing. *Communications of the ACM*, 59(11):56–65, 2016.

[206] Steffen Zeuch, Ankit Chaudhary, Bonaventura Del Monte, Haralampos Gavriilidis, Dimitrios Giouroukis, Sebastian Bress Philipp M. Grulich, Jonas Traub, and Volker Markl. The NebulaStream Platform: Data and application management for the internet of things. In *Conference on Innovative Data Systems Research (CIDR)*, 2020. arXiv 1910.07867; https://arxiv.org/abs/1910.07867.

[207] Steffen Zeuch, Bonaventura Del Monte, Jeyhun Karimov, Clemens Lutz, Manuel Renz, Jonas Traub, Sebastian Breß, Tilmann Rabl, and Volker Markl. Analyzing efficient stream processing on modern hardware. In *Proceedings of the International Conference on Very Large Data Bases (PVLDB)*, 2019.

[208] Yawei Zhao, Deke Guo, Jia Xu, Pin Lv, Tao Chen, and Jianping Yin. CATS: Cooperative allocation of tasks and scheduling of sampling intervals for maximizing data sharing in WSNs. *ACM Transactions on Sensor Networks (TOSN)*, 12(4):29, 2016.

[209] Yanxu Zheng, Sutharshan Rajasegarar, and Christopher Leckie. Parking availability prediction for sensor-enabled car parks in smart cities. In *IEEE International Conference on Intelligent Sensors, Sensor Networks and Information Processing (ISSNIP)*, pages 1–6, 2015.

[210] Wolfgang Ziegler. Incorrect date and time on Raspberry Pi. In *Blog: make stuff and blog about it*, 2017. Accessed Dec. 2018, https://wolfgang-ziegler.com/blog/incorrect-date-and-time-on-raspberrypi.